NEW
CREATIVE
CUISINE

LYNN BEDFORD HALL

NEW
CREATIVE
CUISINE

PHOTOGRAPHY BY ALAIN PROUST

NEW
HOLLAND

First published in the UK in 1989 by
New Holland (Publishers) Ltd
37 Connaught Street, London W2 2AZ
Reprinted in 1993

ISBN 1 85368 082 6 (hbk)
ISBN 1 85368 098 2 (pbk)

Edited by Linda de Villiers
Design by Sydney-Anne Wallace
Cover design by Jennie Hoare
Illustrations by Felicity Harris
Phototypeset by Unifoto (Pty) Ltd
Originated by Unifoto (Pty) Ltd
Printed and bound in Singapore by Tien Wah Press (Pte) Ltd

Photographer's acknowledgements

The photography for a book of this magnitude could not be
undertaken without the assistance of many people. The
publishers and the photographer would like to thank in
particular:

☐ Lesley Cockcroft, ably assisted by Ivy Tingwe, for
preparing and cooking the food
☐ Marine Williams, Nicole Sieff and Lesley Cockcroft for
styling the photographs
☐ Derek Williams and Dick Bomford for their contribution
towards the photography
☐ The following specialist stores for the loan of the latest in
crockery, cutlery and tableware:

A M C Classic	Etcetera
Binnehuis Interiors	Fosters
Boardmans	Garlicks
Bric-A-Brac-Lane	Just Living
Continental China	La Maree
Dice Gift Gallery	Stuttafords

CONTENTS

PREFACE

The majority of the recipes in the *New Creative Cuisine* are from my published works. Paring the selection down to a couple of hundred has been no easy task and many old favourites have had to be side-lined for the simple reason that no cookery book should ever be too fat and heavy to be read in bed or comfortably propped up against a bread-bin. And so, needs must, I have had to choose those that best fit the title.

My basis has been to try and incorporate as many different culinary styles as possible, while still retaining the personal touch which automatically colours the creations of every cook. I certainly have my preferences as regards ingredients and preparation techniques, but at the same time I have tried to take into consideration the frequently changing fashions on the gustatory scene. And so we end up with touches of nouvelle, shades of ethnic cuisine, and a generous portion of vegetarian fare which has become so popular in this health-conscious age. Because natural, unprocessed foods appeal to me very strongly, I have tried to avoid highly processed ingredients and artificial additives, believing that fresh foods, carefully prepared, should not have to be helped along too vigorously.

My selection of recipes ranges from simple, family fare to splendid dishes for elegant entertaining. Because a well-steamed and floured hostess is about as appealing as a stuffed peacock, few of the dishes require much last-minute attention. I have also tried to avoid the temptation of creating dreamy dinner party dishes simply by adding lashings of butter and cream, and find that lower-calorie soured cream or buttermilk can often be successfully substituted and are more in line with the preference, these days, for somewhat lighter fare. The desserts, however, are unashamedly sweet and indulgent.

Where a recipe requires the addition of flour, plain white flour should be used unless otherwise specified. I have also used extra large eggs in every recipe requiring eggs. Because I prefer natural ingredients, I use butter, but margarine may be substituted according to personal conviction.

Happily, eating, drinking and making merry are part of life, and if I can lay claim to have guided, pleased, or even inspired anyone – whether a nervous new cook or an old hand seeking new ideas – then I shall consider this collection truly complete.

Lynn Bedford Hall

Lemon Crumbed Sole

This type of recipe makes it possible to serve crisp, crumbed fish without any last-minute frying. Allow about 3 small fillets per person, and serve with Tartare sauce (page 55) and lemon wedges.

500 g (18 oz) sole fillets
125 g (4 oz) fine cereal crumbs
2.5 ml (¹/₂ tsp) salt
oil for baking

LEMON MAYONNAISE
1 egg
25 ml (5 tsp) lemon juice
2.5 ml (¹/₂ tsp) salt
5 ml (1 tsp) sugar
250 ml (8 fl oz) oil
1 garlic clove, crushed
finely grated rind of ¹/₂ lemon

Begin with the mayonnaise. Put egg, lemon juice, salt, sugar and 25 ml (5 tsp) oil into a blender and blend well. With the motor running, pour in the remaining oil in a slow steady stream. Spoon into a bowl and stir in garlic and lemon rind. Cover and chill for several hours for best flavour.

Dip sole fillets into mayonnaise, coating both sides thoroughly, then coat with crumbs mixed with salt. Chill for at least 1 hour to set crumbs.

Preheat oven to 180 °C (350 °F, gas 4). Heat a thin layer of oil for a few minutes in a large baking dish, then place fillets in dish, turning once in the hot oil. Bake for 10–12 minutes, depending on size.
Serves 4

Smoked Salmon and Tuna Ramekins

An elegant starter for a special dinner which amazingly stretches 90 g (3 oz) smoked salmon to 4–5 servings, depending on the size of the ramekins. Ideally choose smoked salmon with no preservatives or colouring. Quantities are easily doubled.

200 g (7 oz) canned tuna in brine
7.5 ml (1¹/₂ tsp) powdered gelatine
60 ml (4 tbsp) mayonnaise
5 ml (1 tsp) lemon juice
15 ml (1 tbsp) sherry
1 egg white
15 ml (1 tbsp) finely chopped chives
60 ml (4 tbsp) cream, whipped
90 g (3 oz) smoked salmon
black peppercorns

Drain tuna and make up liquid to 100 ml (3¹/₂ fl oz) with water. Sprinkle in gelatine and dissolve over low heat. Add to finely shredded tuna together with mayonnaise, lemon juice and sherry. Purée in blender until smooth, stopping to scrape down the sides. Spoon into a bowl. Whisk egg white with a pinch of salt until stiff, then fold into mixture together with chives and cream. Rinse ramekins and line with smoked salmon slices. Pour in tuna mixture, and chill for a few hours until set. To serve, run a knife round the edges and unmould onto serving plates. Grind a little black pepper over the tops and serve with Melba toast and lemon wedges.
Serves 4.

Fish Cocktail with Tarragon Mayonnaise

A change from prawns in seafood sauce; use fresh salmon, cod or haddock.

800–900 g (1 lb 14 oz–2 lb) firm
  white fish
1 litre (1³/₄ pints) water
1 bay leaf
1 carrot, sliced
small bunch of parsley
a few peppercorns
¹/₂ onion, sliced
5 ml (1 tsp) salt
2 fresh thyme sprigs
25 ml (5 tsp) lemon juice

TARRAGON MAYONNAISE
2 egg yolks
25 ml (5 tsp) tarragon vinegar
5 ml (1 tsp) dried tarragon
2.5 ml (¹/₂ tsp) salt
250 ml (8 fl oz) oil
75 ml (2¹/₂ fl oz) soured cream
30 ml (2 tbsp) chopped chives
15 ml (1 tbsp) capers, drained and
  chopped

Bring all ingredients, from water to lemon juice, to the boil and then simmer, covered, for 10 minutes. Put fish into large saucepan, pour over boiling bouillon (which should just cover fish), bring back to the boil, then cover and simmer very, very gently until just cooked through. Leave to cool in liquid.

Make mayonnaise in advance and chill to develop flavours. Put egg yolks, tarragon vinegar, tarragon, salt and 30 ml (2 tbsp) oil into a blender and blend well. With motor running, slowly pour in the remaining oil. Scoop mayonnaise into a bowl and add cream, chives and capers.

Drain fish thoroughly. Remove any skin and bones, flake, then moisten with mayonnaise. Serve in cocktail glasses or in halved avocados. Serves 8.

Note
If the mayonnaise curdles because the oil has been added too quickly, tip it out, wash and dry the blender container very well. Break in another egg and, with motor running, slowly pour the curdled mixture through the hole in the lid.

Squid Mushroom Salad

Squid marinated in a sharp vinaigrette is squid ruined, so the following dressing is subtle enough not to mask any delicate flavours. The accent in this dish is on the unusual combination of ingredients rather than on the seafood – nevertheless, it is important to use small squid as it has to be cooked in 1 minute. If serving as a starter rather than at a buffet, pile into scallop shells or halved avocados and serve with fingers of buttered brown bread.

2 slim leeks
10 ml (2 tsp) lemon juice
400 g (14 oz) squid tubes, sliced into rings
300 g (11 oz) button mushrooms, sliced
salt
10 ml (2 tsp) mayonnaise

BLENDER DRESSING
100 ml (3¹/₂ fl oz) oil
25 ml (5 tsp) lemon juice
15 ml (1 tbsp) anchovy essence
1 small garlic clove, halved
parsley sprigs
5 ml (1 tsp) sugar
1 small spring onion, chopped
100 ml (3¹/₂ fl oz) buttermilk (optional)

Slice leeks, white parts only, very thinly. Bring a large saucepan of water to the boil and add lemon juice. Drop in squid, leeks and mushrooms and stir to mix, while the water returns to the boil. Boil for about 1 minute, or just until squid stiffens and turns white. Drain well, tip into bowl and pour dressing over while still hot. To make dressing, put all ingredients into a blender and blend well.

Cool salad and then cover and chill overnight. Just before serving, add salt to taste and bind with mayonnaise.
Serves 6 in scallop shells.

Avocados with Lumpfish Roe Mousse

By piping the notoriously rich lumpfish roe mousse into the hollows of small avocados, the temptation to over-indulge is neatly avoided.

10 ml (2 tsp) powdered gelatine
25 ml (5 tsp) cold water
125 ml (4 fl oz) single cream
60 g (2 oz) black lumpfish roe
5 ml (1 tsp) lemon juice
few drops of Tabasco
a little crushed onion
30 ml (2 tsp) mayonnaise
2 egg whites, stiffly whisked
3–4 avocados

Soak gelatine in cold water, then dissolve over low heat. Whip cream, and slowly trickle in melted gelatine. When fairly stiffly whipped, stir in lumpfish roe, lemon juice, Tabasco, onion and mayonnaise. Fold in egg whites, spoon into a bowl and set in the refrigerator.

To serve, pipe the mousse into each avocado half. Serve with lemon wedges, black pepper and Melba toast.
Serves 6–8.

Hint
To make Melba toast, place loaf in freezer for 2–3 hours, then slice bread very thinly. Remove crusts and, if desired, slice into triangles. Arrange in a single layer on a baking sheet and dry out in a very low oven until crisp. Store in an airtight container.

Monkfish with Mushrooms in Cream Sauce (left) and Tuna Mousse (right)

Tuna Mousse

The tangy top layer provides a good contrast to the creamy layer below and makes this a particularly eye-catching dish.

15 ml (1 tbsp) powdered gelatine
250 ml (8 fl oz) chicken stock
5 ml (1 tsp) lemon juice
^{1}/$_2$ pickling onion, grated
15 ml (1 tbsp) tomato sauce
5 ml (1 tsp) Worcester sauce
pinch of sugar
200 g (7 oz) canned tuna, drained and flaked
125 ml (4 fl oz) whipping cream, whipped
2 egg whites, whisked

TOMATO LAYER
170 ml (5^1/$_2$ fl oz) canned tomato juice
185 ml (6 fl oz) mayonnaise
15 ml (1 tbsp) anchovy paste
generous pinch of sugar
10 ml (2 tsp) powdered gelatine
25 ml (5 tsp) cold water

Pour tomato juice into small bowl. Mix mayonnaise, anchovy paste and sugar. Add 45 ml (3 tbsp) to tomato juice, reserve remainder. Whisk well. Soften gelatine in cold water and dissolve over low heat, then stir into tomato-mayonnaise mixture. Pour into 1-litre (1^3/$_4$-pint) mould, and set in refrigerator.

For the mousse, soften gelatine in stock, stir over low heat until dissolved, then pour into a bowl. Add lemon juice, onion, tomato sauce, Worcester sauce, sugar and tuna. Purée in blender until smooth, then return to bowl. Stir in the reserved mayonnaise, then fold in cream and egg whites. Pour carefully on top of first layer, which should be set, and return mould to refrigerator until firm. Unmould and serve with a lightly dressed lettuce and avocado salad.
Serves 8.

Monkfish with Mushrooms in Cream Sauce

Firm in texture, delicate in flavour, monkfish is ideal for hot or cold starters.

800 g (1 lb 14 oz) monkfish fillets
125 ml (4 fl oz) dry white wine
250 ml (8 fl oz) water
1 bay leaf
parsley sprig
^{1}/$_2$ small onion
6 peppercorns
2.5 ml (^{1}/$_2$ tsp) salt
200 g (7 oz) mushrooms, sliced
30g (1 oz) butter
30 ml (2 tbsp) sherry
60 ml (4 tbsp) double cream
10–15 ml (2–3 tsp) French mustard
creamed potatoes
grated Parmesan or Gruyère cheese

WHITE SAUCE
45 g (1^1/$_2$ oz) butter
45 g (1^1/$_2$ oz) flour
250 ml (8 fl oz) warm milk
375 ml (12 fl oz) strained fish stock

Put monkfish, wine, water, bay leaf, parsley, onion, peppercorns and salt in saucepan and poach until just cooked through. Drain and cube fish. Fry mushrooms lightly in butter. Drain on absorbent kitchen paper.

Make a white sauce with butter, flour, milk and fish stock. Season to taste and then stir in fish, mushrooms, sherry, cream and mustard. Spoon into 6 scallop shells or individual baking dishes, surround with a border of creamed potatoes and sprinkle with cheese. Bake at 170 °C (325 °F, gas 3) for 25 minutes.
Serves 6.

Oyster and Cheese Moulds

This is a convenient, store-cupboard starter which will feed a large number of guests. Set in individual ramekins, unmould onto small plates and garnish with spring onions. Serve with black pepper and Melba toast.

15 ml (1 tbsp) powdered gelatine
60 ml (2 tbsp) medium to sweet sherry
200 ml (6¹/₂ fl oz) seasoned chicken stock
250 g (9 oz) low-fat soft cheese
100 ml (3¹/₂ fl oz) thick mayonnaise
2.5 ml (¹/₂ tsp) Worcester sauce
2 spring onions, finely chopped
pinch of sugar
450 g (1 lb) canned oysters in brine
125 ml (4 fl oz) whipping cream, whipped
1 egg white, whisked

Soak gelatine in sherry. Heat chicken stock. Pour onto soaked gelatine and stir until dissolved. Beat together cheese, mayonnaise, Worcester sauce, spring onions and sugar. Slowly beat in stock and gelatine mixture and chill until starting to set.

Drain oysters, dry well on absorbent kitchen paper and chop roughly. Stir into cheese mixture, then fold in cream and egg white. Pour into 10 rinsed ramekins and refrigerate for at least 4 hours. Run a knife around the edges to unmould.
Serves 10.

Avocado Surprise

Set in individual ramekins, turned out and topped with lumpfish roe and soured cream, this is a super starter. The mixture is quite rich, so bear this in mind when planning the rest of the meal.

250 ml (8 fl oz) chicken stock
15 ml (1 tbsp) powdered gelatine
2 very large unbruised avocados
15 ml (1 tbsp) lemon juice
few drops of Tabasco
2.5 ml (¹/₂ tsp) Worcester sauce
pinch each of sugar and celery salt
ground black pepper
45 ml (3 tbsp) mayonnaise
125 ml (4 fl oz) whipping cream, whipped
1 egg white
chilled lumpfish roe
soured cream
finely grated lemon rind

Pour chicken stock into a small saucepan, sprinkle in the gelatine, place over low heat and stir until dissolved without boiling. Using a silver fork, mash avocados with lemon juice. Add Tabasco, Worcester sauce, sugar, celery salt and a few grinds of pepper. Add to stock and purée in blender until smooth. Pour into a bowl. Stir in mayonnaise and fold in the cream. Whisk the egg white until stiff, stir a little into the avocado mixture and then fold in the remainder.

Pour into 6 or 8 rinsed ramekins, cover with plastic wrap and chill for several hours until firm. Run a knife round the edges to unmould. With a teaspoon, scoop a small hollow in the top of each, and drop in a little lumpfish roe. Cover lumpfish roe with a spoonful of soured cream, and then sprinkle with a little lemon rind, or black pepper. Serve on the day it is made with hot toast.
Serves 6–8.

Fish and Shrimp Mousse with Two Sauces

Visually, this is a stunning starter: a pale and delicate fish mousse, set in ramekins, unmoulded and flanked by a ribbon of bright avocado sauce on one side, a pool of light tomato coulis on the other. The combination of flavours is superb, and a further plus is that the creamy textures are achieved without the usual lashings of cream. I have also eliminated egg yolks and used buttermilk, soured cream and egg whites to scale down the possibility of an overly rich beginning to a meal. There is quite a lot of preparation involved, but everything can be completed well in advance – the sauces in the morning, and the mousse even the day before.

250g (9oz) white fish fillets
200 ml (6½ fl oz) water
2 onion slices
45 ml (3 tbsp) white wine
salt
black peppercorns
1 bay leaf
30 g (1 oz) butter
15 g (½ oz) flour
170 ml (5½ fl oz) haddock stock
125 ml (4 fl oz) milk
10 ml (2 tsp) powdered gelatine
45 ml (3 tbsp) thick mayonnaise
100 ml (3½ fl oz) soured cream
200 g (7 oz) canned shrimps
2 egg whites
lemon juice

TOMATO COULIS
10 ml (2 tsp) oil
5 ml (1 tsp) butter
1 onion, chopped
1 leek, sliced
250 g (9 oz) ripe tomatoes,
    skinned, seeded and chopped
45 ml (3 tbsp) water
3 fresh thyme sprigs
salt and ground black pepper
1 bay leaf

2.5 ml (½ tsp) sugar
30 ml (2 tbsp) single cream

AVOCADO SAUCE
1 large, ripe avocado
2.5 ml (½ tsp) lemon juice
200 ml (6½ fl oz) buttermilk
generous pinch of salt
few drops of Worcester sauce
45 ml (3 tbsp) mayonnaise
pinch of sugar

Poach the haddock gently in the water, with onion, wine, seasoning and bay leaf until just cooked. Cool in liquid. Reserve liquid and flake fish very finely. Make a velouté sauce with butter, flour, 125 ml (4 fl oz) poaching liquid and milk. When thickened, add to fish. Soak gelatine in 50 ml (4 tbsp) cooled poaching liquid, dissolve over low heat, and add to fish together with mayonnaise and soured cream. Rinse, dry and roughly chop shrimps, then fold half into mixture. Stiffly whisk egg whites with a pinch of salt

and fold in. Adjust seasoning, add a dash of lemon juice, then spoon into 6 rinsed ramekins and chill.

To make the coulis, heat oil and butter and soften onion and leek. Add tomatoes and remaining ingredients, except cream. Cover and simmer gently for about 15 minutes until soft and thick. Cool. Remove thyme and bay leaf and purée in blender until smooth. Pour into a jug, stir in cream and chill.

For the avocado sauce, dice avocado and place in blender with remaining ingredients. Blend until smooth. If too thick, add a little milk or cream. Spoon into a jug and stir in remaining shrimps. Sink avocado stone in the middle (to preserve the colour), cover and chill.

To serve, unmould ramekins onto serving plates. Pour a pool of avocado sauce on one side, tomato on the other. Garnish with a sprig of fennel or dill. Serves 6.

Salad Niçoise

This salad is usually served on its own, as a first course. It is a popular, somewhat eclectic affair, the ingredients depending on what's in season and on personal preference. It is often dressed just before being eaten, but I like to chill it for a while to give the flavours time to blend.

6–8 anchovy fillets
milk
200 g (7 oz) green beans
1/2 large red pepper
1/2 medium onion
2 medium tomatoes
1/4 cucumber
200 g (7 oz) canned tuna in oil
black olives
hard-boiled eggs (optional)

DRESSING
45 ml (3 tbsp) olive oil
15 ml (1 tbsp) tarragon vinegar
generous pinch of salt
generous pinch of paprika
1 large garlic clove, crushed
5 ml (1 tsp) capers, chopped
pinch of sugar
30 ml (2 tbsp) chopped parsley
6 fresh basil leaves, chopped

Soak anchovies in milk. Trim and slice beans, seed and dice red pepper, and boil together until just tender. Slice onion into rings and skin and slice tomatoes. Pare and slice cucumber very thinly. Drain and flake tuna.

In a flattish bowl layer the beans, red pepper, tuna, onion, tomato slices and cucumber to cover the entire top.

Make the dressing by whisking all the ingredients together with a fork. Pour over salad. Top with drained anchovies, olives and hard-boiled eggs, if using. Cover and chill. Serve with hot French bread. Serves 4–5.

Stuffed Mushrooms Gruyère

A delicious starter for an elegant dinner.

4–6 large brown mushrooms
4 spring onions, chopped
30 g (1 oz) fine fresh wholemeal
**   breadcrumbs**
14 fresh rosemary needles,
**   finely chopped**
2.5 ml (¹/₂ tsp) Worcester sauce
30 ml (2 tbsp) thick mayonnaise
salt and ground black pepper
grated Gruyère cheese
paprika
45 g (1¹/₂ oz) butter
1 small garlic clove, crushed

Remove mushroom stalks and scoop out a little of the centre of each cap. Chop stalks and centres finely and mix with spring onions, breadcrumbs, rosemary, Worcester sauce, mayonnaise and a pinch of salt.

Oil a large baking sheet and arrange mushrooms, hollows up. Season with salt and ground pepper. Top with stuffing mixture and sprinkle with Gruyère cheese and paprika. Combine butter and garlic and put a pat on top of each mushroom. Bake at 180 °C (350 °F, gas 4) for 20 minutes, then serve with a spoonful of the juices over each mushroom, and buttered wholemeal bread. Serves 4–6.

Hint
To peel garlic cloves, pour boiling water over and leave to stand for 5 minutes. Skin will slip off easily.

Stuffed Aubergines

Serve as an unusual first course with hot French bread.

2 medium aubergines
1 large tomato, skinned and
**   chopped**
¹/₂ small onion, finely chopped
45 g (1¹/₂ oz) wholemeal
**   breadcrumbs**
30 ml (2 tbsp) garlic blender
**   mayonnaise (page 69)**
salt and ground black pepper
2.5 ml (¹/₂ tsp) dried basil
pinch of sugar
Feta cheese
30 ml (2 tbsp) oil
black olives to garnish

Boil aubergines in unsalted water for 8–10 minutes or until just softened. Cut in half and remove most of flesh, leaving shells intact. Chop the pulp coarsely and add tomato, onion, breadcrumbs, mayonnaise, seasoning, basil and sugar.

Fill shells and sprinkle liberally with crumbled Feta. Dribble the oil over the aubergines and bake, uncovered, at 170 °C (325 °F, gas 3) for 45 minutes. Leave to cool – the liquid will slowly be absorbed. Serve at room temperature garnished with black olives.
Serves 4.

Avocados Stuffed with Mushrooms and Leeks

Stir-fried leeks and mushrooms, perfumed with rosemary, are marinated in sherry and soy sauce and then spooned into avocado halves. Assemble just before serving, but prepare the filling a few hours in advance. The following quantities are for 4 avocado halves, but can easily be doubled.

2 leeks
45 ml (3 tbsp) oil
150 g (5 oz) brown mushrooms, sliced
rosemary sprig
30 ml (2 tbsp) sweet sherry
15 ml (1 tbsp) soy sauce
ground black pepper
2 avocados, halved
parsley sprigs to garnish

Very finely shred the white parts only of the leeks – you should have about 75 g (2¹/₂ oz) – and add to the hot oil, together with mushrooms and rosemary. Stir-fry over fairly high heat for 1–2 minutes until just beginning to soften and brown.

Spoon into a bowl (including sprig of rosemary) and add sherry, soy sauce and a few grinds of pepper. Cover and cool.

Just before serving, remove rosemary and drain off most of the marinade. Enlarge cavities of halved avocados a little and spoon in filling. Top with a sprig of parsley, and serve with salt and black pepper.
Serves 4.

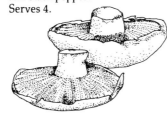

Mushroom Pâté

Serve with savoury biscuits or hot toast.

60 g (2 oz) butter
300 g (11 oz) brown mushrooms, sliced
1 small onion, chopped
1 garlic clove, crushed
pinch of dried thyme
75 g (2¹/₂ oz) butter, diced
25 ml (5 tsp) soy sauce
45 ml (3 tbsp) sweet sherry
ground black pepper
pinch of sugar

Melt 60 g (2 oz) butter and sauté mushrooms, onion, garlic and thyme. When brown and soft, reduce heat to low and add diced butter and remaining ingredients except sugar. Stir until melted, then remove from heat. Add sugar, cool slightly, then pureé, leaving mixture somewhat chunky. Pot, cover with plastic wrap and chill for 24 hours.

Oyster Pâté

Surely the simplest recipe in the book. This delicious pâté is rich, so it goes a long way.

225 g (8 oz) canned oysters in brine
5 ml (1 tsp) lemon juice
1 small onion slice, chopped
ground black pepper
100 g (3¹/₂ oz) butter, melted

Drain oysters and put into blender with remaining ingredients. Blend once or twice to chop coarsely, then pot and chill for about 4 hours. Serve with unbuttered wholemeal bread or hot toast.

Variation
CLAM PÂTÉ
Use 300 g (11 oz) canned clams instead of the oysters.

Green Salad with Pears and Ricotta Balls

This is an unusual salad, interesting enough to be served as a first course, as part of a cold buffet, or with roast chicken. The Ricotta balls, quickly made in a processor, and the pears, add an elegant touch.

NUTTY RICOTTA BALLS
300 g (11 oz) Ricotta cheese
60 g (2 oz) Cheddar cheese, grated
1–2 spring onions, chopped
generous pinch of onion salt
pinch of celery salt
few drops of Tabasco
2.5 ml (1/2 tsp) French mustard
2.5 ml (1/2 tsp) Worcester sauce
parsley sprigs
nuts (almonds, pecans, walnuts or hazels), finely chopped and toasted

DRESSING
75 ml (21/2 fl oz) vegetable oil
30 ml (2 tbsp) olive oil
1 small garlic clove, crushed
30 ml (2 tbsp) lemon juice
generous pinch of dry mustard
generous pinch of salt

SALAD
2 medium pears
250 g (9 oz) broccoli
1 round lettuce
1 avocado

To make the Ricotta balls, put all the ingredients, except nuts, into a processor fitted with the grinding blade. Process until thick and creamy and mixture forms a ball. Spoon into small dish and chill for several hours.

Put ingredients for dressing into large wooden salad bowl, and mix with a fork until creamy.

Peel and core pears and cut into eighths. Add to dressing, toss well and then cover and allow to stand for up to 2 hours.

Steam and chop broccoli. Just before serving, shred lettuce coarsely, and dice avocado. Add broccoli, lettuce and avocado to pears and toss well. Scoop out large teaspoons of chilled Ricotta mixture and roll into 18–24 balls. Roll each ball in chopped nuts and place on top of salad. Serves 6.

Shrimp, Cucumber and Cheese Cream

An unusual, cold and wobbly first course just right on a summer's evening before a special dinner.

¹/₂ cucumber
250 ml (8 fl oz) water
100 ml (3¹/₂ fl oz) white wine
salt
500 g (18 oz) peeled and
    de-veined shrimps
20 ml (4 tsp) powdered gelatine
45 ml (3 tbsp) cold water
250 g (9 oz) low-fat soft cheese
100 ml (3¹/₂ fl oz) thick
    mayonnaise
30 ml (2 tbsp) chopped chives
5 ml (1 tsp) prepared mustard
5 ml (1 tsp) sugar
2 egg whites
125 ml (4 fl oz) whipping cream,
    whipped
30 ml (2 tbsp) mayonnaise
30 ml (2 tbsp) soured cream
few drops of Worcester sauce
pinch of paprika

Pare cucumber, chop into small cubes, then degorge (page 135). Bring water, wine and 2.5 ml (¹/₂ tsp) salt to the boil. Add shrimps and cook for a few minutes until just tender, then drain, reserving the liquid. Sprinkle gelatine onto cold water, leave a few minutes to soften, then stir in 125 ml (4 fl oz) of the reserved hot liquid and stir until gelatine has dissolved. Set aside. Mix cheese with 100 ml (3¹/₂ fl oz) mayonnaise, chives, mustard and sugar. Slowly stir in dissolved gelatine, then add rinsed and well-dried cucumber. Chop half the shrimps and stir into cheese mixture. Stiffly whisk egg whites with a pinch of salt and fold in together with whipped cream. Pour into a rinsed ring mould or 8–10 individual ramekins and set in refrigerator. Mix remaining shrimps with 30 ml (2 tbsp) mayonnaise, soured cream, Worcester sauce and paprika and chill.

To serve, turn out and either spoon shrimp mixture into the centre of the ring mould, or top each ramekin with a spoonful. Serve with Melba toast. Serves 8–10.

Mushrooms with Spinach and Cheese (left) and Brown Mushrooms with Herb Butter (right)

Mushrooms with Spinach and Cheese

These delicious mushrooms may be served in several ways: either as a starter, in which case use large flat mushrooms, one per serving, or use medium-sized brown ones as an accompaniment to grilled steak. These mushrooms may also be served as a vegetarian meal with rice tossed with a nut of butter, toasted almonds and soy sauce.

1 x 250 g (9 oz) packet frozen
   spinach
300 g (11 oz) brown mushrooms
30 ml (2 tbsp) oil
1 onion, chopped
1-2 garlic cloves, crushed
250 g (9 oz) low-fat soft cheese
generous pinch of ground
   nutmeg
generous pinch of dried dill
2.5 ml (^{1}/$_2$ tsp) salt
ground black pepper

1 egg, separated
100 g (3^1/$_2$ oz) Gruyère cheese,
   grated

Thaw spinach completely and drain well in colander. (Frozen spinach takes a long time to thaw, so allow for this. It may be hurried along by immersing the whole packet in cold water.) Remove stalks from mushroom caps and chop finely. Heat oil and lightly fry stalks, onion and garlic. Add spinach and toss a few minutes until mixture is absolutely dry and spinach is cooked. Set aside to cool.

Mix soft cheese, seasonings and egg yolk into spinach mixture. Wipe mushroom caps and arrange on lightly oiled baking dish. Season. Whisk egg white stiffly and fold into spinach mixture. Pile onto mushrooms to cover completely. Sprinkle with Gruyère and bake at 180 °C (350 °F, gas 4) for 25-30 minutes. Serves 4.

Brown Mushrooms with Herb Butter

One of the easiest and most popular of starters and the perfect way of treating large flat mushrooms. Slightly smaller brown mushrooms can be prepared in the same way, and are superb with grilled meat.

6 large brown mushrooms
100 g (3^1/$_2$ oz) butter, softened
2 garlic cloves, crushed
6-8 fresh rosemary needles,
   finely chopped
15 ml (1 tbsp) chopped chives
15 ml (1 tbsp) chopped parsley
5 ml (1 tsp) soy sauce
salt and ground black pepper

Wipe mushrooms. Cut stalks off level with the caps, and chop finely. Arrange caps in a large baking dish. Cream butter with garlic, rosemary, chives, parsley and soy sauce. Divide this

mixture into 6 large pats. Pile the chopped mushroom stalks on top of the caps and season very lightly. Top each mushroom with a pat of the herb butter.

Preheat grill and slide dish underneath. Grill for about 10 minutes until the mushrooms are soft and the butter melted. Serve with fingers of buttered wholemeal bread.
Serves 6.

Chilled Fresh Asparagus Creams

Canned asparagus is useful in salads but the flavour of fresh asparagus is unique. Made with the minimum of ingredients so as not to mask its delicate flavour, the set creams are unmoulded onto small plates and served with mayonnaise.

300 g (11 oz) fresh asparagus
375 ml (12 fl oz) salted water
light chicken stock
10 ml (2 tsp) powdered gelatine
45 ml (3 tbsp) cold water
few drops of lemon juice
4 drops of Tabasco
2 egg whites
100 ml (3$^1/_2$ fl oz) whipping
  cream, whipped
mayonnaise

Rinse asparagus and remove the base of each stalk. If stalks are thick, peel thinly. In a wide, shallow saucepan bring the salted water to the boil, add asparagus in single layer and cook gently for 12 minutes, leaving lid of saucepan slightly tilted. Drain, reserving liquid. Make up reserved liquid to 200 ml (6$^1/_2$ fl oz) with light chicken stock if necessary. Chop asparagus, reserving 6 perfect tips. Purée chopped asparagus and the 200 ml (6$^1/_2$ fl oz) liquid in a blender until smooth, then press through a sieve into a bowl. You should have about 300 ml (10 fl oz) of purée.

Soften gelatine in 45 ml (3 tbsp) cold water and dissolve over low heat. Stir into purée, add lemon juice and Tabasco, then cool, or chill, until mixture thickens. Whisk egg whites with a pinch of salt and fold into mixture together with cream. Adjust seasoning. Pour into 6 rinsed ramekins and allow to set in refrigerator. To serve, run a knife round the edges and unmould onto individual plates. Spread a thin layer of mayonnaise over the tops and place one asparagus tip in the centre of each. If available, place a red oak lettuce leaf at the side, simply for colour.
Serves 6.

Individual Smoked Salmon Cheesecakes (left) and Chicken Liver Pâté (right)

Individual Smoked Salmon Cheesecakes

This light, savoury cheesecake may be set in individual ramekins or on a biscuit crust. Serve with lemon wedges and hot toast.

FILLING
1–2 spring onions
250 g (9 oz) low-fat soft cheese
125 g (4 oz) smoked salmon, finely chopped
100 ml (3¹/₂ fl oz) plain drinking yoghurt
30 ml (2 tbsp) thick mayonnaise
generous pinch of finely grated lemon rind
ground black pepper
10 ml (2 tsp) powdered gelatine
25 ml (5 tsp) cold water
2 egg whites, whisked
125 ml (4 fl oz) whipping cream, whipped

CRUST
125 g (4 oz) savoury cheese biscuits, crushed
60 g (2 oz) butter, melted

Chop spring onions and finely chop a little of the green tops. Mix cheese with salmon, spring onions, yoghurt, mayonnaise, lemon rind and pepper. Soften gelatine in the cold water and dissolve over low heat. Stir gelatine into mixture and fold in egg whites and cream. Pour into individual ramekins, cover and chill for at least 4 hours.

Before serving, grind a little black pepper over each and garnish with lemon rind.

To make the crust, mix crushed biscuits with butter and press onto base of greased 20-cm (8-in) pie dish. Chill. Make filling as described above, pour onto crust, cover and chill for at least 4 hours. Serve sliced in wedges sprinkled with a little ground black pepper.
Serves 6–8.

Chicken Liver Pâté

I thought for a long time before including this recipe, because pâtés on this theme have become standard snack-fare with wholemeal bread. This is, however, such a delicious version that even jaded palates might well be tempted once again.

100 g (3¹/₂ oz) butter
2.5 ml (¹/₂ tsp) dried thyme
2.5 ml (¹/₂ tsp) dried marjoram
1 onion, chopped
500 g (18 oz) chicken livers
2.5 ml (¹/₂ tsp) salt
2 garlic cloves, chopped
generous pinch of ground nutmeg
30 ml (2 tbsp) brandy
60 ml (4 tbsp) sweet sherry
clarified butter (see below)

In a large saucepan melt butter with thyme and marjoram. Fry onion until softened, then add washed, trimmed and sliced chicken livers. Don't overcook, remove from heat when just done, smelling nicely and the gravy beginning to look like gravy. Cool slightly, then spoon into container of blender.

Add remaining ingredients, except clarified butter, and blend until smooth. Pot and pour a little clarified butter over. Mixture will be very soft, but firms up in refrigerator. Chill overnight. Serve with bread, toast fingers or Melba toast. Makes about 400 g (14 oz).

To clarify butter

Cut butter into dice and allow to melt over low heat without browning, skimming off any surface scum. Remove from heat and allow to stand – the yellow liquid which rises to the top is the clarified butter. Cool and strain over pâté.

Leeks with Rosemary Mayonnaise

Leeks with Rosemary Mayonnaise

Buy young, fresh leeks for this unusual starter.

8 leeks
250 ml (8 fl oz) salted chicken stock
2 bay leaves
2 x 7.5 cm (3-in) fresh rosemary sprigs
paprika to garnish

ROSEMARY MAYONNAISE
1 egg
20 ml (4 tsp) lemon juice
2.5 ml (^{1}/$_2$ tsp) salt
200 ml (6^1/$_2$ fl oz) oil
5 ml (1 tsp) sugar
10 ml (2 tsp) Dijon mustard
45 ml (3 tbsp) soured cream

Cut off roots and most of the tops of the leeks, leaving not more than 2.5 cm (1 in) of the green leaves. Remove outside layer. Make a shallow cut down length of leek so that the layers may be opened out slightly. Wash very well to remove grit. Put stock, bay leaves and rosemary sprigs into large frying pan with a lid. Add leeks, bring to boil and simmer, covered, for about 7–10 minutes or until just cooked. Cool in liquid, then drain and chill, reserving rosemary.

To make the mayonnaise, place egg, lemon juice, salt, 30 ml (2 tbsp) oil, sugar and mustard into a blender. Strip needles from the reserved cooked rosemary sprigs and add. Blend well, then with motor running, add remaining oil in a slow steady stream. Tip into small bowl, stir in soured cream, cover and chill for at least 2 hours.

To serve, arrange chilled leeks on serving plates – 2 each should be enough, depending on size. Spoon some mayonnaise down the centre of each serving, and dust with paprika. Serves 4.

Green Bean Salad with Feta Cheese

A favourite bean salad, served as a Greek-style starter, dressed with a herby olive oil dressing and studded with olives and Feta cheese. Use the youngest and slimmest beans you can find, and assemble the salad several hours in advance.

500 g (18 oz) young green beans
2 bay leaves
10 black olives, sliced
1 onion, sliced into rings
1 red pepper, seeded and sliced
Feta cheese

DRESSING
45 ml (3 tbsp) vegetable oil
45 ml (3 tbsp) olive oil
7.5 ml (1^1/$_2$ tsp) dried oregano
25 ml (5 tsp) lemon juice
2.5 ml (^{1}/$_2$ tsp) celery salt
5 ml (1 tsp) thin honey
2 garlic cloves, crushed

First mix ingredients for dressing, cover and stand a few hours for flavour to develop. Shake well before using.

Top and tail beans. Leave them whole if very small, otherwise halve. Poach lightly in a little salted water with the bay leaves. If you tilt the lid of the pot slightly while cooking, you'll retain the bright colour. When just tender, drain well and spoon into a large shallow serving dish. Remove bay leaves and add olives, onion and red pepper.

Pour dressing over, cool, cover and chill for about 4 hours. Sprinkle generously with Feta cheese before serving with chunks of crusty white bread. Serves 4-6.

Asparagus with Lemon Mayonnaise served with French Loaf with Fresh Herb Butter

Asparagus with Lemon Mayonnaise

A timeless old favourite. When asparagus is not in season, substitute slender, young leeks.

300 g (11 oz) fresh asparagus
paprika or chives to garnish

LEMON MAYONNAISE
1 large egg or 2 yolks
25 ml (5 tsp) fresh lemon juice
5 ml (1 tsp) sugar
2.5 ml (¹/₂ tsp) salt
220 ml (7 fl oz) oil
1 garlic clove, crushed
finely grated rind of ¹/₂ lemon
soured cream or whipped cream

To prepare asparagus, rinse gently, then remove base of stalks. If woody, peel thinly. Bring some salted water to the boil in a large shallow saucepan, add asparagus in a single layer and simmer, uncovered, until just tender. Drain and chill.

For the mayonnaise, put egg, lemon juice, sugar, salt and 30 ml (2 tbsp) oil into blender. Blend to mix thoroughly, then with the motor running, pour in remaining oil in a slow, steady stream. Spoon into a small bowl and stir in garlic and lemon rind. Cover and chill for several hours. To thin down before serving, stir in a little soured cream or fold in a few spoonfuls of cream.

Arrange 3–4 asparagus spears on each plate and spoon a ribbon of mayonnaise across each serving. Dust with paprika or sprinkle with snipped chives. Serves 6–8.

French Loaf with Fresh Herb Butter

A welcome change from the ubiquitous garlic bread.

1 large or 2 small French loaves
250 g (9 oz) butter, softened
4 thyme sprigs, chopped
6 sage leaves, chopped
1 oregano sprig, chopped
ground black pepper
30 g (1 oz) parsley, chopped
1 medium onion, grated
5 ml (1 tsp) onion salt
5 ml (1 tsp) prepared mustard

Slice French loaves in 12-mm (¹/₂-in) slices to the base, but not right through. Combine remaining ingredients and butter generously between the slices. Reshape, wrap in foil, leaving the top exposed, and bake at 180 °C (350 °F, gas 4) for 15 minutes. Enough for 30–40 slices.

Tuna Pâté

A tuna pâté with a difference.

6 anchovy fillets
200 g (7 oz) canned tuna in oil
100 g (3¹/₂ oz) butter, melted
10 ml (2 tsp) lemon juice
pinch of sugar
30 ml (2 tbsp) finely chopped parsley
30 ml (2 tbsp) finely chopped chives
30 ml (2 tbsp) thick soured cream

Soak anchovy fillets in milk for 1 hour, then drain. Place in blender with tuna (plus the oil), melted butter, lemon juice and sugar. Blend until smooth, then stir in remaining ingredients. Pot and chill.

Serve at room temperature with Melba toast or unbuttered wholemeal or dark rye bread. Serves about 10 as a snack.

Blue Cheese Mousse

Not everybody likes blue cheese. Used in quantity, it can be very strong and strangely odiferous, rather like old tennis shoes. Used with discretion, however, it adds an interesting tang to a creamy mousse. However, it really depends on personal taste and the type of cheese used, so just taste as you go.

250 g low-fat soft cheese
crumbled blue cheese, starting
    with 15 g ($^1/_2$ oz)
100 ml ($3^1/_2$ fl oz) mayonnaise
2.5 ml ($^1/_2$ tsp) Worcester sauce
2.5 ml ($^1/_2$ tsp) paprika
generous pinch of garlic salt
generous pinch of sugar
15 ml (1 tbsp) powdered gelatine
125 ml (4 fl oz) chicken stock
125 ml (4 fl oz) whipping cream,
    whipped
1 egg white, whisked
30 ml (2 tbsp) finely chopped
    chives

Cream low-fat cheese, blue cheese, mayonnaise, Worcester sauce, paprika, garlic salt and sugar. Soak gelatine in stock, dissolve over low heat, then beat into cheese mixture. Leave until mixture thickens, then fold in cream, egg white and chives. Pour into rinsed mould and chill until set. To unmould, run a knife round the edge and give a gentle shake. Garnish with watercress, parsley, or walnuts. Serve at the end of a meal with biscuits.
Serves 12–14.

Note
Roquefort, the most famous blue-veined cheese, comes from an arid mountain region in France. Here, sheep feed on dry grass and wild herbs and produce a unique, sweet milk from which the cheese is made. Its distinctive flavour develops while the cheese is left to mature inside the limestone caves found in this area.

Potted Roquefort

Potted Cheese with Herbs

Such a simple recipe, but so useful. Use on wholemeal sandwiches, on savoury biscuits, or spread liberally on lightly buttered toast and cooked under the grill until bubbling.

100 ml (3¹/₂ fl oz) milk
60 g (2 oz) butter
150–200 g (5–7 oz) Cheddar cheese, grated
2 eggs, beaten
generous pinch each of dried sage, dry mustard and salt
ground black pepper
1 small garlic clove, peeled
pinch each of sugar and dried thyme

Heat milk and butter in a smallish, heavy saucepan. Add cheese and eggs. Stir over low heat until cheese melts and mixture thickens. Remove from cooker and cool slightly, then pour into blender. Add remaining ingredients and blend until smooth. Spoon into storage container and chill for at least a day before using.
Makes about 250 g (9 oz).

Variation
Heat 10 ml (2 tsp) each butter and oil in a small saucepan and add 1 finely chopped onion and 1 small, skinned and chopped tomato. Cover and sweat over low heat until softened. Beat 2 eggs together with 2.5 ml (¹/₂ tsp) dry mustard. Add to saucepan together with 100 g (3¹/₂ oz) finely grated Gouda cheese. Season with salt and black pepper and cook over low heat, stirring, until mixture thickens and eggs are cooked. Cool and refrigerate.
Makes about 125 g (4 oz).

Potted Roquefort

A splendid addition to the cheese board, either before or after the dessert.

175 g (6 oz) blue cheese
5 ml (1 tsp) Worcester sauce
20 ml (4 tsp) brandy
5 ml (1 tsp) onion salt
100 g (3¹/₂ oz) low-fat smooth cheese
100 ml (3¹/₂ fl oz) double cream
15 ml (1 tbsp) finely chopped parsley
generous pinch of sugar
walnuts to garnish

Grate cheese and mash with remaining ingredients, except walnuts, until smooth. Put into storage container and chill for 12 hours. To serve, form into a square and press halved walnuts all over. Serve with savoury biscuits.
Makes about 200 g (7 oz).

Cream Cheese and Cheddar Roll

250 g (9 oz) cream cheese
225 g (8 oz) Cheddar cheese, very finely grated
2.5 ml (¹/₂ tsp) Worcester sauce
fews drops of Tabasco
15 ml (1 tbsp) brandy
2.5 ml (¹/₂ tsp) French mustard
5 ml (1 tsp) finely grated onion
a little softened butter (optional)
chopped pecan nuts or walnuts

Using a wooden spoon, work all ingredients, except nuts, together until smooth. Roll into a sausage shape (mixture will be fairly soft but firms up in refrigerator), wrap in greaseproof paper and chill overnight. Before serving, roll in nuts until coated.
Makes 20–24 small slices.

Avocado Soup

Not as quick as some avocado soups, but it's reliable and very good, and manages to be smoothly rich without the addition of either egg yolks or cream. May be served either hot or chilled.

30 g (1 oz) butter
45 ml (3 tbsp) flour
375 ml (12 fl oz) hot chicken
    stock
375 ml (12 fl oz) warmed milk
salt and pepper
1 very large or 2 medium, ripe
    but unbruised avocados
10 ml (2 tsp) lemon juice
4 parsley sprigs
1 small spring onion, chopped
pinch of sugar
avocado balls and paprika to
    garnish

Melt butter in saucepan, stir in flour and when absorbed remove from heat and slowly stir in stock and milk. Return to heat and stir until thick and smooth – use a wire whisk to avoid lumps. Season and remove. Mash peeled avocado with lemon juice and add to white sauce together with parsley, spring onion and sugar. Pour into blender and purée until smooth.

To reheat, pour into top of double boiler and stir over simmering water. On no account must the soup boil or even bubble. Check seasoning and serve in individual, heated bowls, garnished with a few avocado balls and a dusting of paprika for colour. Alternatively chill and serve icy cold.
Serves 4–6.

Hint
If this soup is to be refrigerated, sink avocado stone into soup. This helps to preserve the colour.

Gourmet Mushroom Soup

The perennial favourite, but with a difference – here half the mushrooms are cooked and puréed, the rest simmered in the resulting thick broth, finished off with cream and sherry and garnished with fried onion rings.

30 ml (2 tbsp) oil
15 g (^{1}/$_2$ oz) butter
1 onion, chopped
2 leeks, sliced
1 fresh rosemary sprig
300 g (11 oz) brown mushrooms,
    thinly sliced
45 ml (3 tbsp) flour
750 ml (1^1/$_4$ pints) chicken stock
salt and ground black pepper
pinch of ground mace
250 ml (8 fl oz) milk
15 ml (1 tbsp) soy sauce
pinch of sugar
30 ml (2 tbsp) sherry
45 ml (3 tbsp) whipped cream
fried onion rings to garnish

Heat oil and butter, add onion and leeks and allow to soften without browning. Add rosemary and half the mushrooms. Fry gently until soft, then remove rosemary and stir in flour. When well mixed add chicken stock slowly, stirring. Season lightly with salt, pepper and mace. Cover and simmer for 15 minutes. Cool for 10 minutes, then purée until smooth. Return to saucepan, add remaining mushrooms, milk, soy sauce and sugar.

Cover and simmer for 10 minutes, then add sherry and finally swirl in whipped cream. Serve at once garnished with fried onion rings.
Serves 6.

Spiced Pumpkin Soup

A surprisingly lovely soup, smooth and thick, which uses basic ingredients. Serve in individual bowls, top with whipped cream and a sprinkling of paprika, and wait for the compliments.

500 g (18 oz) peeled firm
  pumpkin, cubed
30 ml (2 tbsp) oil
15 g (¹/₂ oz) butter
1 large onion, chopped
2 medium potatoes, peeled and
  cubed
2 carrots, diced
5 ml (1 tsp) ground ginger
5 ml (1 tsp) ground cinnamon
1 litre (1³/₄ pints) chicken stock
250 ml (8 fl oz) milk
5 ml (1 tsp) honey
2.5 ml (¹/₂ tsp) paprika
salt
whipped cream and paprika to
  garnish

Add pumpkin to heated oil and butter, together with onion, potatoes, carrots, ginger and cinnamon. Toss together over low heat for about 5 minutes, then add stock, milk, honey, paprika and salt to taste.
   Bring to boil, half-cover and simmer until vegetables are soft. Cool a little, then purée until smooth. Adjust seasoning, then reheat over low heat, stirring, and serve as suggested.
Serves 6–8.

Cauliflower and Watercress Soup with Blue Cheese Cream

Quite a mouthful, and better than the usual Crème Dubarry. This subtly flavoured vegetable soup, flecked with watercress and topped with savoury whipped cream is very easy to make and grand enough for any dinner party. If you can't find watercress, it may be omitted – but it does add a bit of colour and interest. For a chunkier soup, remove some cauliflower before puréeing soup, then return and reheat gently.

30 ml (2 tbsp) oil
15 g (¹/₂ oz) butter
2 onions, chopped
1 x 500 g (18 oz) cauliflower
1 bunch watercress
1 large potato, peeled and cubed
1 litre (1³/₄ pints) chicken stock
1 bay leaf
500 ml (16 fl oż) milk (skimmed milk may be used)
salt and ground black pepper
pinch of sugar
watercress to garnish

SAVOURY CREAM
125 ml (4 fl oz) double cream
2.5 ml (¹/₂ tsp) Worcester sauce
blue cheese

Make savoury cream in advance and refrigerate. Whip cream with Worcester sauce and cheese – start with a 2.5-cm (1-in) cube and then add more to taste. When thick, cover and chill.

Heat oil and butter in a large saucepan and gently sauté onions. Break cauliflower into florets, wash and add to saucepan. Strip leaves from watercress, wash, then add together with potato. When softened, add stock, bay leaf, milk, seasoning and sugar. The liquid should just cover the vegetables. Half-cover the saucepan and simmer until soft. Remove bay leaf and cool slightly. Purée in blender until smooth. Reheat gently.

To serve, spoon soup into serving bowls and top each serving with a dollop of cream and a sprig of watercress. Serves 6–8.

Quick Minestrone with Pesto

This very simple version of the famous Italian soup is just right for Sunday suppers. A spoonful of pesto stirred into each bowl gives the soup a deliciously different taste. Serve with hot garlic bread.

45 ml (3 tbsp) oil
2 onions, chopped
2 large carrots, diced
2 celery sticks, sliced
1 leek, chopped
2 garlic cloves, crushed
400 g (14 oz) cabbage, shredded
3 tomatoes, skinned and
  chopped
30 ml (2 tbsp) tomato paste
125 g (4 oz) small pasta shells
30 g (1 oz) parsley, chopped
150 g (5 oz) green beans,
  chopped
1.5 litres (2¹/₂ pints) water or
  stock

5 ml (1 tsp) dried oregano
salt and ground black pepper
pinch of sugar
2 bay leaves
pesto (page 31)

Heat oil in a large saucepan and sauté onions, carrots, celery, leek and garlic. When softened, add remaining ingredients, except pesto. Bring to the boil, then cover and simmer for about 1 hour. Remove bay leaves.

If possible, make soup in advance, and reheat for the best flavour. Have the pesto at room temperature and add 5 ml (1 tsp) to each serving.
Serves 8.

Note

If desired, a small triangle of toast may be floated on the soup, and topped with a spoonful of pesto.

Courgette and Green Pepper Soup

A most delicate and delicious soup, which contains neither potatoes, egg yolks nor cream. It is lower in calories than most smooth soups, and yet the texture is beautifully creamy.

30 ml (2 tbsp) oil
1 large green pepper, seeded and
  diced
1 small onion, chopped
2 leeks, sliced
500 g (18 oz) courgettes
1 bay leaf
750 ml (1¹/₄ pints) chicken stock
few parsley sprigs
2.5 ml (¹/₂ tsp) salt
45 g (1¹/₂ oz) skimmed milk
  powder
125 ml (4 fl oz) milk

Heat oil in a large saucepan and add green pepper, onion and leeks. Cover saucepan and sweat over low heat until softened. Add trimmed, pared and sliced courgettes and toss to mix, then add bay leaf, stock, parsley and salt. Cover and simmer for about 20 minutes until vegetables are soft.

Blend milk powder with milk, add to soup, then purée in blender. Adjust seasoning and reheat without boiling, or cool and chill. Serve garnished with green pepper and sliced courgettes.
Serves 4–6.

Fish and Mussel Soup

A hearty and delicious soup, just right for an informal supper and great served with Anchovy French bread.

30 ml (2 tbsp) oil
15 g (¹/₂ oz) butter
1 large onion, chopped
1 garlic clove, crushed
3 tomatoes, skinned and
  chopped
2 carrots, finely diced
2 potatoes, peeled and diced
45 ml (3 tbsp) chopped parsley
400 g (14oz) fresh or frozen
  white fish fillets
1 litre (1¾ pints) fish stock (see
  below)
1 bay leaf
5 ml (1 tsp) dried dill
salt and ground black pepper
pinch of sugar
275 g (10 oz) canned mussels
45 ml (3 tbsp) sherry

Heat oil and butter in a large saucepan and soften onion and garlic. Add tomatoes, carrots, potatoes and parsley. When vegetables are softened, place fish on top, then add stock, bay leaf, dill, seasoning and sugar. Cover and simmer for about 20 minutes until cooked. When cool enough to handle, remove fish and discard skin and bones, if any, then flake it and return to saucepan. Reheat without boiling, adding mussels plus their liquid and sherry.
Serves 6 generously.

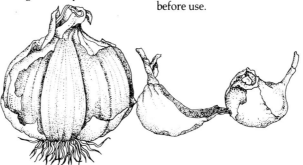

Fish Stock

750-900 g (1³/₄–2 lb) fish
  trimmings
1 onion, sliced
a few parsley sprigs
1 bay leaf
salt
1 small carrot
6 black peppercorns
150 ml (5 fl oz) white wine
1 litre (1³/₄ pints) water

Combine all the ingredients and simmer for 45 minutes. Strain before use.

Anchovy French Bread

250 g (9 oz) unsalted butter
60 g (2 oz) canned anchovies
pinch of paprika
45 ml (3 tbsp) finely chopped
  parsley
a few drops of lemon juice
1 French loaf

Mash butter with remaining ingredients, except bread. Slice bread to base, but not right through, in 15-mm (³/₄-in) slices, and spread generously with anchovy butter. Wrap in foil, leaving top exposed. Bake at 180 °C (350 °F, gas 4) for 15–20 minutes.

Hint

To remove excess saltiness, soak anchovies in milk before using.

Lentil and Vegetable Soup

This is a nourishing, speedy and meatless soup. Low in cost, it is a meal in itself served with wholemeal bread and cheese and perfect for Sunday suppers. Use red lentils, which cook to a pulp very quickly. Do not soak them, simply rinse them.

45 ml (3 tbsp) oil
1 large onion, chopped
1–2 garlic cloves, crushed
2.5 ml (^{1}/$_2$ tsp) dried thyme
2 large carrots, coarsely grated
200 g (7 oz) red lentils
1.5 litres (2^3/$_4$ pints) stock or 1.5 litres (2^3/$_4$ pints) water with 15 ml (1 tbsp) Marmite
45 g (1^1/$_2$ oz) parsley, chopped
1 bay leaf
225 g (8 oz) cabbage, shredded
15 ml (1 tbsp) tomato paste
5 ml (1 tsp) each salt and sugar
5 ml (1 tsp) Worcester sauce

Heat the oil in a large saucepan and add onion, garlic, thyme and carrots. Stir-fry for a few minutes and then add remaining ingredients. Bring to the boil, then cover and simmer for 20 minutes, stirring once or twice. For best flavour, allow to cool and then reheat before serving. Remove bay leaf and adjust seasoning. Serve with 5 ml (1 tsp) pesto (page 31) stirred into each serving, and Cheddar thins.
Serves 6.

Cheddar Thins

Crisp, savoury biscuits which go well with most soups.

225 g (8 oz) Cheddar cheese, coarsely grated
125 g (4 oz) butter
225 g (8 oz) flour
2.5 ml (^{1}/$_2$ tsp) salt
5 ml (1 tsp) dry mustard
paprika or sesame seeds

Cream cheese and butter. Add flour sifted with salt and mustard. Knead well until smooth. Roll into two 4-cm (1^1/$_2$-in) diameter sausages and wrap in greaseproof paper. Chill for 2–3 hours. Slice into 5-mm (^{1}/$_4$-in) thick rounds.
    Arrange on lightly oiled baking sheet and sprinkle with paprika or sesame seeds. Bake at 180 °C (350 °F, gas 4) for about 12 minutes. Allow to crisp for a few seconds before removing to a cake rack to cool. Makes 60.

Traditional Pesto

125 g (4 oz) fresh basil leaves
45 g (1^1/$_2$ oz) parsley sprigs
2 garlic cloves, chopped
45 ml (3 tbsp) chopped walnuts or pine nuts
60 g (2 oz) Parmesan cheese, grated
15 g (^{1}/$_2$ oz) butter, softened (optional)
about 75 ml (2^1/$_2$ fl oz) olive oil
salt and ground black pepper

Using the grinding blade, process all the ingredients except the oil and seasoning. With the motor running, slowly add oil in a steady stream to make a thick green purée. Season, then spoon into jars, run a thin film of oil over the top and refrigerate.

Carrot and Orange Soup

A cold, creamy, surprising soup with a lovely colour.

30 ml (2 tbsp) oil
a nut of butter
6–8 carrots, pared and diced
1 large onion, sliced
2 medium potatoes, cubed
1 litre (1³/₄ pints) chicken stock
500 ml (16 fl oz) milk
grated rind of 1 small orange
salt
2.5 ml (¹/₂ tsp) paprika
1 bay leaf
4 parsley sprigs
fresh orange juice (optional)
250 ml (8 fl oz) single cream or
    milk
whipped cream
thin strips of orange rind
snipped chives

Heat oil and butter in large saucepan and add carrots, onions and potatoes. Allow to soften without browning, then add stock, milk, orange rind, salt, paprika, bay leaf and parsley. Half-cover saucepan and simmer until vegetables are soft. Cool, remove bay leaf, and purée in blender until smooth. The addition of freshly squeezed orange juice at this stage is optional – it will sharpen the flavour somewhat, and up to 125 ml (4 fl oz) may be added.

Stir in cream, or milk (or 125 ml (4 fl oz) of each), adjust seasoning, then chill thoroughly. Serve in cold bowls, garnished with whipped cream, thin strips of orange rind and snipped chives.
Serves 8.

Chilled Courgette and Cucumber Soup

Delicate in both flavour and colour and lightly spiked with mint.

30 ml (2 tbsp) oil
15 g ($^1/_2$ oz) butter
400 g (14 oz) courgettes, peeled and sliced
1 onion, chopped
$^1/_2$ large cucumber, peeled and diced
1 large potato, peeled and diced
750 ml (1$^1/_4$ pints) chicken stock
250 ml (8 fl oz) milk
2 bay leaves
finely grated rind of 1 small lemon
a few parsley sprigs
salt and ground black pepper
pinch of sugar
10 fresh mint leaves

Heat oil and butter in a large saucepan and add courgettes, onion and cucumber. Allow to soften without browning. Add potato, stock, milk, bay leaves, lemon rind, parsley, seasonings and sugar.

Half-cover and simmer for about 25 minutes until soft. Cool, remove bay leaves, and add mint leaves. Purée in a blender until smooth. Adjust seasoning and chill thoroughly.

Serve in chilled soup bowls, garnished with lightly whipped cream and finely grated courgette.
Serves 6–8.

Iced Celery Soup

Madame de Pompadour, it is said, used to drink hot celery soup to rouse her passions. That's why I feel it's safer to serve this soup cold.

30 ml (2 tbsp) oil
nut of butter
5 celery sticks, chopped
1 large onion or 4 leeks, chopped
2 large potatoes, peeled and cubed
45 g (1$^1/_2$ oz) parsley, chopped
750 ml (1$^1/_4$ pints) seasoned chicken stock
250 ml (8 fl oz) milk
generous pinch of celery salt
1 bay leaf
2.5 ml ($^1/_2$ tsp) dried basil
pinch of sugar
125 ml (4 fl oz) single cream

Heat oil and butter in a large saucepan and add celery, onion or leeks, potatoes and parsley. Sauté gently for 5 minutes, tossing now and then. Add remaining ingredients, except cream, cover saucepan, tilt lid slightly, and simmer gently for about 20 minutes until vegetables are very soft.

Cool soup slightly, remove bay leaf and purée in blender until smooth. Pour into storage container, stir in cream, and chill very well before serving in chilled bowls.
Serves 8.

Hint

To serve hot, return soup to saucepan after puréeing. Reheat gently and swirl in cream. Stir until very hot, without boiling.

Tomato Salad with Soured Cream and Blue Cheese or Basil

Very good with curry or grills.

$^1/_2$ large onion, thinly sliced
    into rings
3 large, firm tomatoes, thinly
    sliced
salt and ground black pepper
sugar
100 ml ($3^1/_2$ fl oz) soured cream
nut of blue cheese
5 ml (1 tsp) brandy
snipped chives

Blanch onion rings by pouring
boiling water over, leaving for
5 minutes and then draining.
Spread half tomato slices over
bottom of smallish, shallow salad
bowl. Cover with half the onion
slices. Sprinkle with salt, pepper
and sugar. Repeat tomato and
onion layers and season.
    Whisk cream and cheese
together until cream stiffens and
cheese is thoroughly broken up.
Stir in brandy. Taste and add
more blue cheese, if desired.
Alternatively, omit blue cheese
and add about 8 chopped fresh
basil leaves to the soured cream
and brandy. Spoon over tomato-
onion slices, sprinkle with chives
and chill for 30 minutes. Don't
leave this standing for too long
because it will weep.
Serves 4.

Hint
Blue cheese adds a tasty tang to
a green bean salad. Combine
400 g (14 oz) cooked beans with
chopped, blanched onion and red
pepper. Season and add grated
blue cheese to taste. Mix 45 ml
(3 tbsp) French dressing
(page 47) with 25 ml (5 tsp)
soured cream. Toss with hot
vegetables, cool, then cover
and chill.

Chinese Cabbage and Fennel Salad with Sherry Dressing

Chinese Cabbage and Fennel Salad with Sherry Dressing

A marvellous mixture of raw salad ingredients – particularly good with pork.

500 g (18 oz) Chinese cabbage, shredded
250 g (9 oz) courgettes, scrubbed and thinly sliced
2 leeks, thinly shredded
150 g (5 oz) mung bean sprouts
1 bulb fennel, thinly sliced
toasted almonds to garnish (optional)

DRESSING
60 ml (4 tbsp) oil
5 ml (1 tsp) lemon juice
30 ml (2 tbsp) sherry
generous pinch of ground ginger
pinch of sugar
35 ml (7 tsp) soy sauce

Put cabbage into a large bowl and add courgettes, leeks and sprouts. Blanch fennel in boiling water for 2 minutes, drain and add to rest of salad.

Mix oil, lemon juice, sherry, ginger and sugar and pour over vegetables, tossing until glistening. Cover and leave for 1–2 hours. Just before serving, add soy sauce and toss well. Garnish with toasted almonds, if desired.
Serves 6.

Note
The bulbous Florentine fennel is the one used in cooking, and is not to be confused with wild fennel. Trim the root end and top, remove the outer layer, and scrub the bulb.

Cheese and Cucumber Mould

Surround with marinated mushrooms and serve as an eye-catching salad at a cold buffet.

1 medium cucumber
250 g (9 oz) low-fat soft cheese
125 ml (4 fl oz) mayonnaise
125 ml (4 fl oz) soured cream
5 ml (1 tsp) sugar
20 ml (4 tsp) powdered gelatine
125 ml (4 fl oz) chicken stock
generous pinch of celery salt
2.5 ml ($^1/_2$ tsp) dried dill
30 ml (2 tbsp) chopped chives
45 ml (3 tbsp) finely chopped parsley
2 egg whites, stiffly whisked

Peel, slice, seed and chop cucumber finely, reserving a chunk to slice into thin rings for the garnish.

Beat together low-fat cheese, mayonnaise, soured cream and sugar. Sprinkle gelatine over stock to soften, then stir over low heat to dissolve gelatine. Cool slightly and beat into cheese mixture. Add celery salt and dill. Stir in cucumber, chives and parsley, then fold in egg whites. Pour into a rinsed soufflé dish and set in refrigerator. Unmould when firm and garnish with reserved cucumber. Serves 8.

Hint
To make marinated mushrooms, heat 30 ml (2 tbsp) oil and 30 g (1 oz) butter and fry 400 g (14 oz) small, white button mushrooms. When brown and soft, remove with slotted spoon to serving dish. To pan juices add 1 medium onion, grated, 1–2 crushed garlic cloves, 100 ml ($3^1/_2$ fl oz) white wine, 2.5 ml ($^1/_2$ tsp) each paprika, salt and sugar. Simmer, stirring, for 2 minutes. Add 10 ml (2 tsp) basil. Pour over mushrooms, cool, cover and chill.

Green Bean, Cucumber, Feta and Nut Salad

Easy to prepare in advance, this attractive, special-occasion salad should be served in a large, shallow dish. It is particularly good with grilled chicken or garlicky lamb.

500 g (18 oz) young, slender
 green beans
2 large fresh rosemary sprigs
1/3 cucumber, cut in julienne
salt and ground black pepper
Feta cheese
pecan nuts

DRESSING
25 ml (5 tsp) lemon juice
2.5 ml (1/2 tsp) prepared mustard
generous pinch of salt
1 garlic clove
2 parsley sprigs
1 spring onion, chopped
100 ml (31/2 fl oz) oil

Top, tail and halve beans and cook, with rosemary, in a minimum amount of water. Leave pan half-covered to retain the bright colour, and don't overcook. Arrange beans in salad bowl, add cucumber. Finely chop a little of the rosemary and add to beans together with seasoning.
  Blend all the ingredients for the dressing in a blender, pour over vegetables, toss to coat and then leave, covered, to marinate for a few hours. Just before serving, top generously with crumbled Feta and sprinkle with chopped pecan nuts.
Serves 6–8.

Hints
Feta is a salty cheese and it is advisable to rinse and pat dry before using.

The flavour of pecan nuts is enhanced by toasting them lightly in the oven.

Courgette Salad with Sprouts, Apples and Almonds

A crunchy, nutritious raw salad, good as part of a cold buffet.

250 g (9 oz) courgettes, peeled
   and coarsely grated
225 g (8 oz) lentil sprouts
2 Granny Smith apples, peeled
   and coarsely grated
30 g (1 oz) seedless raisins
toasted, flaked almonds

DRESSING
100 ml (3¹/₂ fl oz) oil
45 ml (3 tbsp) lemon juice
15 ml (1 tbsp) soy sauce
1 garlic clove, halved
10 ml (2 tsp) honey
1 pickling onion, quartered
30 ml (2 tbsp) mayonnaise
a few parsley sprigs

Mix courgettes with sprouts, apples and raisins.

Put all ingredients for dressing into blender and blend until creamy. Toss vegetables with dressing, spoon into salad bowl, cover with plastic wrap and chill for several hours. Scatter almonds over top of salad just before serving.
Serves 6.

Hint
Growing your own sprouts is easy. Buy a perforated top for a jar (or use cheese cloth and an elastic band) and mung beans, lentils, alfalfa and so on from your nearest health food shop. Rinse and soak 90 g (3 oz) in the jar overnight. Next day drain and place jar in a cupboard at an angle so that all the water will run off. Rinse and drain sprouts twice a day. Once sprouted, rinse, dry well and refrigerate.

Tomato Salad with Basil and Italian Cheese

The simplest of salads, brought to life with fresh basil. Serve as a side dish with pasta, or add black olives and anchovies and serve as a light starter.

4 firm, medium-sized tomatoes
1 onion, thinly sliced into rings
25 ml (5 tsp) finely chopped
   fresh basil (firmly packed to
   measure)
ground black pepper
sugar
Mozzarella, coarsely grated

DRESSING
30 ml (2 tbsp) oil (garlic,
   preferably)
10 ml (2 tsp) lemon juice
pinch each of salt, sugar and dry
   mustard

Plunge tomatoes into boiling water, leave for a few minutes, then slip off skins and slice thinly. Pour boiling water over onion slices, stand for 5 minutes, then drain. Arrange tomatoes and onions on flat salad dish and sprinkle with basil. Grind over a little pepper and sprinkle with a little sugar to bring out the flavour. Cover thinly with grated cheese. If preparing in advance, cover and leave.

Mix together ingredients for dressing and pour over salad 15 minutes before serving.
Do not toss.
Serves 4–6.

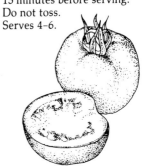

Brown Rice Salad with Mushrooms

Brown Rice Salad with Mushrooms

Specially good with cold chicken. I like unpolished rice for this salad, but quick-cooking, white rice can be substituted, in which case simply adjust the cooking time, and reduce stock to 750 ml (1¹/₄ pints).

300 g (11 oz) brown rice
2.5 ml (¹/₂ tsp) salt
800 ml (26 fl oz) chicken stock
5 ml (1 tsp) dried tarragon
30 ml (2 tbsp) oil
30 g (1 oz) butter
250–300 g (9–11 oz) brown mushrooms, sliced
1 green pepper, seeded and diced
25 ml (5 tsp) soy sauce
ground black pepper
60 g (2 oz) parsley, finely chopped
6 spring onions, chopped

Put rice, salt, stock and tarragon into a saucepan, bring to the boil, cover, turn heat to very low and leave for 50 minutes without looking.

Meanwhile prepare mushrooms: Heat oil and butter and add mushrooms and green pepper. Sauté until just softened, remove from heat, add soy sauce and pepper to taste, then cover and stand until rice is cooked. Spoon rice into large bowl – the grains should be separate and dry. Using a fork, add mushroom mixture, including all the juices, and toss. Add parsley and spring onions, then cover and cool, or chill until required. Serves 8.

Note

Wipe cultivated mushrooms clean with a damp cloth, or carefully wash under running water, with the gill side down. Wipe dry and use immediately. Do not soak or wash mushrooms before storing.

Greek Salad

Perfect with roast lamb, or Stifado (page 77), or served as a first course, in which case include a handful of crisply fried croûtons.

2 garlic cloves
45 ml (3 tbsp) olive oil
15 ml (1 tbsp) lemon juice
2.5 ml (¹/₂ tsp) salt
ground black pepper
Feta cheese
half a small lettuce, coarsely shredded
12–18 stoned black olives, sliced
1 large tomato, chopped
¹/₄ cucumber
1 green pepper
1 medium onion, thinly sliced into rings
pinch of sugar
croûtons (optional)

Crush garlic directly into wooden salad bowl. Add oil. Using a wooden spoon, stir in lemon juice, salt and pepper. Add as much crumbled Feta as you like, cover and stand for an hour or so. Just before serving add lettuce, olives, tomato, and peeled, seeded and diced cucumber.

Slice green pepper into thin strips and discard seeds. Place in a bowl with onion and sugar, cover with boiling water and stand for a few minutes. Drain, add to salad and toss well. Add croûtons at this stage if desired. Serves 4–6.

Green Salad with Herb Croûtons

Green Salad with Herb Croûtons

A crisp, green salad that is slightly more interesting than the usual tossed salad. Most of the preparation can be done in advance.

1 small head lettuce
$^1/_2$ small bunch young spinach
1 large avocado, cubed
4 spring onions, chopped
1 garlic clove, crushed
2.5 ml ($^1/_2$ tsp) salt
15 ml (1 tbsp) lemon juice
2.5 ml ($^1/_2$ tsp) Worcester sauce
45 ml (3 tbsp) oil
sliced hard-boiled egg to garnish

CROÛTONS
2 thick slices stale white bread
30 ml (2 tbsp) oil
30 g (1 oz) butter
5 ml (1 tsp) mixed dried herbs
onion salt

Wash and shred lettuce and spinach – have these two in roughly equal quantities. Add avocado and spring onions. Into a wooden salad bowl put garlic, salt, lemon juice and Worcester sauce. Stir in oil, add greens and toss. Top with herb croûtons and toss again. Garnish with sliced hard-boiled egg.

To make croûtons, remove crusts from bread and cut into small cubes. Heat oil, butter and dried herbs and fry bread cubes until brown. Drain on absorbent kitchen paper and sprinkle with onion salt.

To make in advance, prepare and chill greens, except avocado. Have dressing standing ready in salad bowl. Make croûtons and set aside. Combine just before dinner, and garnish with hard-boiled egg.
Serves 6.

Broccoli Salad with Creamy Curry Dressing

A chunky, colourful salad which looks particularly attractive served in one of those shallow, pizza-type earthenware dishes. It makes an eye-catching addition to any cold buffet.

500–600 g (18 oz-1 lb 5 oz) broccoli
salt and ground black pepper
1 red pepper, seeded
2 leeks, thinly sliced
2.5–5 ml ($^1/_2$-1 tsp) curry powder
2.5–5 ml ($^1/_2$-1 tsp) turmeric
10 ml (2 tsp) boiling water
125 ml (4 fl oz) thick mayonnaise
125 ml (4 fl oz) buttermilk
toasted flaked almonds

Cut away lower tough ends of broccoli stalks. Chop stems coarsely and break off florets. Poach stems in a little boiling water until softened. Add florets and cook until just tender, keeping lid of saucepan tilted (this retains the bright colour). When just cooked, drain, if necessary, spoon into salad bowl and season.

Cut pepper into thin strips. Pour boiling water over leeks and pepper to blanch, stand for a few minutes, drain and spoon on top of broccoli. Put curry powder and turmeric in a cup, pour over the boiling water and stand for 5 minutes, then stir into mayonnaise mixed with buttermilk. Pour over vegetables and sprinkle generously with almonds. May be chilled for an hour or two before serving.
Serves 6.

Green Salad with Walnuts

A crisp and crunchy salad with a
light, creamy dressing.

250 g (9 oz) lettuce, shredded
250 g (9 oz) young spinach
$^1/_2$ cucumber, peeled and diced
1 apple, peeled and diced
1 celery stick, thinly sliced
60 g (2 oz) walnuts, chopped

DRESSING
45 g (1$^1/_2$ oz) blue cheese
45 ml (3 tbsp) oil
125 ml (4 fl oz) buttermilk
a few drops of Worcester sauce

Make dressing first. Crumble
cheese into a bowl and mash
with a fork. Slowly mix in oil.
When this becomes a smooth
paste, stir in buttermilk and
Worcester sauce. Whisk well
with a rotary whisk, cover and
chill for 1–2 hours.
   Put lettuce and spinach into
salad bowl. Add cucumber, apple
and celery. Toss to mix and then
pour dressing over. Sprinkle
with walnuts, and serve.
Serves 4–6.

Variation

GREEN SALAD WITH YOGHURT
DRESSING
A light, refreshing salad to serve
with curry.

DRESSING
200 ml (6$^1/_2$ fl oz) drinking
   yoghurt
30 ml (2 tbsp) oil
5 ml (1 tsp) lemon juice
generous pinch of paprika
$^1/_2$ medium onion, thinly sliced
45 ml (3 tbsp) chopped parsley
5 ml (1 tsp) sugar
1 garlic clove crushed with
   generous pinch of salt

Put dressing ingredients into a
wooden salad bowl, stir well,
then cover and leave for about 2
hours. When ready to serve, add
green salad leaves and toss well.
Serves 4–6.

Chinese Green Salad with Ginger and Almonds

A combination of crisp green leaves, ginger and soy sauce, this salad is marvellous with pork dishes, or may even be served as a light starter.

750 g (1³/₄ lb) Chinese cabbage, shredded
250 g (9 oz) courgettes, scrubbed and thinly sliced
2 leeks, thinly sliced
2 knobs preserved ginger, cut in slivers
25 ml (5 tsp) soy sauce
25 ml (5 tsp) ginger syrup
25 ml (5 tsp) oil
5 ml (1 tsp) lemon juice
halved, toasted almonds

Toss cabbage, courgettes, leeks and ginger in a large bowl. Mix soy sauce and ginger syrup, add to vegetables and mix well. Mix oil with lemon juice and add. Toss until glistening, then cover securely and stand for about 2–3 hours.
   Spoon into a salad bowl, and top with almonds.
Serves 6–8.

Spinach, Mushroom and Blue Cheese Salad

A fresh, raw salad with a lovely tang.

1 bunch young spinach
¹/₂ bunch spring onions, chopped
125 g (4 oz) mushrooms, sliced

DRESSING
2 x 2.5-cm (1-in) cubes blue cheese (or more to taste)
1 garlic clove, crushed
75 ml (2¹/₂ fl oz) oil (half olive, if liked)
30 ml (2 tbsp) tarragon or garlic vinegar
5 ml (1 tsp) Worcester sauce
salt
ground black pepper
pinch of sugar

Begin with the dressing. Grate cheese coarsely into wooden salad bowl. Add remaining ingredients, stir to mix and allow to stand for at least 30 minutes.
   Wash spinach, discard ribs and stems, then dry and shred – you should have about 400 g (14 oz). Add to dressing together with spring onions and mushrooms. Toss well, then cover and leave for 15 minutes, to allow flavours to blend, before serving. Serves 6.

Variation

HERB DRESSING
An alternative dressing may be made with fresh basil.

Blend 100 ml (3¹/₂ fl oz) oil, 25 ml (5 tsp) lemon juice, generous pinch of salt, 2.5 ml (¹/₂ tsp) sugar, 5 ml (1 tsp) Dijon mustard, few parsley sprigs, 1–2 chopped garlic cloves, 12 fresh basil leaves. Pour into a jar, cover and leave for 1 hour. Shake well before using.

Mushroom Bean Salad with Sherry Dressing

Choose slim, young green beans to make this salad, which goes particularly well with steak or chicken.

250 ml (8 fl oz) seasoned chicken stock
5 ml (1 tsp) dried marjoram
250 g (9 oz) green beans, trimmed and halved
1 onion, sliced into rings
200 g (7 oz) mushrooms, sliced
nut of butter
hard-boiled eggs, marjoram sprigs or toasted almonds to garnish

DRESSING
30 ml (2 tbsp) oil
30 ml (2 tbsp) sweet sherry
15 ml (1 tbsp) soy sauce
pinch of salt

Put stock into a saucepan, rub marjoram to crush, and add. Bring to boil, then add beans, onion, mushrooms and butter. Cook, partially covered, until just tender, tossing once or twice. Using a slotted spoon, remove to shallow salad bowl.
Mix ingredients for dressing and pour over warm vegetables. Cool, cover and chill for about 4 hours. Garnish just before serving.
Serves 4–6.

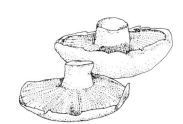

Broccoli and Mushroom Salad with Creamy Cheese Dressing

A colourful and nourishing salad to set off a spread at a cold buffet. The combination of lightly cooked broccoli with raw mushrooms is delicious, but green beans, red peppers and/or cauliflower would make good alternatives.

500 g (18 oz) broccoli
salt and ground black pepper
300 g (11 oz) white or brown mushrooms, wiped and sliced
2 spring onions
250 g (9 oz) low-fat soft cheese
170 ml (5½ fl oz) buttermilk or plain drinking yoghurt
45 ml (3 tbsp) thick mayonnaise
45 ml (3 tbsp) chopped parsley
5–10 ml (1–2 tsp) honey

generous pinch of celery salt
1–2 pickled gherkins, chopped
paprika
chopped walnuts or toasted almonds

Trim broccoli and slice lengthways. Poach in a little boiling water until just tender. Drain, chop coarsely and arrange in large, shallow bowl. Season, then add mushrooms. Chop spring onions, including a little of the tops, and combine with the remaining ingredients, except paprika and nuts, using a wooden spoon, not a blender. Pour over vegetables, mixing very lightly to coat thoroughly. Dust with paprika and top with nuts. Cover and set aside for an hour or two, or chill until required. Serve at room temperature.
Serves 6–8.

Mushroom Salad

Soaked in a little sherry-flavoured dressing, these mushrooms can be served as a super, low-calorie side dish, tossed with green leaves and extra dressing to make a special salad, or enriched with a little soured cream or yoghurt and then piled into avocado halves as a delicate starter.

300 g (11 oz) button mushrooms, wiped and thinly sliced
6 slim spring onions, finely chopped

MARINADE
30 ml (2 tbsp) olive oil
30 ml (2 tbsp) vegetable oil
45 ml (3 tbsp) sherry
15 ml (1 tbsp) soy sauce
pinch of sugar
ground black pepper

Spoon mushrooms into a large, shallow salad bowl. Add spring onions. Mix ingredients for marinade, pour over mushrooms, toss to moisten and then cover and chill, preferably overnight.
Serves 6–8 as a starter or will fill 8–10 avocado halves.

Pineapple Rice Salad

200 g (7 oz) long-grain white rice
500 ml (16 fl oz) salted water
250 g (9 oz) canned pineapple pieces in natural juice
75 ml (2^1/$_2$ fl oz) oil
2.5 ml (^{1}/$_2$ tsp) dry mustard
15 ml (1 tbsp) soy sauce
1 green pepper, seeded and finely chopped
1 celery stick, thinly sliced
45 g (1^1/$_2$ oz) seedless raisins

Put rice into saucepan, add water and bring to the boil. Cover and simmer on very low heat for about 20 minutes, until cooked.
Meanwhile, make the dressing. Drain pineapple and reserve 45 ml (3 tbsp) of the juice. Mix oil, mustard, soy sauce and pineapple juice. Tip cooked rice into bowl and immediately fork in the dressing. Add green pepper, celery and raisins. Chop pineapple and add. Allow to cool, then cover and chill for a few hours. Serves 6–8.

Mushroom Salad

Bulgar Salad with Tomatoes and Black Olives

Bulgar wheat is used extensively in the Middle East. The grains are first soaked and then toasted, after which they need only be soaked in water. It makes a delicious and unusual salad and can also be served as a light first course, with cheese or with hummus and pitta bread.

250 g (9 oz) bulgar wheat
6 small spring onions, finely chopped
30 g (1 oz) parsley, finely chopped
30 ml (2 tbsp) fresh mint, finely chopped
2 medium tomatoes, chopped
black olives, sliced
lettuce, mint and sliced cucumber to garnish

DRESSING
45 ml (3 tbsp) vegetable oil
45 ml (3 tbsp) olive oil
30 ml (2 tbsp) lemon juice
1 garlic clove, crushed
salt and ground black pepper
2.5 ml ($^1/_2$ tsp) dried oregano

Mix ingredients for dressing first and stand for several hours to blend flavours.

Soak bulgar wheat in water to cover generously for about 1 hour. Drain in colander, and squeeze out excess moisture with hands. Put into a large bowl and add spring onions, parsley and mint. Pour over prepared dressing, toss, cover and stand 30 minutes. Adjust seasoning and then fold in tomatoes and olives. Serve garnished with lettuce, mint and sliced cucumber.
Serves 6.

Broccoli, Leek and Carrot Salad with Orange Dressing

A colourful salad, with a light and subtle dressing.

450 g (1 lb) broccoli florets
3 leeks
5 carrots, cut in julienne
salt and ground black pepper

DRESSING
100 ml (3¹/₂ fl oz) oil
100 ml (3¹/₂ fl oz) fresh orange juice
generous pinch of finely grated orange rind
generous pinch of salt
2.5 ml (¹/₂ tsp) prepared mustard
2.5 ml (¹/₂ tsp) honey
5 ml (1 tsp) finely chopped parsley

Trim broccoli and divide thinly lengthways. Wash and slice leeks, white parts only. Cook broccoli, leeks and carrots in a minimum amount of boiling water in a large saucepan until tender-crisp. Drain if necessary and spoon into large, shallow salad bowl. Season.

Mix ingredients for dressing and pour over hot salad ingredients, using just enough dressing to moisten vegetables thoroughly. Allow to cool, tossing gently once or twice. Cover and stand for about 1 hour before serving. Serves 8.

Hint
Vegetables such as broccoli and green beans, especially when served as a salad, should be bright green and crisp. Keep the lid of the saucepan tilted to retain the colour.

Stir-fried Green Bean Salad with Pecan Nuts

Use the most slender, youngest French beans you can find for this super salad, which is particularly good to serve with beef or tongue.

500 g (18 oz) green beans
45 ml (3 tbsp) oil
2 garlic cloves, crushed
15 ml (1 tbsp) soy sauce
45 ml (3 tbsp) sherry
2.5 ml (¹/₂ tsp) dried basil
60 g (2 oz) pecan nuts, coarsely chopped

Top and tail beans and halve if necessary. Heat oil in a large frying pan and stir-fry beans and garlic for about 5 minutes. Reduce heat and add soy sauce, sherry and basil. Cover and cook over very low heat, stirring occasionally, until just tender. Spoon into shallow salad bowl, including juices, and toss in pecans. Cool, cover and stand for about 1 hour before serving. Serves 4–6.

Hint
To retain the freshness of shelled nuts, put them in the freezer immediately after purchasing.

Green Bean, Red Pepper and Anchovy Salad

Green Bean, Red Pepper and Anchovy Salad

This bright, robust salad goes particularly well with pasta dishes but may also be served as a light first course. It is important not to overcook the vegetables – the beans should retain their cheerful colour and the pepper and onion rings be blanched only briefly to take the edge off their bite.

500 g (18 oz) young green beans
1 red pepper
1 onion, thinly sliced
60 g (2 oz) canned rolled fillets
    of anchovy with capers

DRESSING
45 ml (3 tbsp) vegetable oil
25 ml (5 tsp) olive oil
25 ml (5 tsp) lemon juice
generous pinch of salt

2.5 ml (¹/₂ tsp) sugar
2.5 ml (¹/₂ tsp) dried tarragon

Top, tail and halve beans, or if very slender leave them whole. Cook in a minimum amount of salted water until just tender – leave lid of saucepan tilted to retain colour. Drain in a colander. Don't be tempted to refresh under cold water as they'll absorb the dressing better if hot. While beans are cooking, seed and cut red pepper into thin strips. Pour boiling water over pepper and onion, stand for 2 minutes, then drain. Spoon vegetables into a shallow salad dish.

Mix ingredients for dressing and pour over hot vegetables. When cool, cover and chill several hours to allow dressing to be absorbed. Soak anchovies in milk for 15 minutes to remove excess salt and arrange on top of salad just before serving.
Serves 4–6.

Chinese Rice Salad with Almonds

A super combination of different salad ingredients, flavours and textures. I prefer using brown rice but white may be substituted.

200 g (7 oz) brown rice
300 g (10 oz) lentil sprouts
225 g (8 oz) canned water
    chestnuts, drained and sliced
2 celery sticks, finely chopped
4–6 spring onions, chopped
250 g (9 oz) canned pineapple
    rings in natural juice
100 g (3¹/₂ oz) toasted flaked
    almonds

DRESSING
45 ml (3 tbsp) oil
25 ml (5 tsp) soy sauce
1 knob root ginger, peeled and
    grated
5 ml (1 tsp) sugar
10 ml (2 tsp) lemon juice

First mix together the dressing ingredients, then boil rice as usual until fluffy and dry. Toss dressing with rice while still hot. Add lentil sprouts, water chestnuts, celery and spring onions. Drain pineapple and reserve 100 ml (3¹/₂ fl oz) of the juice. Pat dry and cube 4 rings of pineapple and add to rice mixture. Moisten with reserved pineapple juice, then cover and chill for a few hours or overnight.

To serve, pile onto serving dish and top with almonds.
Serves 8.

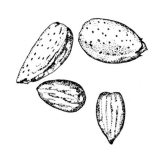

(Clockwise) Creamy French Dressing with Herbs, Blender Mayonnaise, Green Mayonnaise with Fresh Herbs and French Dressing with Wine and Herbs.

Green Mayonnaise with Fresh Herbs

Gives a colourful lift to cold chicken, fish, and chilled starters such as asparagus or leeks.

6 spinach leaves
small handful of chopped
　parsley
4 fresh tarragon sprigs
4 small fresh marjoram sprigs
10 basil leaves
250 ml (8 fl oz) mayonnaise

Boil spinach, parsley, tarragon, marjoram and basil rapidly for 2 minutes in a small saucepan. Drain well, pat dry and chop finely, discarding marjoram stems. Add to mayonnaise and blend briefly. Chill well to allow flavour to develop before using. Makes 250 ml (8 fl oz).

Blender Mayonnaise

Made in seconds, this mayonnaise is easily doubled if larger quantities are required.

1 extra large egg or 2 yolks
　(for a thicker consistency)
2.5 ml ($^{1}/_{2}$ tsp) salt
2.5 ml ($^{1}/_{2}$ tsp) dry mustard
25 ml (5 tsp) tarragon vinegar or
　lemon juice
250 ml (8 fl oz) oil
5 ml (1 tsp) sugar
1 garlic clove, chopped

Put egg, salt, mustard, vinegar, 25 ml (5 tsp) oil, sugar and garlic into a blender. Blend well and then, with motor running, slowly pour in remaining oil through the hole in the lid. You should have a smooth, creamy mayonnaise.
　For a lighter mayonnaise, stir in a little soured cream, yoghurt or buttermilk.
Makes 300 ml (10 fl oz).

French Dressing with Wine and Herbs

A nice change from ordinary vinaigrette and good with most green salads.

125 ml (4 fl oz) oil
45 ml (3 tbsp) good red wine
15 ml (1 tbsp) lemon juice
generous pinch of salt
5 ml (1 tsp) sugar
15 ml (1 tbsp) chopped mixed
　fresh herbs (sage, thyme,
　basil, marjoram)
45 ml (3 tbsp) chopped parsley

Put all the ingredients into a screw-top jar, shake and stand briefly before using – if left too long the fresh herbs could turn bitter.
Makes 200 ml (6$^{1}/_{2}$ fl oz) or enough for 1 very large salad.

Creamy French Dressing with Herbs

The addition of wine and buttermilk makes a lovely, light dressing that is lower in calories than most. Use on any green salad, but before adding, toss the salad ingredients with a dash of oil first so that the dressing will cling to the leaves.

125 ml (4 fl oz) each oil, dry
　white wine and buttermilk
5 ml (1 tsp) honey
2.5 ml ($^{1}/_{2}$ tsp) dried oregano
2.5 ml ($^{1}/_{2}$ tsp) dried tarragon
2 garlic cloves, crushed
generous pinch of celery salt

Shake all the ingredients in a screw-top jar and leave to stand for at least 1 hour before using. Use when freshly made, as it does not keep well.
Makes 375 ml (12 fl oz) .

Chicken and Prawn Paella

The following is a scaled-down version of an authentic paella, using easily available ingredients.

2.5 ml (¹/₂ tsp) saffron threads
750 g (1³/₄ lb) chicken wings or
    drumsticks
30 ml (2 tbsp) vegetable oil
30 ml (2 tbsp) olive oil
2 onions, chopped
2 garlic cloves, crushed
1 red pepper, seeded and diced
300 g (11 oz) long-grain white
    rice
about 1 litre (1³/₄ pints) hot
    chicken stock
100 ml (3¹/₂ fl oz) white wine
400 g (14 oz) canned tomatoes,
    chopped
salt and ground black pepper
400 g (14 oz) pink peeled frozen
    prawns, de-veined
150 g (5 oz) large prawns with
    shells
nut of butter
a few drops of lemon juice
generous pinch of paprika
225 g (8 oz) canned mussels in
    brine
12 black olives, sliced
175 g (6 oz) green peas
    (optional)

Soak saffron in 30 ml (2 tbsp) hot water for 1 hour. If using chicken wings, trim off tips. Heat oils in large frying pan and brown chicken well. Remove. To pan juices add onion, garlic and pepper and stir until softened. Add rice and toss until glistening. Add 600 ml (1 pint) stock and the wine, and when boiling add tomatoes plus juice, and saffron. Pour into your largest baking dish, add chicken and seasoning, then cover and bake at 170 °C (325 °F, gas 3) for 1 hour. Remove. The rice should be tender and the liquid absorbed. Add another 250 ml (8 fl oz) stock and bake for 30 minutes or until chicken is very tender.

Meanwhile cook peeled prawns according to packet directions. Fry large prawns with shells in butter with lemon juice and paprika. Drain and rinse mussels. Add shelled prawns, mussels, olives (and peas, if using) to rice mixture, and arrange fried prawns on the top. If mixture seems dry, add more stock. Cover and heat through for about 30 minutes. Serves 6.

Squid Casserole with Mushrooms

400 g (14 oz) squid
30 ml (2 tbsp) oil
15 g (½ oz) butter
1 onion, chopped
2 garlic cloves, crushed
1 red pepper, seeded and diced
150 g (5 oz) mushrooms, wiped and sliced
2 large beefsteak tomatoes, skinned and chopped
45 ml (3 tbsp) sherry
15 ml (1 tbsp) soy sauce
ground black pepper
pinch of sugar
beurre manié or 15 ml (1 tbsp) cornflour mixed with little soured cream

Dry squid and slice if necessary. Heat oil and butter, add squid and toss for a few minutes until it stiffens and turns white, then remove to baking dish. Add a little more oil to the pan, and lower heat. Add onion and allow to soften before adding garlic, red pepper, mushrooms, tomatoes, sherry, soy sauce, pepper and sugar. Stir briefly, until just bubbling and juicy, and then pour over squid.

Cover and bake at 170 °C (325 °F, gas 3) for about 1 hour 15 minutes, until squid is tender and a good gravy has formed. Thicken with beurre manié or cornflour mixture and return to oven, uncovered, for 15 minutes. Serve on rice with a green salad. Serves 4.

Oriental Squid

750 g (1¾ lb) squid
45 ml (3 tbsp) oil
30 ml (2 tbsp) whisky
1 large bunch spring onions, chopped
1 onion, chopped
2 garlic cloves, crushed
300 g (11 oz) brown mushrooms, wiped and sliced
60 ml (4 tbsp) flour
500 ml (16 fl oz) chicken stock
200 ml (6½ fl oz) white wine
30 ml (2 tbsp) soy sauce
small knob root ginger, peeled and grated
a few drops of lemon juice

Slice squid into thin rings, pat dry and fry in hot oil in large saucepan for a few minutes or until just stiffening and turning white. Flame with warmed whisky, remove from pan with slotted spoon and set aside.

To pan add a dash of oil if necessary and add spring onions, onion, garlic and mushrooms. Toss for a few minutes until glistening, then sprinkle in flour and slowly add stock, wine, soy sauce, ginger, lemon juice and squid. Cover and simmer very slowly for approximately 50 minutes, stirring occasionally. Adjust seasoning, and serve on a bed of rice, with peas and a crisp salad. Serves 6.

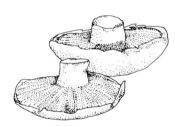

Lobster Salad

Lobster Salad

This is a salad for a special summer luncheon: lobster tails piled with diced lobster flesh, doused with a dash of vermouth and then tossed with a creamy dressing lightly flavoured with tarragon. Surround with rice and Raw mushroom salad (page 43) and add the prettiest of garnishes: red leaf lettuce, cherry tomatoes, sprays of tarragon.

Allow one cooked lobster per serving. Place on its back and cut down the middle. Squeeze tail to snap covering membranes and then snip them off. Carefully pull out alimentary canal which runs down the length of the lobster. Remove flesh from body, tail and legs, discarding body and head and all soft matter and entrails. Keep the tail and flatten gently to maintain its shape. Rinse flesh and tail and pat dry. Dice flesh. Each lobster should provide about 125 g (4 oz). Put into glass bowl and pour over 10 ml (2 tsp) dry vermouth per lobster. Cover and chill for about 2 hours. Fold Mayonnaise dressing (see below) into each serving of chilled lobster flesh, pile into reserved tails and serve as suggested.

MAYONNAISE DRESSING
7.5 ml (1¹/₂ tsp) dried tarragon
20 ml (4 tsp) boiling water
100 ml (3¹/₂ fl oz) thick
  mayonnaise
45 ml (3 tbsp) soured cream
2.5 ml (¹/₂ tsp) Dijon mustard
pinch of sugar

Place tarragon in a cup, pour over boiling water, cover and allow to steep for about 1 hour. Strain the flavoured liquid into mayonnaise and stir in soured cream, mustard and sugar. Makes enough for 4 small salads.

Seafood Risotto

Serving seafood on its own can be expensive. The solution is to mix it with other ingredients, as in the following recipe in which shrimps are combined with rice, cooked Italian-style. This is a simple, easily prepared dish, wide open to variations, with but one imperative – a risotto must include Parmesan cheese.

30 ml (2 tbsp) oil
butter
1 large onion, chopped
2 garlic cloves, crushed
300 g (11 oz) mushrooms, wiped and sliced
250 g (9 oz) long-grain white rice
600 ml (19 fl oz) hot chicken stock
100 ml (3¹/₂ fl oz) white wine
2.5 ml (¹/₂ tsp) turmeric
salt and ground black pepper
400 g (14 oz) canned shrimps in brine, drained and rinsed
grated Parmesan cheese

Heat oil and 30 g (1 oz) butter in a large frying pan. Add onion and garlic and fry gently until softened. Add rice and mushrooms and toss until coated with oil. Slowly add heated stock, half the wine, turmeric, salt and pepper. Cover and simmer for 25–30 minutes on very low heat. Add remaining wine, the shrimps, 45 ml (3 tbsp) Parmesan cheese and a knob of butter. Using a fork, toss until well mixed and heated through. Serve with peas, or a tossed salad, and extra Parmesan to sprinkle on each serving. Serves 4.

Seafood Sauce for Pasta

Seafood Sauce for Pasta

A great dish for informal entertaining. Add a salad and grated Parmesan for sprinkling, and if you want to stretch it beyond 6 servings, simply increase the amount of pasta.

800 g (1 lb 14 oz) filleted firm white fish
375 ml (12 fl oz) water
2 bay leaves
salt
10 ml (2 tsp) lemon juice
400 g (14 oz) squid
45 ml (3 tbsp) oil
2 onions, chopped
1 green pepper, seeded and diced
2 garlic cloves, crushed
45 ml (3 tbsp) flour
100 ml (3¹/₂ fl oz) white wine
400 g (14 oz) tomatoes, skinned and chopped
2.5 ml (¹/₂ tsp) each salt and paprika
25 ml (5 tsp) tomato paste
2.5 ml (¹/₂ tsp) dried oregano
2.5 ml (¹/₂ tsp) dried basil
5 ml (1 tsp) sugar
900 g (2 lb) cooked mussels in shells
300 g (11 oz) ribbon noodles

Place fish fillets flat in a large pan. Add water, bay leaves, a little salt and lemon juice. Poach until just cooked, then leave to cool in liquid. Remove skin, any bones and dark flesh, and flake. Strain stock and reserve.

Slice squid into thin rings. Heat oil and sauté onion, green pepper and garlic. Add squid and toss over fairly low heat just until it stiffens. Sprinkle in flour, stir to mix, then add 250 ml (8 fl oz) reserved fish stock, wine, tomatoes and remaining ingredients, except mussels and noodles. Bring to the boil, then cover and simmer very slowly, stirring occasionally, for about 45 minutes or until sauce is thick and squid tender. Add flaked fish and a little more stock. Cover and simmer slowly for 10–15 minutes while you boil the pasta.

Adjust seasoning (it could need another pinch of sugar), then spoon into a large baking dish. Rinse mussels and place round edge, then put in oven at 170 °C (325 °F, gas 3) just to heat through very briefly.

To cook the pasta, boil the noodles in plenty of salted water until just done. Drain and toss with a little oil to keep the strands separate.
Serves 6–8.

Clam Sauce

15 ml (1 tbsp) vegetable oil
15 ml (1 tbsp) olive oil
1 onion, chopped
1 celery stick, finely chopped
2 garlic cloves, crushed
400 g (14 oz) canned tomatoes, chopped
45 ml (3 tbsp) dry vermouth
salt and ground black pepper
generous pinch of dried oregano
generous pinch of dried basil
45 ml (3 tbsp) chopped parsley
575 g (1¹/₄ lb) canned clams in water, drained

Heat oil in large frying pan and sauté onion, celery and garlic. When soft, add tomatoes plus their juice, and remaining ingredients, except clams. Cover and simmer gently for 20 minutes. Add clams and heat through. Serve on pasta with grated Parmesan cheese.
Serves 4.

Mussel Quiche

PROCESSOR PASTRY
175 g (6 oz) flour
generous pinch of salt
100 g (3¹/₂ oz) butter, diced
5 ml (1 tsp) lemon juice
45 ml (3 tbsp) cold water

FILLING
20 ml (4 tsp) oil
2 slim leeks, finely chopped
3 eggs
250 ml (8 fl oz) milk
125 ml (4 fl oz) single cream
generous pinch of freshly grated nutmeg
2.5 ml (¹/₂ tsp) salt
5 ml (1 tsp) flour
225 g (8 oz) canned mussels in brine, drained and coarsely chopped
paprika

To make pastry, use grinding blade of processor and mix flour, salt and butter until well blended. With motor running, slowly add lemon juice and water through feed tube, and continue to blend until mixture forms a ball. Wrap and chill for 1 hour, then roll out and line a 25-cm (10-in) diameter, deep, fluted flan tin. Cover pastry with greaseproof paper and fill to the brim with dried beans. Preheat oven to 200 °C (400 °F, gas 6) and heat a large baking sheet. Place flan tin on baking sheet and bake blind for 10 minutes. Remove paper and beans and bake for 5 minutes longer.

For the filling, heat oil and add leeks. Cover and sweat slowly until soft. Drain on absorbent kitchen paper. Beat eggs, milk, cream, nutmeg and salt. Brush base of pastry crust with 5 ml (1 tsp) flour. Arrange leeks and mussels on base. Carefully pour egg mixture over and dust with paprika. Place tin on baking sheet and bake for 35–40 minutes until just set.
Serves 6–8.

Fish and Shrimp Casserole

Simply the quickest of fishy dishes using a firm fish, a can of soup and a can of shrimps, all baked together, then topped with a buttery crumble.

750 g (1³/₄ lb) filleted fish
salt and ground black pepper
lemon juice
200 g (7 oz) canned shrimps in brine
425 g (15 oz) canned asparagus soup
45 ml (3 tbsp) dry vermouth
45 ml (3 tbsp) double cream or soured cream

TOPPING
30 g (1 oz) butter
90 g (3 oz) fine, stale white breadcrumbs
30 ml (2 tbsp) grated Parmesan cheese

Cut fish into 4 equal pieces, dry well and arrange close together in buttered baking dish. Season, then dribble each piece with a little lemon juice. Drain and rinse shrimps and scatter over fish. Stir soup with vermouth and cream or soured cream until smooth, pour over fish and bake, uncovered, at 180 °C (350 °F, gas 4) for about 35 minutes or until fish is just cooked through.

Meanwhile, make topping. Melt butter in small frying pan. Add breadcrumbs and toss over medium heat until lightly browned and crisp. Mix in Parmesan, sprinkle over fish and return to oven for 5 minutes to heat through. Serve with new potatoes and brightly coloured vegetables such as broccoli and glazed baby carrots, or, more simply, with lemon-flavoured rice and a green salad.
Serves 4.

Fish, Cheese and Asparagus Casserole

A simple old favourite which is given airs by topping with puff pastry fleurons before serving.

4 x 200g (7oz) white fish
    fillets
salt and ground black pepper
lemon juice
400 g (14 oz) canned asparagus
    spears
4–6 spring onions, finely
    chopped

SAUCE
milk
45 g (1¹⁄₂ oz) butter
45 ml (3 tbsp) flour
5 ml (1 tsp) dry mustard
salt and pepper
150 g (5 oz) Cheddar cheese,
    coarsely grated
30 ml (2 tbsp) sherry

FLEURONS
puff pastry
1 egg, beaten
paprika

Arrange fish in greased
30 x 20-cm (12 x 8-in) baking
dish. Season and sprinkle each
piece with a few drops lemon
juice. Drain asparagus and
reserve liquid. Dot fish with
chopped asparagus spears and
spring onions.
    To make the sauce, make up
asparagus liquid to 500 ml
(16 fl oz) with milk. Melt butter
and stir in flour and mustard.
Remove from heat and slowly
add the 500 ml (16 fl oz) liquid.
Return to cooker and cook,
stirring, until sauce is smooth
and thick. Season, stir in cheese
and sherry and pour over fish.
Bake, uncovered, at 200 °C
(400 °F, gas 6) for about
30 minutes or until fish is
cooked through. Top with
fleurons before serving, or
simply sprinkle with a little
grated Parmesan cheese before
baking.
    To make fleurons, cut puff
pastry into small crescents or
rounds. Brush with beaten egg,
dust with paprika and bake at
200 °C (400 °F, gas 6) on
moistened baking sheet for
10–15 minutes until risen and
lightly browned.
Serves 4–5.

Fish Fillets in Cream Sauce

The light creamy sauce used in this recipe enhances the delicate flavour of fresh succulent fish. Serve the fillets on a pool of sauce, or pour it over and sprinkle with very finely grated lemon rind.

4 x 200 g (7 oz) pieces of firm white fish

POACHING LIQUID
375 ml (12 fl oz) water
1 small onion, chopped
few parsley sprigs
100 ml (3¹/₂ fl oz) white wine
salt and a few black peppercorns

CREAM SAUCE
45 g (1¹/₂ oz) butter
45 ml (3 tbsp) flour
375 ml (12 fl oz) reserved poaching liquid
1 egg yolk
100-125 ml (3¹/₂-4 fl oz) double cream
10 ml (2 tsp) lemon juice
30 ml (2 tbsp) finely chopped parsley
salt and pepper

Bring ingredients for poaching liquid to the boil in a large pan and simmer for 5 minutes. Add fish fillets, cover and simmer until just cooked. Carefully remove to serving platter, cover with greaseproof paper and keep warm. Strain stock.

To make the sauce, melt butter, add flour and cook for 1 minute. Slowly add hot reserved stock and simmer, stirring, for a few minutes. Beat egg yolk and cream, add a little of the hot sauce, then return to saucepan and heat through, stirring, without boiling, until thickened. Remove from heat, add lemon juice and parsley, adjust seasoning, pour over fish and serve immediately. Braised fennel makes a good accompaniment.
Serves 4.

Hint
Having bought your fish, unwrap it as soon as you get home. Spread out on large plate, salt it, and keep in coldest part of refrigerator. Never re-freeze thawed fish.

Crumbed Baked Fish

This is the easiest and most convenient way of 'frying' fish.

750 g (1³/₄ lb) skinned, filleted fish
salt and ground black pepper
125 ml (4 fl oz) mayonnaise
125 g (4 oz) cornflake crumbs

If using frozen fish, thaw, skin and dry very well with absorbent kitchen paper. Season, then coat both sides with mayonnaise. Roll in crushed cornflakes and chill for at least 1 hour to set crumbs.

To bake, cover bottom of baking sheet with a shallow layer of oil. Preheat oven to 180 °C (350 °F, gas 4) and heat baking sheet until hot. Turn fillets once in hot oil and then bake for about 20 minutes or until cooked. Serve with lemon wedges and Sauce tartare. Serves 4.

Sauce Tartare

125 ml (4 fl oz) mayonnaise
5 ml (1 tsp) finely chopped gherkin
2.5 ml (¹/₂ tsp) chopped capers
5 ml (1 tsp) chopped chives
10 (2 tsp) chopped parsley
2.5 ml (¹/₂ tsp) Dijon mustard
pinch of sugar
hard-boiled white of egg, shredded (optional)

Combine ingredients and chill. Makes about 125 ml (4 fl oz).

Baked Fish with Mushrooms and Buttermilk

In this dish, floured fish fillets are baked in a savoury vegetable sauce enriched with a little buttermilk, instead of cream.

4 x 175 g (6 oz) skinned fish fillets
45 ml (3 tbsp) flour
2.5 ml (¹/₂ tsp) each salt and paprika
45 ml (3 tbsp) oil
1 onion, chopped
1 red pepper, seeded and diced
300 g (11 oz) white or brown mushrooms, wiped and sliced
15 ml (1 tbsp) soy sauce
ground black pepper
about 125 ml (4 fl oz) buttermilk
225 g (8 oz) canned mussels (optional)

Coat fish with mixture of flour, salt and paprika, and arrange in lightly greased baking dish to fit. Heat oil and sauté onion, red pepper and mushrooms. When soft, season with soy sauce and pepper. Stir in enough buttermilk to moisten, then pour evenly over fish. Bake, uncovered, at 180 °C (350 °F, gas 4) for 20–25 minutes or until fish is cooked through. If using mussels, drain and rinse and add to the dish 5 minutes before serving.
Serves 4.

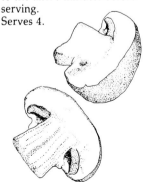

Greek-Style Fillets of Fish

In this casserole, fish is baked in a robustly flavoured sauce. The result is high on colour, low in cost. Serve with rice and/or small potatoes tossed in melted butter, and a spinach salad topped with crumbled Feta.

800 g (1lb 14oz) filleted white fish
2 large onions
30 ml (2 tbsp) vegetable oil
30 ml (2 tbsp) olive oil
2 garlic cloves, crushed
250 g (9 oz) aubergine, cubed
1 green pepper, seeded and diced
350 g (12 oz) tomatoes, skinned and chopped
45 ml (3 tbsp) chopped parsley
2.5–5 ml (¹/₂–1 tsp) dried oregano
170 ml (5¹/₂ fl oz) white wine
salt and ground black pepper
pinch of sugar
black olives

If using a pack of frozen fillets, thaw in milk. Dry well and place in a large baking dish in a single layer. Season lightly. Slice onions into thin rings. Heat oils in a large saucepan and sauté onions, garlic, aubergine and green pepper for a few minutes.

Add tomatoes, parsley, oregano, wine, seasoning and sugar. Cover and simmer for 20 minutes stirring occasionally. The mixture should be thick and juicy. Pour over fish and bake, uncovered, at 170 °C (325 °F, gas 3) for 35–40 minutes until fish is cooked. Add a handful of black olives 5 minutes before end of baking time.
Serves 4.

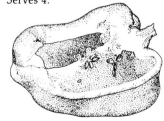

Low-Calorie Fish Dish

No crumbing and frying, no eggs, no cream – this fish is poached and blanketed with a light, delicately flavoured sauce.

1 kg (2¹/₄ lb) filleted firm white fish
400 ml (13 fl oz) water
a few onion slices
100 ml (3¹/₂ fl oz) white wine
salt
2 bay leaves
thinly sliced orange to garnish

SAUCE
45 ml (3 tbsp) oil
1 large onion, finely chopped
45 ml (3 tbsp) flour
300 ml (10 fl oz) reserved poaching liquid
250 ml (8 fl oz) fresh orange juice
45 ml (3 tbsp) chopped parsley
5 ml (1 tsp) French mustard

5–10 ml (1–2 tsp) sugar
100 ml (3¹/₂ fl oz) buttermilk
pinch of salt

Remove skin from fish, slice into portions and place in large pan. Add water, onion, wine, salt and bay leaves, bring to boil and simmer gently until just cooked. Drain and arrange in baking dish to fit in single layer. Reserve 300 ml (10 fl oz) of the poaching liquid.

Heat oil and sauté onion. Sprinkle in flour, then slowly stir in reserved liquid and orange juice. When sauce thickens, add remaining ingredients and simmer briefly. Adjust seasoning, pour over fish and heat through, uncovered, at 180 °C (350 °F, gas 4) for about 10 minutes or until just beginning to bubble. Garnish with thinly sliced orange.

Serve with new potatoes and steamed broccoli.
Serves 6.

Whole Barbecued Fish

This is a basic recipe, using simple ingredients. If you have fresh herbs at hand, tuck them inside the fish to add interest – but be circumspect, for the fresh fish flavour should not be masked. Succulence is the aim, and the marinade will take care of that.

The fire must be very deep and very low, and the fish should not be salted until near the end of the cooking period.

1.8–2 kg (4–4¹/₂ lb) hake or
   bass, gutted and scaled

MARINADE
125 ml (4 fl oz) white wine
125 ml (4 fl oz) oil
2 garlic cloves, crushed
5 ml (1 tsp) dry mustard
5 ml (1 tsp) paprika
10 ml (2 tsp) Worcester sauce
1 large onion, coarsely grated
45 ml (3 tbsp) chopped parsley
7.5–10 ml (1¹/₂-2 tsp) dried dill

Mix ingredients for marinade. Place fish in a large glass or earthenware dish, pour marinade over, spooning some into the cavity, and leave for 2 hours, turning a few times.

Oil the grid well before barbecuing, and cook the fish very slowly for about 45 minutes, basting often and turning grid regularly. Any remaining marinade may be spooned over each serving. Serve with Barbecued mushrooms.
Serves about 6.

Barbecued Mushrooms

Large, brown mushrooms make a splendid accompaniment.

Brush with melted butter spiked with crushed garlic, or alternatively brush with rosemary-flavoured oil, and barbecue on the grid until cooked.

Grilled Golden-Topped Cod

Deliciously juicy, these butter-brushed fillets are grilled and then finished off with a soufflé topping which melts to a rich golden-brown.

4 x 250 g (9 oz) skinless cod
   fillets
5 ml (1 tsp) salt
20 ml (4 tsp) flour
2.5 ml ($^1/_2$ tsp) dried dill
30 g (1 oz) butter, melted
15 ml (1 tbsp) lemon juice
125 ml (4 fl oz) thick
   mayonnaise
60 g (2 oz) Cheddar cheese,
   grated
5 ml (1 tsp) French mustard
1 egg white, stiffly whisked

Dust fish with a mixture of salt, flour and dill. Place in ovenproof dish to fit and brush top with butter mixed with lemon juice.

Grill until top turns white (this takes only a few minutes), then turn carefully.

Mix mayonnaise, cheese and mustard and fold in egg white. Spread over fish pieces and grill until golden brown. Do not position too close to the grill, as the mayonnaise mixture scorches easily. Serve with new potatoes and beans or a salad.
Serves 4.

Note
When grilling the mayonnaise-topped fish, watch carefully, and remove as soon as it melts and turns colour.

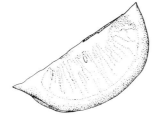

Baked Fish with Almonds

There's no frying with this dish, and it's very easy to assemble. Any firm fish will do, as long as it's filleted and skinless.

30 ml (2 tbsp) oil
30 g (1 oz) butter
2 garlic cloves, crushed
4 x 180 g (6 oz) fish fillets
salt
paprika
20 ml (4 tsp) soy sauce
finely chopped parsley
1 onion, coarsely grated
60 g (2 oz) almonds, flaked

Preheat oven to 180 °C (350 °F, gas 4). Melt oil and butter in a baking dish. Add garlic and put in oven to heat. Remove when hot and turn fish once in buttery mixture. Sprinkle each piece lightly with salt and paprika and spoon 5 ml (1 tsp) soy sauce over each. Sprinkle with a little parsley and onion. Finally, top each piece with 15 g ($^1/_2$ oz) almonds. Bake, uncovered, for about 25 minutes until cooked, basting once or twice.

Pour buttery juices over each portion and serve with Orange carrots (page 131), a green salad and boiled new potatoes.
Serves 4.

Fish with Cucumber Cream Sauce

Fish with Cucumber Cream Sauce

Any firm fish fillets can be used for this dish, and they may be grilled, poached or baked, with the sauce served over the top or underneath.

600 g (1 lb 5 oz) filleted firm white fish
fresh dill or cucumber twists to garnish

SAUCE
cucumber
15 g (¹/₂ oz) butter
2.5 ml (¹/₂ tsp) dried dill
10 ml (2 tsp) flour
250 ml (8 fl oz) fish stock (page 30)
2 egg yolks
10 ml (2 tsp) chopped capers
15 ml (1 tbsp) sherry
125 ml (4 fl oz) soured cream or fresh cream
salt and ground black pepper

Grill, poach or bake fish as desired.

To make the sauce, peel and cube enough cucumber to make up 125 g (4 oz), discarding the seeds. Heat butter, add cucumber, sprinkle in dill and sauté gently until softened, shaking pan occasionally. Sprinkle in flour, then stir in stock. Beat together egg yolks, capers, sherry and soured cream or cream and add to pan. Stir until thickened. Adjust seasoning and, if desired, sharpen with a dash of lemon juice.

Garnish the dish with fresh dill, if available, or thin twists of cucumber and serve with rice tossed with fried mushrooms. Serves 3–4.

Hint
You can use frozen fish steaks but thaw them in milk for that fresh-from-the-sea flavour, and be sure to dry them well before baking.

Fish Baked in Cucumber Sauce

A simple, yet tasty, budget fish dish.

750g (1³/₄ lb) skinned white fish fillets
milk
salt and ground black pepper
30 g (1 oz) butter
10 ml (2 tsp) oil
6 spring onions, chopped
¹/₂ large cucumber, peeled and diced
2.5 ml (¹/₂ tsp) dried dill
30 g (1 oz) parsely, finely chopped
generous pinch of celery salt
45 ml (3 tbsp) flour
grated Cheddar or Gruyère cheese

Place fish in shallow oven dish and pour over 250 ml (8 fl oz) milk. Season and bake at 180°C (350 °F, gas 4) until just done.

Remove fish to lightly buttered baking dish and add enough milk to poaching liquid to give you 500 ml (16 fl oz). Set aside. In a smallish saucepan heat butter and oil. Add spring onions and toss until coated, then add cucumber (you should have 225 g (8 oz)). Add dill, parsley and celery salt. Cover and cook for about 10 minutes on a low heat, shaking saucepan occasionally until vegetables are soft. Sprinkle in flour and slowly stir in the 500 ml (16 fl oz) milk. When sauce is thick, check seasoning – it might need a pinch of salt, a dash of lemon juice or a little sugar – and pour over the fish.

Sprinkle with a little grated cheese and bake until just heated through and cheese has started to melt.
Serves 4.

Poor Man's Thermidor

Cod with Mushrooms and Soured Cream

The fish cooks slowly in the juices from the onions and mushrooms, and the result is both delicate and delicious.

1 kg (2¼ lb) cod
30 ml (2 tbsp) flour
2.5 ml (½ tsp) salt
2.5 ml (½ tsp) paprika
30 g (1 oz) butter
30 ml (2 tbsp) oil
1 large onion, chopped
300 g (11 oz) mushrooms, wiped and sliced
10 ml (2 tsp) soy sauce
170–200 ml (5½–8 fl oz) soured cream
25 ml (5 tsp) sherry
grated Parmesan or Mozzarella cheese

Skin and fillet fish so that you have two good pieces, totalling about 750 g (1¾ lb). Mix flour, salt and paprika and dust fish on both sides. Arrange in lightly buttered dish to fit really closely, but without actually overlapping.

Heat butter and oil and soften onion and mushrooms. When just beginning to shrink, remove from heat, add soy sauce and pour over fish. Combine soured cream and sherry in the warm pan, then dribble over fish, sprinkle with chosen cheese and bake, uncovered, at 180 °C (350 °F, gas 4) for about 40 minutes. Serve with buttered rice and peas, or a salad and new potatoes. Serves 4.

Hint

If commercially soured cream is unobtainable, fresh cream may be soured by adding a dash of vinegar or a little lemon juice. This cream will, however, be higher in calories than the cultured product.

Poor Man's Thermidor

This is the sort of dish that looks so inviting in a beautiful casserole set on a hot tray at an informal party: chunks of firm, poached fish in a creamy mushroom and cheese sauce accompanied by a bowl of saffron rice and a green salad, this is one of the nicest of fork suppers.

550 g (1 lb 3 oz) chunks of poached, filleted firm white fish
45 g (1½ oz) butter
45 g (1½ oz) flour
750 ml (1¼ pints) hot milk
salt and pepper
30 ml (2 tbsp) oil
1 onion, finely chopped
300 g (11 oz) white mushrooms, wiped and sliced
100 ml (3½ fl oz) tomato purée
5–10 ml (1–2 tsp) French mustard
125 g (4 oz) Cheddar cheese, grated
20 ml (4 tsp) brandy

The fish should be in neat pieces, with all bones and skin carefully removed. Melt butter, stir in flour, remove from heat and slowly add hot milk. Return to heat and cook until smooth and thickened. Season and set aside. Heat oil in frying pan, add onion and mushrooms and fry gently until soft, then increase heat to remove any moisture. Add to white sauce together with tomato purée, mustard, cheese, brandy and the fish. Adjust seasoning.

Turn mixture into a buttered 30 x 20-cm (12 x 8-in) casserole, cover and heat through at 170 °C (325 °F, gas 3) for about 30 minutes, then serve as suggested.
Serves 6.

Salmon in Pastry

**400 g (14 oz) canned pink
  salmon**
125 ml (4 fl oz) soured cream
1 celery stick, finely chopped
30 ml (2 tbsp) chopped parsley
**45 ml (3 tbsp) finely chopped
  spring onions**
3 hard-boiled eggs, chopped
salt and ground black pepper
5 ml (1 tsp) lemon juice
400 g (14 oz) puff pastry
1 egg, beaten

SAUCE
150 ml (5 fl oz) soured cream
**100 ml (3¹/₂ fl oz) thick
  mayonnaise**
**2.5 ml (¹/₂ tsp) finely grated
  lemon rind**
10 ml (2 tsp) lemon juice
pinch of sugar

Drain and flake salmon,
discarding skin and bones. Mix
with soured cream, celery,
parsley, spring onions, hard-
boiled eggs, seasoning and lemon
juice. Roll pastry out lightly on
floured board into a long
rectangle and divide in two,
making one piece about
23 x 17 cm (9 x 7 in) and the
other slightly larger. Spoon
salmon filling onto smaller piece,
moisten edges of pastry and
cover with the second piece. Seal
edges, and scallop to make a
raised edge. Brush with beaten
egg, prick top, and decorate with
any pastry trimmings. Lift
carefully onto a large, moistened
baking sheet and bake at 200 °C
(400 °F, gas 6) for 35 minutes
until puffed and golden brown.
Transfer to warmed platter, or
allow to cool. Serve with the
sauce and a salad.
    Combine all the ingredients
for the sauce. If serving the pie
hot, heat sauce gently in top of
double boiler. To serve cold,
simply stir ingredients until
blended. Serves 6.

Rainbow Trout with Vermouth and Almonds

**A sophisticated way of treating
trout: baked in vermouth and
butter, topped with toasted
almonds and garnished with
slices of lemon. Serve this
splendid dish with tiny potatoes
and the simplest of salads.**

6 rainbow trout
45 ml (3 tbsp) flour
5 ml (1 tsp) salt
2.5 ml (¹/₂ tsp) paprika
100 g (3¹/₂ oz) butter
**10 ml (2 tsp) finely grated lemon
  rind**
4 pickling onions, grated
45 ml (3 tbsp) snipped chives
250 ml (8 fl oz) dry vermouth
blanched, flaked almonds

Clean trout. Wipe with a damp
cloth and pat dry. Dust trout
with flour mixed with salt and
paprika and place side by side in
1 or 2 buttered baking dishes.
Cream butter with lemon rind,
onions and chives. Divide into 12
portions. Place one portion
inside the cavity of each fish and
spread the rest over the top.
Pour the vermouth over. Cover
and bake at 180 °C (350 °F,
gas 4) for about 25 minutes or
until just cooked. Brown almonds
in the oven at the same time and
remove when lightly toasted.
    To serve, top each trout
generously with almonds and
spoon juices over each serving.
Serves 6.

Chicken Chow

Serving Chinese food to guests is tricky, because of last-minute stir-frying. Therefore I've worked out a Chinese-type dish which can be assembled and semi-cooked in advance. This breaks all the rules, of course, but it's a good and useful recipe.

1 small chicken
water
a few parsley sprigs
1 bay leaf
1 onion, halved
salt
1 small cucumber, peeled and
  diced
5 spring onions, chopped, or
  2 leeks, thinly sliced
200 g (7 oz) mushrooms, thinly
  sliced
175 g (6 oz) mung bean sprouts
1 large green pepper, seeded and
  thinly shredded
2 celery sticks, thinly sliced
45 ml (3 tbsp) oil
45 ml (3 tbsp) soy sauce
45 ml (3 tbsp) flour
45 ml (3 tbsp) sherry
toasted almonds

Poach chicken in plenty of water with herbs, onion and salt. Strip flesh from bones and dice enough to give you 450–500 g (1 lb–18 oz). Reserve 375 ml (12 fl oz) stock.

Mix together cucumber, spring onions or leeks, mushrooms, sprouts, green pepper and celery. Heat oil in large Chinese wok or in heavy frying pan and sauté vegetables briskly over high heat for 2–3 minutes, turning constantly with a wooden spoon. Spoon into large baking dish, add cubed chicken and toss.

Whisk together reserved stock, soy sauce, flour and sherry and pour over chicken mixture. At this stage you can leave it for a while, covered, in a cool place.

To serve, preheat oven to 200°C (400°F, gas 6) and bake, uncovered for 20 minutes, stirring once after 10 minutes. Spoon onto brown rice in Chinese bowls and sprinkle with almonds.
Serves 6–8.

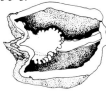

Crunchy Rice and Chicken Salad

The crunchy rice adds an interesting texture to this salad, which is quite different from the usual chicken mayonnaise.

45 ml (3 tbsp) oil
25 ml (5 tsp) lemon juice
15 ml (1 tbsp) honey
425 g (15 oz) hot, cooked brown rice
2 celery sticks, chopped
1 leek, finely sliced
45 ml (3 tbsp) chopped parsley
150 g (5 oz) peeled and cubed cucumber
100 g (3¹/₂ oz) mung bean sprouts
salt and ground black pepper
1 chicken
parsley sprigs
1 bay leaf
1 onion, halved
350 g (12 oz) canned pineapple rings in natural juices

250 ml (8 fl oz) thick mayonnaise
10 ml (2 tsp) soy sauce
2.5–5 ml (¹/₂–1 tsp) ground ginger
toasted almonds

Mix oil, lemon juice and honey and fork into hot rice. Add celery, leek, parsley, cucumber and sprouts. Adjust seasoning, cover and chill.

Poach chicken in plenty of water with parsley, bay leaf, onion and salt. Cool chicken in liquid, then strip flesh from bones, and dice, discarding skin. Drain pineapple and reserve juice. Chop 3–4 rings into small pieces and add to chicken. Mix mayonnaise with soy sauce, ginger and a little of the reserved pineapple juice to taste. Toss this dressing with chicken and pineapple, cover and chill.

To serve, make a border of rice, spoon chicken into centre, and sprinkle with almonds.
Serves 6–8.

Chicken Baked with Soy Sauce and Sherry

Another aromatic and quickly prepared chicken dish. Serve this one with a salad and baked potatoes topped with a creamy mushroom sauce.

1 kg (2¹/₄ lb) chicken pieces
oil for frying
1 large onion, coarsely grated
3 garlic cloves, crushed
1 knob root ginger, peeled and grated
30 ml (2 tbsp) oil
45 ml (3 tbsp) soy sauce
45 ml (3 tbsp) sweet sherry
5 ml (1 tsp) curry powder

Cut chicken breasts in half, if large, and remove excess fat from thighs. Brown on both sides in a little oil, then transfer to baking dish in single layer, close together and skin-side down. Sprinkle over onion, garlic and ginger. Mix remaining ingredients together and pour over chicken. Do not season. Bake at 180°C (350°F, gas 4) for 45 minutes, then reduce heat to 170°C (325°F, gas 3), turn chicken and continue baking for about 30 minutes until well browned and tender. Serve with the juices spooned over each serving.
Serves 5–6.

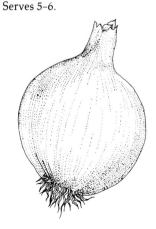

Devilled Chicken

Another quick and easy recipe.
Serve this tangy chicken with
baked potatoes and soured cream
and a salad. As the chicken
bakes at a low temperature,
don't use large potatoes as they
won't cook through – I simply
roll small to medium ones in oil,
place in a baking dish, and by the
time the chicken is ready
they should be done too.

1 kg (2¹/₄ lb) chicken pieces
salt and pepper
oil
45 ml (3 tbsp) chutney
45 ml (3 tbsp) tomato sauce
10 ml (2 tsp) Worcester sauce
5 ml (1 tsp) curry powder
5 ml (1 tsp) prepared mustard
1 large onion, coarsely grated
2 garlic cloves, crushed
butter

Cut chicken breasts in half if
large and remove excess fat

from thighs. Season lightly and
place, skin-side up, in a shallow
baking dish brushed with oil.
Mix together the chutney,
tomato sauce, Worcester sauce,
curry powder, mustard, onion
and garlic. Spread over chicken.
   Bake, uncovered, at 170°C
(325°F, gas 3) for 1 hour. Dot
with butter and continue baking
until chicken is cooked through
and a deep, rich colour.
Serves 4 generously.

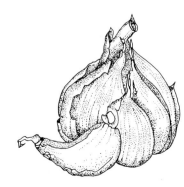

Spicy Chicken Curry

30 ml (2 tbsp) oil
1.25 kg (2³/₄ lb) chicken pieces
salt and ground black pepper
2 large onions, chopped
2 garlic cloves, crushed
2 cooking apples, peeled and
   diced
1 knob root ginger, peeled and
   grated
45 ml (3 tbsp) flour
15 ml (1 tbsp) curry powder (or
   to taste)
5 ml (1 tsp) turmeric
5 ml (1 tsp) ground cinnamon
5 ml (1 tsp) ground coriander
2.5 ml (¹/₂ tsp) ground cumin
500 ml (16 fl oz) seasoned
   chicken stock
60 g (2 oz) sultanas
15 ml (1 tbsp) honey
25 ml (5 tsp) tomato paste
25 ml (5 tsp) chutney
finely grated rind of ¹/₂ lemon
2 bay leaves

Heat oil in saucepan and brown
chicken on both sides. Transfer
to large baking dish and season.
Add a little more oil to saucepan
if necessary and sauté onions,
garlic, apples and ginger. When
softened, sprinkle in flour, curry
powder and spices. Slowly add
stock and stir until boiling. Stir
in sultanas, honey, tomato paste,
chutney and lemon rind. Spoon
over chicken, tuck in bay leaves,
cover and bake at 170°C (325°F,
gas 3) for about 1 hour 30
minutes or until tender.
   If desired, enrich gravy with a
little cream or soured cream, or
sharpen with lemon juice or
yoghurt, and serve with rice and
a tomato and onion salad.
Serves 6.

Chicken with Mushrooms and Soured Cream

A simple, satisfying casserole which never seems to lose its appeal. In this dish the mushrooms are not fried beforehand, which means that the chicken cooks gently in the juices.

1 kg (2¹/₄ lb) chicken pieces
5 ml (1 tsp) paprika
45 ml (3 tbsp) oil
salt and ground black pepper
1 large onion, chopped
2 garlic cloves, crushed
45 ml (3 tbsp) flour
250 ml (8 fl oz) hot chicken stock
300 g (11 oz) brown mushrooms, wiped and sliced
125 ml (4 fl oz) soured cream
25 ml (5 tsp) sweet sherry
20 ml (4 tsp) soy sauce

Trim off any bits of fat from chicken pieces. Dust with paprika. Heat oil and fry chicken on both sides until lightly browned. Remove to baking dish to fit closely in a single layer, skin-side up, and season lightly. To fat in pan add onion and garlic and sauté lightly. Stir in flour and slowly add hot stock. When thickened, remove from heat and add mushrooms, soured cream, sherry and soy sauce. Pour over chicken and bake, uncovered, at 170 °C (325 °F, gas 3) for 1 hour 20 minutes, or until tender, and gravy is thick and nut-brown. Serve with Oriental rice (see below). Serves 5–6.

Oriental Rice

200 g (7 oz) long-grain rice
500 ml (16 fl oz) water or stock
2.5 ml (¹/₂ tsp) salt
45 ml (3 tbsp) finely chopped parsley
4 spring onions, chopped
25 ml (5 tsp) soy sauce
45 g (1¹/₂ oz) toasted flaked almonds
nut of butter

Put rice into saucepan with water and salt and bring to the boil. Cover and cook on low heat until dry and fluffy. Fork in remaining ingredients and turn into heated serving dish. Serves 5–6.

Chicken Breasts Duxelle with Whisky Cream Sauce

These breasts are stuffed, flamed in whisky, poached, then covered in a creamy sauce and topped with toasted almonds. Duxelle is the French name for a simple mixture of mushrooms, spring onions and herbs fried in butter, used to enhance a variety of sauces, soups and stuffings.

4 x 125 g (4 oz) filleted, skinless
  chicken breasts
15 ml (1 tbsp) oil
salt and ground black pepper
15 ml (1 tbsp) whisky, warmed
45 ml (3 tbsp) white wine
45 ml (3 tbsp) water
chicken stock or water

DUXELLE
150 g (5 oz) brown mushrooms,
  very finely chopped

45 g (1¹/₂ oz) butter
6 spring onions, chopped
1 small carrot, diced
5 ml (1 tsp) finely chopped fresh
  rosemary needles
salt and ground black pepper

SAUCE
30 g (1 oz) butter
30 ml (2 tbsp) flour
250 ml (8 fl oz) reserved chicken
  stock
150 ml (5 fl oz) single cream,
  soured cream, or half and half
5 ml (1 tsp) French mustard
10 ml (2 tsp) whisky
1 egg yolk
pinch of sugar (if using soured
  cream)
toasted flaked almonds

Begin with the duxelle: squeeze mushrooms in absorbent kitchen paper until very dry. Heat butter, and fry mushrooms, spring onions, carrot and herbs over medium heat for about 15 minutes, turning with wooden spoon, until dry and shrunken and richly browned. Remove from heat and season. Set aside.

Either cut pockets in chicken breasts by slicing horizontally, but not right through, and opening out, or flatten gently with a mallet. Be careful not to tear the flesh.

Divide duxelle equally between the four breasts. Either stuff pocket or spoon down length of one side of breast and fold over, then pinch to close. It is not necessary to tie or skewer them. Heat oil and seal breasts on both sides without browning, turning once, carefully, with a spatula. Season breasts, and then flame with whisky. Add wine and water. Cover and poach over low heat for about 20 minutes or until just tender. Do not boil rapidly, or overcook, or they will toughen. Remove breasts to small baking dish to fit fairly snugly, and make up pan juices to 250 ml (8 fl oz) with stock or water.

To make sauce, melt butter, stir in flour, cook 1 minute then slowly add hot stock and stir until thickened. Mix together cream/soured cream, mustard, whisky, egg yolk and pinch of sugar. Pour on a little of the hot sauce, stir to mix, then return to saucepan and heat, stirring, until thickened. Do not boil. Pour over chicken and sprinkle generously with toasted almonds.

Cover and heat through at 170 °C (325 °F, gas 3) for 20–30 minutes. Serve with rice tossed with stir-fried, grated courgettes, and a green salad. Serves 4.

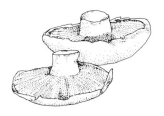

Chicken Breasts with Tarragon and Mustard Cream Sauce

These breast fillets are coated with a creamy velouté sauce with just a hint of tarragon.

15 ml (1 tbsp) oil
4 x 125 g (4 oz) filleted, skinless chicken breasts
45 ml (3 tbsp) white wine chicken stock
salt and ground black pepper
30 g (1 oz) butter
5 ml (1 tsp) dried tarragon
30 ml (2 tbsp) flour
250 ml (8 fl oz) reserved chicken stock
1 egg yolk
100 ml (3¹/₂ fl oz) single cream or soured cream
5 ml (1 tsp) French mustard
paprika

Heat oil and seal breasts quickly on both sides – don't allow to brown. Add wine and 45 ml (3 tbsp) stock, cover and poach gently for about 20 minutes or until cooked. Transfer to warm platter, season and keep warm. Measure pan juices and make up to 250 ml (8 fl oz) with hot chicken stock.

Make a velouté sauce by melting butter with tarragon. Stir in flour and cook for a few seconds without browning. Remove from heat and gradually stir in stock, then simmer, stirring, until thickened. Mix together egg yolk, cream and mustard. Pour sauce through a small sieve (to strain out tarragon) into the egg mixture, then return to saucepan and stir over low heat to cook egg without boiling. Adjust seasoning, pour over breasts, and sprinkle with paprika.
Serves 4.

Chicken Niblets

These spicy chicken wings make a delicious party snack or can be served as a main course with rice tossed with fried mushrooms. An added bonus is that they can be prepared in advance.

16 chicken wings
125 g (4 oz) butter
20 ml (4 tsp) soy sauce
125 g (4 oz) flour
5 ml (1 tsp) garlic salt
5 ml (1 tsp) curry powder
2.5 ml (¹/₂ tsp) ground ginger
2.5 ml (¹/₂ tsp) paprika
2.5 ml (¹/₂ tsp) ground coriander
oil for baking

Slice tips off chicken wings and separate each wing at the joint with poultry shears, being careful not to cut through the bone. This will give you 32 neat little pieces. Melt butter and add soy sauce. Mix flour with

remaining ingredients except oil.

Using a pastry brush, brush each joint with butter and soy sauce mixture, then roll in seasoned flour. Chill thoroughly – all day if you like. To bake, cover base of one very large or two medium, shallow baking dishes with a thin layer of oil. Place in oven for a few minutes to heat, then arrange chicken in a single layer, closely but not overlapping. Cover and bake at 170 °C (325 °F, gas 3) for 1 hour, then uncover and bake for further 10 minutes.
Serves 8.

The following are all variations on the crumbed chicken theme. These are singularly useful recipes because they can, or rather **must**, be prepared in advance and then baked just before dinner, without any need for constant attention or basting. Serve with baked potatoes, soured cream and a salad for a complete meal.

Sesame Chicken

45 g (1¹/₂ oz) sesame seeds
75 g (2¹/₂ oz) finely crushed
   toasted breadcrumbs
2.5 ml (¹/₂ tsp) celery salt
2.5 ml (¹/₂ tsp) dried thyme
5 ml (1 tsp) ground coriander
25 ml (5 tsp) soy sauce
75 ml (2¹/₂ fl oz) thick
   mayonnaise
2 garlic cloves, crushed
about 1.25 kg (2³/₄ lb) chicken
   pieces
oil for baking

Mix sesame seeds, breadcrumbs, celery salt, thyme and coriander on a large plate. Mix soy sauce, mayonnaise and garlic. Remove wing tips from chicken pieces and cut breasts in half if large. Using a pastry brush, brush chicken with mayonnaise mixture, then coat with crumb mixture – there will be enough for quite a thick coating. Chill for at least 2 hours.

To bake, heat a thin film of oil in a large baking dish. Turn chicken once in hot oil and arrange skin-side down. Bake, uncovered, at 200 °C (400 °F, gas 6) for 15 minutes. Reduce heat to 170 °C (325 °F, gas 3) and bake for 30 minutes. Turn pieces over and continue baking for about 20 minutes more until crisp, golden brown and tender. Serves 6.

Mustard-Baked Chicken with Honey and Almonds

Coated with a buttery mustard mixture and then baked until richly browned, this is a quickly prepared chicken dish with a delicious flavour.

800–900 g (1 lb 14 oz–2 lb)
   chicken pieces, preferably
   thighs
45 g (1¹/₂ oz) butter, softened
15 ml (1 tbsp) honey
25 ml (5 tsp) French mustard
2.5 ml (¹/₂ tsp) salt
45 ml (3 tbsp) fine, fresh white
   breadcrumbs
5 ml (1 tsp) lemon juice
chopped, toasted almonds

Remove excess fat from thighs and arrange on plate, skin-side up. Cream butter with remaining ingredients, except almonds. Cover top of each piece of chicken thickly with butter mixture, and refrigerate for several hours.

To bake, place chicken pieces in lightly oiled baking dish. Bake at 170 °C (325 °F, gas 3) for 30 minutes. Baste well, then bake until tender and well-browned, about 60 minutes more, basting twice. Add a little water to dish if necessary to prevent scorching and to keep chicken moist. Sprinkle almonds over each piece 10 minutes before end of baking period, and baste before returning to oven.

To serve, spoon succulent juices over each serving, or pour into a saucepan and use to make a light gravy.
Serves 4–5.

Hint
To blanch almonds, place in a small saucepan, cover with cold water and just bring to the boil. When cool enough to handle, the skins should slip off easily.

Crumbed Chicken with Tarragon and Garlic

This chicken dish is enhanced by garlic mayonnaise, which should be made at least a few hours in advance, and chilled.

8 x 125 g (4 oz) chicken thighs
75 g (2¹/₂ oz) fine cereal or toasted breadcrumbs
2.5 ml (¹/₂ tsp) garlic salt
2.5 ml (¹/₂ tsp) salt
7.5–10 ml (1¹/₂–2 tsp) dried tarragon

GARLIC BLENDER MAYONNAISE
1 egg
2.5 ml (¹/₂ tsp) salt
220 ml (7 fl oz) oil
25 ml (5 tsp) tarragon vinegar
2.5 ml (¹/₂ tsp) sugar
4 garlic cloves, peeled

First make the mayonnaise: Put egg, salt, 30 ml (2 tbsp) oil, vinegar, sugar and garlic into blender and blend well, then, with motor running, slowly add remaining oil through the hole in the top. Chill.

Remove any fat from thighs and coat thoroughly with mayonnaise – you'll need about two-thirds of the batch. Mix remaining ingredients on a large plate, coat chicken in crumbs, then chill for at least 1 hour to set.

To bake, heat a little oil in a baking dish and arrange chicken quite closely. Cover and bake at 170 °C (325 °F, gas 3) for 1 hour, then uncover and bake 15 minutes longer. Serve with spinach and blue cheese salad. Serves 8.

Crumbed Parmesan Chicken Wings

16 x 75 g (2¹/₂ oz) chicken wings
125 ml (4 fl oz) mayonnaise
3–4 garlic cloves, crushed
5 ml (1 tsp) Worcester sauce
75 g (2¹/₂ oz) fine, toasted breadcrumbs
75 g (2¹/₂ oz) Parmesan cheese, finely grated
5 ml (1 tsp) salt
ground black pepper
10 ml (2 tsp) dried oregano
oil for baking

Remove and discard wing-tips. Using poultry scissors and cutting between bones at the top, divide wings in half. Mix mayonnaise, garlic and Worcester sauce on large plate. Mix remaining ingredients, except oil, on another large plate.

Using a pastry brush, coat chicken wings with mayonnaise mixture, then roll in crumb mixture, coating well. Chill for at least 1 hour to set crumbs.

To bake, cover bases of two large baking dishes with a thin layer of oil and place in 170 °C (325 °F, gas 3) oven until hot. Turn wings once in hot oil and then bake, uncovered, for about 45 minutes, or until brown and crisp.

Serve as a cocktail snack or for a light supper, with baked potatoes or rolls and a salad. Serves 4 as supper or 16 as a snack.

Hint
Toasted breadcrumbs may be bought at some supermarkets. To make your own, place thin slices of bread, crusts removed, on a baking sheet and place in a low oven until golden brown and crisp. Place in a plastic bag and crush with a rolling pin until the desired consistency is reached.

Stuffed Roast Chicken with Herbs

The following is possibly my favourite way of treating roast chicken. The addition of just a few simple ingredients adds a wonderful flavour, and the smell as it roasts brings everyone to the kitchen.

30 g (1 oz) butter
30 ml (2 tbsp) oil
2 garlic cloves, crushed
1 small onion, grated
2.5 ml ($^1/_2$ tsp) each dried thyme, basil and oregano
15 ml (1 tbsp) soy sauce
1 x 2 kg (4$^1/_2$ lb) chicken
salt and ground pepper
2 small fresh rosemary sprigs
375 ml (12 fl oz) chicken stock or water

STUFFING
150 g (5 oz) cooked rice
1 small onion, chopped
30 ml (2 tbsp) chopped parsley
generous pinch of salt
45 ml (3 tbsp) chopped toasted walnuts or brazil nuts
30 ml (2 tbsp) reserved herb-butter mixture

Heat butter and oil until just melted. Add garlic, onion, dried herbs and soy sauce. Mix well, reserving 30 ml (2 tbsp) to add to the stuffing ingredients.

Wipe chicken inside and out with vinegar-water and dry well. Remove all fat and nick out oil gland in parson's nose. Combine all ingredients for stuffing, stuff body cavity, then truss. Season lightly and brush with remaining herb-butter mixture – there should be just enough to coat it lightly all over.

Place chicken on rack in roasting pan. Add rosemary and stock or water to pan. Roast at 170 °C (325 °F, gas 3) for about 2 hours 45 minutes, basting a few times. Cover top loosely with a tent of foil, shiny-side up, when it has browned sufficiently, and add more stock or water to roasting pan whenever necessary.

When done remove to serving platter and leave in warming drawer for about 15 minutes. Make a gravy from juices, and serve with roast potatoes and colourful vegetables. Serves 6.

Chicken Breasts in Curry-Cream Sauce

A smooth sauce blankets the chicken in this dish which can be assembled beforehand and baked when required. Served with Orange sultana rice (opposite), it's an easy but elegant version of curried chicken.

45 ml (3 tbsp) oil
15 g (¹/₂ oz) butter
2 onions, finely chopped
10 ml (2 tsp) curry powder (or more to taste)
5 ml (1 tsp) each ground ginger, ground cinnamon, ground cumin, ground coriander and turmeric
8 x 100 g (3¹/₂ oz) filleted, skinless chicken breasts
salt and ground black pepper
100 ml (3¹/₂ fl oz) water
45 ml (3 tbsp) cornflour
250 ml (8 fl oz) chicken stock
200 ml (6¹/₂ fl oz) soured cream
45 ml (3 tbsp) sherry
toasted almonds
paprika

Heat oil and butter in large, heavy frying pan. Add onions and allow to soften over low heat without browning. Stir in curry powder and all spices, and when well mixed turn heat down low and arrange breasts on top. Season, add water, cover and cook gently until tender, turning after 15 minutes. When done, transfer to baking dish to fit closely.

Whisk together cornflour, stock, cream and sherry and add to pan juices, which should measure about 250 ml (8 fl oz). Stir until thickened, season, pour over chicken and bake, uncovered, at 170 °C (325 °F, gas 3) for 30–40 minutes. Sprinkle with toasted almonds and paprika and serve.
Serves 8.

Orange Sultana Rice

200 g (7 oz) quick-cooking rice
250 ml (8 fl oz) fresh orange juice, strained
250 ml (8 fl oz) water
1 cinnamon stick
45 g (1¹/₂ oz) sultanas
2.5 ml (¹/₂ tsp) salt
5 ml (1 tsp) finely grated lemon or orange rind
chopped parsley

Put all the ingredients, except parsley, into a saucepan. Bring to the boil, stir once, then cover and simmer on lowest heat for 25–30 minutes, without looking or stirring. Remove cinnamon stick and fork in parsley.
Serves 6.

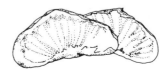

The Shah's Chicken Curry

The Shah liked mild and aromatic curries.

1 kg (2¹/₄ lb) chicken pieces
15 g (¹/₂ oz) butter
15 ml (1 tbsp) oil
2 cinnamon sticks
2 large onions, chopped
2 garlic cloves, crushed
2 bay leaves
1 knob root ginger, peeled and grated
10 ml (2 tsp) curry powder
2.5 ml (¹/₂ tsp) ground cumin
45 ml (3 tbsp) flour
500 ml (16 fl oz) hot seasoned chicken stock
2 tomatoes, chopped
5 ml (1 tsp) honey
2.5 ml (¹/₂ tsp) salt
10 ml (2 tsp) lemon juice
60 g (2 oz) sultanas
100 ml (3¹/₂ fl oz) buttermilk, cream or soured cream

Remove any fat from chicken and cut breasts in half if large. Heat butter and oil, add cinnamon sticks and brown chicken on both sides. If necessary, do chicken in batches, but leave cinnamon sticks in frying pan. As chicken browns, transfer pieces to baking dish.

To pan juices and cinnamon sticks add onions, garlic, bay leaves, root ginger, curry powder and cumin and toss together for a minute over low heat. Sprinkle in flour, stir to mix, then slowly stir in stock. Add tomatoes, honey, salt, lemon juice and sultanas. Bring to the boil, stirring, then pour over the chicken. Bake, covered, at 170 °C (325 °F, gas 3) for about 1¹/₂ hours, by which time chicken should be tender and sauce nicely thickened. Remove cinnamon sticks and bay leaves. Swirl in buttermilk (do not stir) and return to low oven for 5 minutes to heat through without boiling.

Garnish with a sprinkling of chopped coriander and serve with Spiced rice and little bowls of coconut, chutney, sliced bananas and toasted almonds. Serves 4–6.

Spiced Rice

30 g (1 oz) butter
30 ml (2 tbsp) oil
300 g (11 oz) white long-grain rice
1 onion, chopped
5 ml (1 tsp) masala paste
2.5 ml (¹/₂ tsp) turmeric
4 whole cloves
750 ml (1¹/₄ pints) hot chicken stock
45 ml (3 tbsp) sultanas
4 cardamom pods, split
1 cinnamon stick
2 bay leaves
8 peppercorns

Heat butter and oil and add rice, onion, masala, turmeric and cloves. Fry lightly, stirring with a fork. Slowly add hot stock and then remaining ingredients. Cover pot with a tea towel and then with a lid, and simmer very gently for about 25 minutes until liquid has been absorbed. Discard spices. Serves 6–8.

Chicken Casserole

A simple, tasty casserole using everyday ingredients.

30 ml (2 tbsp) oil
2 large onions, chopped
2 garlic cloves, crushed
2 carrots, finely diced
1 kg (2¹/₄ lb) chicken pieces
salt and ground black pepper
400 g (14 oz) canned tomato
    soup
125 ml (4 fl oz) water
45 ml (3 tbsp) sherry
15 ml (1 tbsp) honey
25 ml (5 tsp) Worcester sauce
30 g (1 oz) parsley, chopped
15 ml (1 tbsp) brown vinegar
5 ml (1 tsp) prepared mustard
2.5 ml (¹/₂ tsp) dried oregano
generous pinch of cinnamon
soured cream and snipped chives
    to garnish

Heat oil in large frying pan and sauté onions, garlic and carrots. Transfer to large baking dish. Add a little oil to frying pan if necessary and brown chicken lightly on both sides. Arrange on top of vegetables and season lightly.

Pour off any fat remaining in pan and add remaining ingredients, except soured cream and chives. Mix well and pour over chicken. Cover and bake at 170 °C (325 °F, gas 3) for about 1 hour 30 minutes until tender. For a thicker gravy, bake uncovered for a further 15 minutes. Swirl in a few spoonfuls of soured cream and sprinkle with chives. Serve with rice.
Serves 4–6.

Hints
Keep peeled cloves of garlic on hand by storing them in a jar of oil in the refrigerator. Use the flavoured oil for salad dressings.

Cartons of soured cream and cottage cheese are best stored upside-down in the refrigerator.

Duck with Orange Liqueur Sauce

This duck is first roasted, then carved and simmered in the orange-flavoured sauce.

1 x 2 kg (4¼ lb) duck (weighed with giblets and neck)
salt and ground black pepper
1 onion, peeled
½ unpeeled orange, quartered
5 ml (1 tsp) ground ginger
150 ml (5 fl oz) orange liqueur
250 ml (8 fl oz) fresh orange juice
500 ml (16 fl oz) giblet stock
peel of ½ orange, cut into thin strips
30 ml (2 tbsp) cornflour
15 ml (1 tbsp) soy sauce

Wipe duck inside and out with vinegar-water. Nick out point of gland in tail, squeeze the little glands on either side, and remove loose fat in body cavity and at neck end. Season body cavity and stuff with whole onion and orange quarters. Rub duck with ginger and 5 ml (1 tsp) salt, truss, and prick well all over. Place breast side up on rack in roasting pan and roast at 200 °C (400 °F, gas 6) for 30 minutes. Pour off fat and add a little water to roasting pan. Prick duck again all over, pour over 45 ml (3 tbsp) orange liqueur, reduce heat to 180 °C (350 °F, gas 4) and roast for 1 hour. Pour over another 45 ml (3 tbsp) orange liqueur, prick well, add more water to roasting pan if necessary and continue roasting for about an hour until tender and browned. To test, prick between leg and thigh – juices should run clear. If cooked, but not sufficiently browned, turn on griller for a few minutes. Set duck aside while making sauce.

Heat orange juice, giblet stock and peel. Boil 5 minutes, then add 60 ml (4 tbsp) orange liqueur mixed with cornflour and soy sauce. Boil until thickened, then adjust seasoning – if it needs salt add a little more soy sauce.

Carve duck into neat pieces and arrange in baking dish. Pour sauce over and bake, uncovered, at 170 °C (325 °F, gas 3) for 30 minutes until hot and bubbling. Serve with boiled new potatoes, peas and carrots. Serves 4.

Almond Chicken Salad

Quite different from the usual chicken mayonnaise, this salad uses filleted chicken breasts, lightly poached and drenched with a creamy buttermilk dressing. For a richer flavour, use more cream. Serve with Brown rice salad with mushrooms (page 38).

6 x 100 g (3¹/₂ oz) filleted,
   skinless chicken breasts
oil
45 ml (3 tbsp) water
45 ml (3 tbsp) sherry
1 small onion
2 bay leaves
5 ml (1 tsp) salt
paprika and toasted, flaked
   almonds to garnish

BUTTERMILK-LEMON DRESSING
250 ml (8 fl oz) buttermilk
170 ml (5¹/₂ fl oz) double cream
45 ml (3 tbsp) reserved stock
3 egg yolks
very generous pinch of finely
   grated lemon rind
generous pinch of salt

Seal breasts on both sides with a little oil in a large frying pan – do not allow to brown. Add water, sherry, onion, bay leaves and salt, cover and simmer for about 20 minutes. Cool in the stock, remove chicken and slice lengthways, into long, thin strips. Reserve stock. Mix ingredients for dressing in the top of a double boiler, whisk until smooth, then stir over simmering water until mixture is slightly thickened and coats back of spoon. Adjust seasoning and then pour, while warm, over chicken. When cool, cover and refrigerate. Just before serving, sprinkle with paprika and toasted, flaked almonds.
Serves 6.

Coronation Turkey

A succulent and moist Boxing Day salad using left-over turkey breast, a little jellied turkey stock, and a creamy dressing.

500 g (18 oz) turkey breast
250 ml (8 fl oz) jellied stock
toasted almonds

CURRY DRESSING
15 g (¹/₂ oz) butter
15 ml (1 tbsp) oil
1 small onion, chopped
15 ml (1 tbsp) curry powder
2.5 ml (¹/₂ tsp) ground cinnamon
2.5 ml (¹/₂ tsp) ground ginger
150 ml (5 fl oz) turkey stock
15 ml (1 tbsp) tomato paste
30 ml (2 tbsp) chutney
250 ml (8 fl oz) mayonnaise
75 ml (2¹/₂ fl oz) soured cream
pinch of sugar

First make the dressing: in a small saucepan heat butter and oil and lightly fry onion. Stir in curry powder and spices, cook for 1 minute, then add stock, tomato paste and chutney. Simmer, covered, for 5 minutes, then strain into a bowl, pressing through with the back of a spoon. Cool, then stir in mayonnaise, soured cream and a pinch of sugar. Cover and chill to blend flavours.

To assemble, arrange turkey strips on flat platter, dot with jellied stock and toss lightly. Pour over about 250 ml (8 fl oz) dressing and top with almonds. Serve at once, or lightly chilled, with brown rice tossed with French dressing (page 47), chopped spring onions and celery.
Serves 6.

Hint
Avoid weeping when chopping onions by chilling them thoroughly in the fridge beforehand.

Casserole of Steak, Wine and Mushrooms

This is a robustly flavoured dish which should be made in advance, left to cool, and then reheated for best results. It is important to use a good cut, rump or Porterhouse, and a reasonably good red wine.

30 ml (2 tbsp) oil
nut of butter
6 x 200 g (7 oz) thick slices steak
prepared mustard
2 onions, chopped
2 garlic cloves, crushed
45 ml (3 tbsp) flour
250 ml (8 fl oz) red wine
250 ml (8 fl oz) stock
2.5 ml (^{1}/$_2$ tsp) each dried thyme, basil and oregano
125 ml (4 fl oz) tomato purée
salt and ground black pepper
pinch of sugar
300 g (11 oz) brown mushrooms, sliced chopped parsley to garnish

Heat oil and butter in frying pan and brown steaks quickly on both sides. Transfer to baking dish in single layer, and spread each steak with a little prepared mustard. In same frying pan, soften onions and garlic over low heat. Sprinkle in flour and slowly stir in wine, stock, herbs, tomato purée, seasoning and sugar. Bring to the boil, stirring, and when thickened pour over steak, cover securely and bake at 170 °C (325 °F, gas 3) for 1^1/$_4$ hours.

Lightly sauté mushrooms in a little oil. Add to steak, cover and bake another 30 minutes. Cool, and if necessary, skim fat. Reheat at 170 °C (325 °F, gas 3) until hot and bubbling. Sprinkle with parsley and serve with small glazed onions, jacket potatoes and a green vegetable. Serves 6.

Hint
On informal occasions, serve the casserole with buttered noodles and a green bean salad. Toss young, cooked beans with sliced onion, red pepper and vinaigrette dressing. Fry breadcrumbs until crisp in oil with a clove of crushed garlic, and then mix with grated Gruyére cheese. Just before serving, sprinkle crumb mixture over beans.

Stifado

Stifado

This is a highly flavoured, peasant-type Greek stew for which I like to use beef shin for added succulence.

45 ml (3 tbsp) flour
10 ml (2 tsp) salt
5 ml (1 tsp) paprika
5 ml (1 tsp) dried oregano
30 ml (2 tbsp) oil
1 kg (2¼ lb) best quality beef shin cut in slices, 2.5 cm (1 in) thick
24 pickling onions, peeled
250 ml (8 fl oz) beef stock
30 ml (2 tbsp) tomato paste
15 ml (1 tbsp) brown sugar
2 garlic cloves, crushed
2 bay leaves
1 cinnamon stick
3 whole cloves
170 ml (5½ fl oz) red wine
100 ml (3½ fl oz) soured cream

Mix flour, salt, paprika and oregano and coat shin on both sides, reserving any that remains. Heat oil and brown meat lightly on both sides. Remove to baking dish in single layer. Brown onions in same frying pan, adding a little more oil if necessary. Transfer to baking dish with meat when golden brown. Drain off any fat from pan, then add stock, tomato paste, sugar, garlic, bay leaves, cinnamon, cloves and red wine mixed with remaining flour mixture. Bring to the boil and pour over meat. Check that spices are lying in the gravy and not on the shin. Cover and bake at 170 °C (325 °F, gas 3) for 1½ hours or until tender. Cool. Remove bay leaves, cloves and cinnamon 40 minutes before serving. The gravy should be fairly thick and quite generous in quantity, but if not add 100 ml (3½ fl oz) stock before reheating at 170 °C (325 °F, gas 3). Before serving swirl in soured cream, and garnish with parsley. Serves 4–5.

Aromatic Beef Curry

A beef stew of a different kind is the following aromatic curry.

30 g (1 oz) butter
30 ml (2 tbsp) oil
2 large onions, sliced
2 tart apples, peeled and diced
15 ml (1 tbsp) curry powder
2 garlic cloves, crushed
5 ml (1 tsp) each turmeric, ground cinnamon and cumin
750 g (1¾ lb) boneless chuck steak, cubed
7.5 ml (1½ tsp) salt
45 ml (3 tbsp) mild chutney
25 ml (5 tsp) brown vinegar
15 ml (1 tbsp) brown sugar
200 ml (6½ fl oz) tomato purée
250 ml (8 fl oz) water
2 bay leaves
45 g (1½ oz) dessicated coconut
60 g (2 oz) sultanas
single cream (optional)

Heat butter and oil and fry onions and apples. Add curry powder, garlic, spices and beef. When browned, turn off heat and stir in remaining ingredients, except sultanas. Spoon into a large baking dish and bake, covered, at 170 °C (325 °F, gas 3) for 1½ hours. Add more water or stock if necessary, and the sultanas. Cover and bake for further 30 minutes or until very tender. If using, swirl in cream just before serving. Serves 6.

Roast Rump with Chasseur-Style Sauce

1 x 2.5 kg (5¹/₂ lb) boneless beef
  rump
2 garlic cloves, peeled and thinly
  sliced
10 ml (2 tsp) salt
10 ml (2 tsp) dry mustard
10 ml (2 tsp) brown sugar
5 ml (1 tsp) dried oregano
5 ml (1 tsp) dried sage
30 ml (2 tbsp) flour

SAUCE
30 ml (2 tbsp) oil
200 g (7 oz) mushrooms, wiped
  and sliced
1 onion, chopped
30 ml (2 tbsp) flour
100 ml (3¹/₂ fl oz) white wine
250 ml (8 fl oz) chicken stock
15 ml (1 tbsp) tomato paste
2.5 ml (¹/₂ tsp) salt
2.5 ml (¹/₂ tsp) sugar
5 ml (1 tsp) Worcester sauce
45 ml (3 tbsp) soured cream

Make deep slits in the joint and
insert garlic. Mix dry ingredients
and rub all over meat. Allow to
stand for 4 hours. Place on rack
over a little water and roast at
170 °C (325 °F, gas 3) for about
2¹/₄ hours for medium rare. No
need to baste, but after 1¹/₂ hours
cover loosely with a tent of foil,
shiny-side out, to stop further
browning. When cooked to your
liking, transfer to warming oven,
and stand while making sauce.
    Heat oil and fry mushrooms
and onion. When softened add
flour, cook for a minute, stirring,
then add remaining ingredients,
except soured cream. Simmer,
uncovered, for 10–15 minutes
until thick. Stir in soured cream.
Serve this herby rump with
robust sauce with Casserole of
potatoes and onions.
Serves about 10.

Casserole of Potatoes and Onions

**This old-fashioned dish of
potatoes layered with onions
and baked in stock is easy to
assemble and good with almost
any main course.**

600 g (1 lb 5 oz) potatoes,
  scrubbed and thinly sliced
2 onions, thinly sliced
2 garlic cloves, crushed
2.5 ml (¹/₂ tsp) mixed dried
  herbs
salt and ground black pepper
45 g (1¹/₂ oz) butter
375 ml (12 fl oz) stock
paprika

Cover base of deep, 20-cm (8-in)
pie dish with half the potatoes –
there is no need to grease the
dish. Cover with onions, garlic
and herbs. Season. Dot with half
the butter, then cover with
remaining potatoes. Dot with

remaining butter. Pour stock
over, using chicken if serving
with white meat or fish, or beef
stock for red meat (10 ml (2 tsp)
Marmite dissolved in 375 ml
(12 fl oz) hot water does very
well.) Dust top with paprika and
bake, uncovered, at 180 °C
(350 °F, gas 4) for about 1 hour,
until potatoes are soft and
succulent.
Serves 5–6.

Note

**If meat is being cooked at
170 °C (325 °F, gas 3), bake
potato and onion casserole at
the same temperature, but
increase the baking time by
30 minutes.**

Roast Sirloin with Herb Butter

A splendid way of preparing steaks for a special meal, this tenderized sirloin is brushed with a savoury butter before roasting, and may be carved into thick steaks (if preferred) rather than thin slices. There is no need to bother with gravy, either, as the buttery juices are simply spooned over each serving. A bowl of soured cream flavoured with horseradish, mustard, or green peppercorns makes an excellent accompaniment.

1.25–1.5 kg (2³/₄–3 lb) rolled
   sirloin
buttermilk

HERB BUTTER
45 g (1¹/₂ oz) butter
2 garlic cloves, crushed
5 ml (1 tsp) dry mustard
20 g (³/₄ oz) parsley, chopped
45 ml (3 tbsp) chopped chives
2.5 ml (¹/₂ tsp) dried thyme
2.5 ml (¹/₂ tsp) dried oregano
5 ml (1 tsp) salt

Remove strings, any fat, and the thin outer skin, and put joint in a glass or earthenware dish to fit. Pour over enough buttermilk to coat generously, and marinate in refrigerator for 12–24 hours. Dry very well with absorbent kitchen paper. Open out, or if necessary butterfly the sirloin by cutting in half horizontally, three-quarters of the way through, and then folding open like a book. Score inside quite deeply, in a diamond pattern.

Cream butter with remaining ingredients and spread two-thirds over scored meat. Roll up and spread remaining butter mixture over the top. (It is not always necessary to tie up again, it depends on the way in which it has been cut.) Place flat in roasting pan and roast at 170 °C (325 °F, gas 3) for about 1 hour. Switch off oven and leave for 15 minutes before carving. Serve with Baked fried potatoes (page 132) and a salad.
Serves 6–8.

Meat Ball Stroganoff

Serve these meat balls in a mushroom sauce on ribbon noodles with a green salad.

500 g (18 oz) lean minced beef (or a mixture of pork, veal and beef)
60 g (2 oz) fresh breadcrumbs (see note)
1 onion, grated
1 garlic clove, crushed
2.5 ml ($^1/_2$ tsp) dried thyme
1 egg, beaten
generous pinch of salt
10 ml (2 tsp) soy sauce
30 ml (2 tbsp) oil

SAUCE
1 onion, chopped
300 g (11 oz) brown mushrooms, wiped and sliced
30 ml (2 tbsp) flour
250 ml (8 fl oz) beef stock
100 ml ($3^1/_2$ fl oz) thick soured cream
15 ml (1 tbsp) soy sauce

Mix mince with breadcrumbs, onion, garlic, thyme, egg, salt and soy sauce and form into about 16 small balls. Heat oil in large pan and fry meat balls over low heat until browned on all sides. Remove. In fat in pan, sauté onion and mushrooms. When mushrooms are browned and have drawn juices, sprinkle in flour. Slowly stir in stock and when thickened, add cream and soy sauce. Return meat balls and simmer, half-covered, until cooked through.
Serves 4 generously.

Note
Cut thick slices of day-old bread, remove crusts, then cube. Reduce to crumbs in a food processor or blender.

Oven-Baked Spicy Steak

500–600 g (18 oz–1 lb 5 oz) good quality steaks
oil
salt and ground black pepper
2 onions, chopped
2 garlic cloves, crushed
45 ml (3 tbsp) tomato sauce
20 ml (4 tsp) Worcester sauce
30 ml (2 tbsp) chutney
5 ml (1 tsp) brown sugar
5 ml (1 tsp) prepared mustard
75 ml ($2^1/_2$ fl oz) red wine

Beat steaks well with a mallet and brown on both sides in a little oil. Transfer to shallow baking dish, and season. Add a little more oil to frying pan if necessary, and sauté onions and garlic. Remove pan from heat, and stir in remaining ingredients. Mix well, pour over steak, and bake, uncovered, at 170 °C (325 °F, gas 3) for about 1 hour or until tender. Serve with a crisp salad and baked potatoes with soured cream. Serves 3–4.

Hint
Baked potatoes are always a good accompaniment to steak. Normally, however, they are baked in a hot oven, whereas meaty casseroles are often baked at 170 °C (325 °F, gas 3). This problem can be overcome by starting the potatoes off ahead, at 200 °C (400 °F, gas 6), and then allowing them to finish baking at the lower temperature with the meat dish.

Steak au Poivre Vert

or Steak with green peppercorn sauce – a richer and milder version of the popular Steak with black pepper.

4 x 150 g (5 oz) thick slices fillet steak
oil for frying
25 ml (5 tsp) brandy
salt
nut of butter
4–6 spring onions, chopped
15 ml (1 tbsp) green peppercorns, rinsed and drained
200–250 ml (6¹/₂–8 fl oz) single cream or soured cream (or half and half)
10 ml (2 tsp) Dijon mustard
pinch of sugar

Smear base of a heavy frying pan with just a very little oil and fry steak until done to your liking, turning once, without piercing. Stand back and flame with warmed brandy, shaking pan until flame dies. Salt lightly, transfer to platter and keep warm. Add nut of butter to pan and sauté spring onions. When softened, add peppercorns, cream or soured cream, mustard and sugar. Stir until just heated and well blended, then add any steak juices that escaped while it was standing. Mix well, pour over steak and serve at once. Serves 4.

Hint

Use a pair of tongs to turn steaks or chops. If the meat is pierced, natural juices will be lost.

Piquant Porterhouse

A rather classy stew. Even though this steak is not grilled, a top quality cut, such as rump or Porterhouse should still be used.

30 ml (2 tbsp) oil
4 x 125 g (4 oz) Porterhouse steaks
1 large onion, chopped
1–2 garlic cloves, crushed
generous pinch of dried oregano
pinch of thyme
30 ml (2 tbsp) flour
100 ml (3¹/₂ fl oz) port
45 ml (3 tbsp) tomato sauce
10 ml (2 tsp) Worcester sauce
5 ml (1 tsp) prepared mustard
15 ml (1 tbsp) brown sugar
15 ml (1 tbsp) brown vinegar
2 whole cloves
salt and ground black pepper
single cream (optional)

Heat oil in large, heavy frying pan and quickly brown steaks on both sides. Remove and set aside. Lower heat and add onion, garlic and herbs. When onion is softened, mix flour with port and add to pan together with steaks and remaining ingredients. Stir to mix, bring to the boil, then turn heat down to very low. Cover and simmer for about 40 minutes, turning once. When steak is tender and gravy thick, remove cloves. Stir the cream into the gravy if desired. Serve with noodles and a crisp salad. Serves 4.

Minced Beef Roll

Mozzarella cheese and canned chilli tomatoes give ordinary meat loaf a new look and an Italian flavour.

500 g (18 oz) lean minced beef
2.5 ml (¹/₂ tsp) salt
1 onion, coarsely grated
2 garlic cloves, crushed
30 g (1 oz) fine, fresh wholemeal
　breadcrumbs
1 egg, lightly beaten
2.5 ml (¹/₂ tsp) dried thyme
2.5 ml (¹/₂ tsp) dried oregano
15 ml (1 tbsp) Worcester sauce
45 ml (3 tbsp) chopped parsley
400 g (14 oz) canned chilli
　tomatoes
Mozzarella cheese

Mix all ingredients well, except chilli tomatoes and Mozzarella. Press mince mixture out on a sheet of greaseproof paper into a rectangle measuring 30 x 20 cm (12 x 8 in). Spread with half chilli tomatoes and sprinkle with 125 g (4 oz) coarsely grated Mozzarella. With the help of the paper, roll up from the long edge, like a Swiss roll. Place, seam-side down, on an oiled Swiss roll tin a little larger than the meat roll. Bake at 170 °C (325 °F, gas 3) for 30 minutes. Remove from oven and spread remaining chilli tomatoes over the top, and then arrange thin slices of Mozzarella, side by side, to cover the top completely. Return to oven and bake for 30 minutes more.

　Serve in thick slices with baked potatoes and soured cream, a mushroom gravy, or simply with mash and vegetables.
Serves 6.

Marinated Steak with Mustard Butter

Use small T-bone, rump or fillet steaks for this succulent dish.

900 g (2 lb) steak, sliced

MUSTARD BUTTER
60 g (2 oz) butter
30 ml (2 tbsp) chopped chives
15 ml (1 tbsp) French mustard
few drops of lemon juice
pinch of sugar

MARINADE
45 ml (3 tbsp) red wine
25 ml (5 tsp) soy sauce
1 medium onion, grated
30 ml (2 tbsp) oil
5 ml (1 tsp) dried oregano
2 garlic cloves, crushed

First make mustard butter: Cream all ingredients together, form into a roll, wrap in greaseproof paper and chill.

Arrange steaks in glass dish in single layer. Mix ingredients for marinade and pour over steak. Leave for 3–4 hours, turning occasionally. To cook, don't wipe steaks dry. Fry in heavy, ungreased frying pan, and pour over any remaining marinade when browned. Do not season.

　Serve with a slice of mustard butter on each steak.
Serves 4–6.

Roast Fillet of Beef with Mushrooms and Wine

1 kg (2¹/₄ lb) beef fillet
2 garlic cloves, slivered
5 ml (1 tsp) dry mustard
2.5 ml (¹/₂ tsp) paprika
30 ml (2 tbsp) oil
salt and ground black pepper
1 onion, chopped
200 g (7 oz) mushrooms, wiped and sliced
6 thyme sprigs, chopped
125 ml (4 fl oz) red wine
2.5 ml (¹/₂ tsp) salt
2.5 ml (¹/₂ tsp) sugar
soured cream (optional)

Spike meat all over with garlic. Rub with mustard and paprika and brown gently on all sides in hot oil. Transfer to small roasting pan that is a little larger than the meat, and season lightly.

In the same pan, fry onion, mushrooms and thyme. When beginning to brown, remove from heat and add wine, salt and sugar. Pour over fillet and roast at 170 °C (325 °F, gas 3) for about 1 hour 10 minutes for rare. Remove meat to serving platter and stand in warm place for 5 minutes.

Serve the gravy thickened, reduced, or with the addition of a little soured cream.
Serves 6–8.

Note

The only really accurate method of judging whether meat is done is to use a thermometer, as so many factors affect the amount of cooking time required.

Marinated T-Bone Steaks with Herbs

It's the marinade that makes this dish special, so don't be tempted to make any sauces.

1.25 kg (2³/₄ lb) T- bone steaks

MARINADE
30 ml (2 tbsp) oil
30 ml (2 tbsp) lemon juice
10 ml (2 tsp) French mustard
30 ml (2 tbsp) chopped mixed fresh herbs

Mix marinade ingredients and spoon on both sides of steak. Leave about 4 hours, turning occasionally. Pan-fry in relays, if necessary adding the merest little dashes of water or white wine to the pan if browning too fast. Season as you turn.
Serves 3–4.

Fillet Steak with Port and Mustard

4 x 150 g (5 oz) fillet steaks
15 g (¹/₂ oz) butter
10 ml (2 tsp) oil
salt and ground black pepper
45 ml (3 tbsp) single cream

MARINADE
45 ml (3 tbsp) port
10 ml (2 tsp) French mustard
10 ml (2 tsp) Worcester sauce
2–3 garlic cloves, crushed

Mix marinade ingredients. Pour over steaks and leave for 5–6 hours, turning once. Melt butter and oil in heavy pan. Pat steaks dry, reserving marinade. Brown steaks and season lightly. Remove to warmed dish. To pad add reserved marinade and the cream. Swirl around quickly, pour over steaks and serve immediately.
Serves 4.

Roast Sirloin with Green Peppercorn Sauce

This recipe is for a small sirloin, on the bone. Choose a piece with a good undercut of fillet and give it the following careful treatment. To ensure tenderness, the joint is first marinated and then roasted at a low temperature. It should be rare on the inside and darkly browned on the outside due to the soy-mustard baste. It is given a further lift with the tangy soured cream sauce.

1 x 1 kg (2¼ lb) piece sirloin on the bone
10 ml (2 tsp) dry mustard
2 garlic cloves, crushed
15 ml (1 tbsp) soy sauce
15 ml (1 tbsp) oil
1 fresh rosemary sprig
salt and ground black pepper

MARINADE
45 ml (3 tbsp) oil
45 ml (3 tbsp) lemon juice
100 ml (3½ fl oz) red wine
1 small onion, chopped
2 bay leaves

SOURED CREAM SAUCE
250 ml (8 fl oz) soured cream
1 egg yolk plus 2.5 ml (½ tsp) cornflour or 2 egg yolks
10 ml (2 tsp) green peppercorns, drained and rinsed
5 ml (1 tsp) French mustard
10 ml (2 tsp) brandy
pinch of salt
pinch of sugar

Remove any excess fat from meat and place in glass dish. Mix oil, lemon juice and wine and pour over meat. Add onion and bay leaves. Marinate for a few hours at room temperature if kitchen is cool, otherwise place in refrigerator. Turn occasionally.

To roast, pat meat dry. Mix mustard, garlic, soy sauce and oil and brush all over meat. Place on rack in roasting pan, put rosemary on top, and pour a little water in at the side to prevent scorching. Roast at 170 °C (325 °F, gas 3) for 1½ hours, adding a little more water as necessary. Season lightly towards end of roasting period. Stand in warming drawer to allow juices to settle.

Put all sauce ingredients into a small saucepan and heat slowly, stirring with a balloon whisk to mix, and then a wooden spoon. Stir until mixture thickens, but do not allow to boil. Serve sauce separately.

Carve joint upper side downwards, towards the bone, in thin slices. Cut fillet separately.
Serves 4.

Marinade for Steak on the Barbecue

30 ml (2 tbsp) chutney
30 ml (2 tbsp) tomato sauce
25 ml (5 tsp) Worcester sauce
5 ml (1 tsp) prepared mustard
5 ml (1 tsp) brown sugar
10 ml (2 tsp) brown vinegar
1 onion, chopped
2 garlic cloves, crushed

Arrange 675 g (1½ lb) rump steak in non-metallic dish. Mix ingredients for marinade, pour over steak and leave for 6 hours, turning twice. Makes about 100 ml (3½ fl oz).

Frosted Meat Loaf

The potato 'frosting' and a home-made tomato sauce or mushroom gravy add to the appearance and flavour of this meat loaf variation.

125 ml (4 fl oz) milk
1 egg
45 g (1¹/₂ oz) quick-cooking porridge oats
30 ml (2 tbsp) oil
2 onions, chopped
500 g (18 oz) minced beef
15 ml (1 tbsp) Worcester sauce
30 ml (2 tbsp) tomato sauce
45 ml (3 tbsp) chopped parsley
1 medium carrot, coarsely grated
5 ml (1 tsp) salt
5 ml (1 tsp) mixed dried herbs

FROSTING
6 medium potatoes, boiled and mashed
about 100 ml (3¹/₂ fl oz) milk, heated
30 g (1 oz) butter
1 egg yolk
salt and pepper

Beat milk with egg, add porridge oats and leave to soak for 10 minutes. Heat oil and fry onions until lightly browned. Mix remaining ingredients, then add fried onion and milk mixture. Combine thoroughly and pack firmly into an oiled 25 x 7.5 x 6-cm (10 x 3 x 2¹/₂-in) loaf tin. Bake at 180 °C (350 °F, gas 4) for 1 hour. Stand for about 10 minutes or until juices are absorbed, then unmould onto a flat, warmed serving dish.

Beat mashed potato with hot milk, butter and egg yolk until fluffy and creamy. Season, then swirl over the entire loaf, top and sides, and return to the oven at the same temperature for 15–20 minutes. Serve with a green vegetable and maybe pumpkin baked in the oven at the same time.
Serves 6.

Casseroled Rump with Port

A type of ragoût with a full-bodied flavour, which is excellent served peasant-style with hot bread or noodles, a salad and a good burgundy. It should be made well in advance, cooled and refrigerated to allow the flavours to mature.

1 x 750 g (1³/₄ lb) piece of rump steak, well-trimmed
oil
nut of butter
salt and ground black pepper
1 large onion, chopped
1 green pepper, seeded and diced
200 g (7 oz) brown mushrooms, wiped and sliced
45 ml (3 tbsp) flour
200 ml (6¹/₂ fl oz) port
200 ml (6¹/₂ fl oz) seasoned beef stock
pinch of sugar
2 whole cloves
2 garlic cloves, crushed
2.5 ml (¹/₂ tsp) dried oregano

Cut rump into biggish pieces, about 5 x 7.5-cm (2 x 3-in), and brown briefly over high heat in a large heavy frying pan just slicked with oil. Remove steak to baking dish, arrange in single layer, and season. To frying pan, add a little more oil and a nut of butter and fry onion, green pepper and mushrooms. When softened and beginning to smell good, spoon over steak.

To pan juices, add flour and stir until nut-brown. Slowly add port, stock, sugar and cloves. Stir well, and when hot and thick, pour over steak. Cover and bake at 170 °C (325 °F, gas 3) for 30 minutes. Add garlic and oregano and bake for another 30 minutes. Remove and cool.

Refrigerate all day, but remove in time for baking dish to reach room temperature. Reheat, uncovered, at 170 °C (325 °F, gas 3) for about 50 minutes, by which time gravy will be thickened and slightly reduced. Remove cloves before serving as suggested, or with new potatoes, spinach and courgettes.
Serves 4.

Fillet Steak with Sherry and Cream

So quick, and so good.

600 g (1 lb 5 oz) fillet steak
ground black pepper
crushed garlic
15 ml (1 tbsp) oil
5 ml (1 tsp) butter
salt
125 ml (4 fl oz) single cream or
   soured cream
5 ml (1 tsp) French mustard (or
   more to taste)
25 ml (5 tsp) sweet sherry
pinch of sugar if using
   soured cream

If the fillet is in one piece, slice into 4 and cut horizontally three-quarters of the way through the middle and open out like a book. Sprinkle each piece with pepper and garlic. Heat oil and butter in heavy frying pan and brown steak quickly on both sides. Salt as you turn. Mix single cream or soured cream with remaining ingredients, then pour over steaks when nearly done, and simmer until very hot, stirring gently. Allow sauce to reduce and thicken slightly.

Spoon steaks onto serving dish, pour sauce over and serve at once, with new potatoes and a simple tossed salad.
Serves 4.

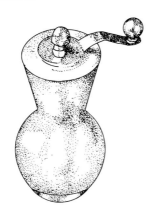

Braised Silverside of Beef

This lean boneless cut needs to be spiked with herb butter before being slowly simmered in a richly flavoured stock. Vegetables are added towards the end of the cooking period and served round the meat.

1 x 1.5 kg (3 lb) piece of
   silverside
45 g (1½ oz) butter
2 garlic cloves, crushed
5 ml (1 tsp) mixed dried herbs
5 ml (1 tsp) salt
5 ml (1 tsp) dry mustard
2.5 ml (½ tsp) paprika
30 ml (2 tbsp) oil
2 onions, chopped
250 ml (8 fl oz) beef stock,
   heated
125 ml (4 fl oz) red wine
125 ml (4 fl oz) tomato purée
2 bay leaves
10 ml (2 tsp) Worcester sauce
10 ml (2 tsp) brown sugar
new potatoes and baby carrots

Trim off any loose bits of sinew or fat from joint. Cream butter with garlic and herbs and place in freezer to harden. Make small slits in joint and stuff with slices of the herb butter. Rub outside of meat with salt, mustard and paprika. Heat oil in a large saucepan and brown meat and onions over low heat. Add stock, wine, tomato purée, bay leaves, Worcester sauce and sugar. Bring to a slow boil and then cover and simmer very gently for about 2 hours, or until meat is tender, turning twice. Add prepared vegetables and simmer until cooked.

Remove meat to large serving platter and surround with potatoes and carrots. Thicken gravy with a mixture of flour and water. Ladle a few spoonfuls over the joint and serve the remainder separately.
Serves 6.

Tipsy Steak

One of the nicest ways of doing steak – flamed with brandy and then smothered in butter and sherry.

30 g (1 oz) butter
1 garlic clove, crushed
15 ml (1 tbsp) chopped chives
2.5 ml (¹/₂ tsp) Worcester sauce
4 x 175 g (6 oz) rump or fillet
  steaks
paprika
25 ml (5 tsp) brandy, warmed
salt and ground black pepper
45 ml (3 tbsp) sherry

Cream together butter, garlic, chives and Worcester sauce. Allow to stand for several hours.

Brush heavy frying pan with a little oil (or use a non-stick pan) and heat. Sprinkle steak on both sides with paprika, and then fry on both sides until done to taste. Pour over brandy and flame, while you stand well clear. Remove steaks to heated platter and season lightly.

To frying pan, add sherry and the butter mixture. Stir until melted, then pour over steaks and serve at once.
Serves 4.

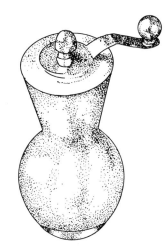

Easy Fillet Steaks

This useful recipe meets the challenge of serving slices of rare fillet without any last-minute frying.

600–700 g (1 lb 5 oz – 1³/₄ lb)
  fillet steak
oil for frying
salt and ground black pepper

SAVOURY BUTTER
100 g (3¹/₂ oz) butter, softened
2.5 ml (¹/₂ tsp) French mustard
2 garlic cloves, crushed
15 ml (1 tbsp) chopped chives
15 ml (1 tbsp) chopped fresh
  oregano or a generous pinch
  of dried
2.5 ml (¹/₂ tsp) Worcester sauce

First make the savoury butter: Cream butter with remaining ingredients. Roll into a sausage shape, wrap in greaseproof paper and chill.

Cut fillet into 15-mm (³/₄ -in) slices, then sear steaks over high heat in a heavy frying pan smeared with oil, for about 15 seconds per side. Be careful not to pierce when turning. Remove to ovenproof serving platter and leave, covered loosely.

Fifteen minutes before serving, season steaks lightly, and top each slice with a round of herb butter. Bake at 220 °C (425 °F, gas 7) for about 10 minutes, but the time does depend on the thickness of the meat and the degree of rareness required. Remove and leave in warming oven for 5 minutes for juices to settle. Serve with the buttery juices spooned over and tiny new potatoes.
Serves 4–6.

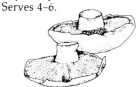

Chinese Stroganoff

In this dish – a combination of Russian Beef stroganoff and Chinese Steamed beef – everything is cooked together without any previous frying, which means that, not only is it simple to prepare, but also none of the flavour is lost.

1 kg (2¹/₄ lb) fillet of beef
1 large onion, coarsely grated
2 garlic cloves, crushed
300 g (11 oz) mushrooms, sliced
300 ml (10 fl oz) chicken stock
45 ml (3 tbsp) soy sauce
45 ml (3 tbsp) dry white wine
30 g (1 oz) cornflour
5 ml (1 tsp) dry mustard
30 ml (2 tbsp) oil
200 ml (6¹/₂ fl oz) soured cream

Slice fillet into thin strips across the grain. Divide between two medium, or one large, shallow baking dish, arranging in a single layer. Add onion, garlic and mushrooms. Whisk together stock, soy sauce, wine, cornflour, mustard and oil. Pour over meat and mushrooms, stir gently to moisten, then cover and stand for 3 hours.

Uncover and bake at 180 °C (350 °F, gas 4) for about 35 minutes, or until meat is cooked and gravy thick and brown. Swirl in cream and return to oven for 5 minutes to heat through. Serve with Chinese-style noodles (below). Serves 8.

Chinese-Style Noodles

250 g (9 oz) very small ring noodles
100 ml (3¹/₂ fl oz) oil
2 bunches spring onions, chopped
2 green peppers, seeded and diced
2 knobs root ginger, peeled and grated
800 g (1 lb 14 oz) canned bean sprouts, rinsed and drained
60-75 ml (4-5 tbsp) soy sauce

Boil noodles in plenty of salted water. Heat oil in a large, deep saucepan. Add spring onions, green pepper and ginger and stir-fry until tender-crisp. Drain noodles and toss with a spoon of oil. Add to vegetables and, keeping the heat low, fork in the sprouts and soy sauce to taste. Serve immediately.
Serves 8.

Bobotie

I like minced beef for this dish.
Lamb can too often be fatty,
unless it's left-over leg, which,
no matter what you do to it, will
always taste like left-over leg.
The following version is smooth
and moist and a favourite in our
house. It's even good cold.
Traditionally, this Dutch dish
should also include a handful of
quartered almonds, although I
don't think they make any
difference to the flavour.

1 fairly thick slice bread (white
    or brown)
375 ml (12 fl oz) milk
30 ml (2 tbsp) oil
15 g ($^1/_2$ oz) butter
2 onions, sliced
2 garlic cloves, crushed
25 ml (5 tsp) curry powder
10 ml (2 tsp) salt
30 ml (2 tbsp) chutney
15 ml (1 tbsp) smooth
    apricot jam
15 ml (1 tbsp) Worcester sauce
5 ml (1 tsp) turmeric
25 ml (5 tsp) brown vinegar
1 kg (2$^1/_4$ lb) minced beef
60 g (2 oz) sultanas
3 eggs
pinch of salt
pinch of turmeric
bay leaves

Remove crusts and soak bread
in milk. Heat oil and butter in
large pan and fry onions and
garlic. When onions are soft, add
curry powder, salt, chutney, jam,
Worcester sauce, turmeric and
vinegar and mix well. Drain,
mash bread and reserve milk.
Add bread to pan together with
mince and sultanas. Cook over
low heat, stirring, and when
meat begins to turn brown,
remove from heat. Add 1 beaten
egg, mix well, then spoon into a
greased, 30 x 15-cm (12 x 6-in)
baking dish and level the top.
   Beat remaining eggs with
reserved milk, you should have
300 ml (10 fl oz), and the salt
and turmeric. Pour over meat
mixture and put a few bay leaves
on top. Stand dish in a larger
pan of water (this is important
to prevent drying out) and bake,
uncovered, at 180 °C (350 °F,
gas 4) for 1 hour or until set.
Serve with rice, coconut,
chutney, nuts and bananas.
Serves 8.

Biriani with Lentils

Biriani is a Malay dish usually prepared with rice and mutton. This is a simple variation, spicy rather than hot.

30 ml (2 tbsp) oil
1 large onion, sliced
2 garlic cloves, crushed
1 fat cinnamon stick
2 bay leaves
4 cardomom pods, split
2.5 ml (¹/₂ tsp) ground cumin
10 ml (2 tsp) ground coriander
1 knob root ginger, peeled and crushed
10 ml (2 tsp) biriani paste
750 g (1³/₄ lb) minced beef
250 g (9 oz) brown lentils, soaked overnight
10 ml (2 tsp) lemon juice
5 ml (1 tsp) salt
650 ml (21 fl oz) stock
30 ml (2 tbsp) tomato paste
pinch of sugar

Heat oil in large saucepan and add onion and garlic. When browned, add all the spices and stir for a minute or two, then add mince. Keep stirring, and when meat is no longer pink, add drained lentils and remaining ingredients. Cover and simmer very gently for 45 minutes, then remove bay leaves, cinnamon and cardamom pods. Raise the heat and simmer uncovered for about 5 minutes until excess liquid has evaporated. Adjust seasoning and serve with Spiced yellow rice or Spiced raisins (see below). Serves 8.

Spiced Yellow Rice

300 g (11 oz) rinsed brown rice
1 litre (1³/₄ pints) water
5 ml (1 tsp) salt
5 ml (1 tsp) sugar
2.5 ml (¹/₂ tsp) turmeric
generous pinch of ground cloves
oil
75 g (2¹/₂ oz) seedless raisins

Put all ingredients except raisins into large saucepan, bring to the boil, then cover and simmer until rice is tender. Rinse, then steam in colander with raisins until dry and fluffy.
Serves about 8.

Spiced Raisins

300 g (11 oz) seedless raisins
2.5 ml (¹/₂ oz) ground cinnamon
100 ml (3¹/₂ fl oz) brown vinegar
100 ml (3¹/₂ fl oz) water
45 ml (3 tbsp) brown sugar
generous pinch of ground cloves
2.5 ml (¹/₂ tsp) ground ginger
2 bay leaves

Simmer all the ingredients in a covered saucepan for 30 minutes. Spoon into a bowl and cool. Remove bay leaves before serving.

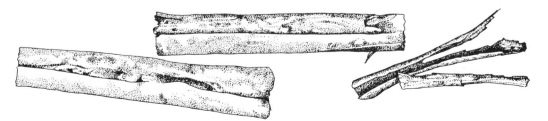

Stuffed Aubergines with Mince and Feta

A favourite way of serving mince, simmered in red wine, piled into aubergine cases, baked and topped with Feta cheese. This dish can be assembled in advance and set aside until an hour before serving. Serve simply with a green salad and crusty bread.

4 x 125 g (4 oz) small, firm
   aubergines
salt
30 ml (2 tbsp) oil
1 onion, finely chopped
1 green pepper, seeded and diced
250 g (9 oz) lean minced beef
   or lamb
1–2 garlic cloves, crushed
5 ml (1 tsp) dried oregano
100 ml (3$^{1}/_{2}$ fl oz) red wine
100 ml (3$^{1}/_{2}$ fl oz) water
30 ml (2 tbsp) tomato paste
salt and ground black pepper
pinch of sugar
2 bay leaves
Feta cheese

SAUCE
250 ml (8 fl oz) beef stock
30 ml (2 tbsp) tomato paste
pinch of sugar

Cut stem end from aubergines, slice in half, scoop out and dice flesh finely, leaving cases about 15 mm ($^{3}/_{4}$ in) thick. Sprinkle cases with salt and stand while making stuffing.

Heat oil and fry onion and green pepper. Add meat and stir until no longer pink. Add garlic, aubergine flesh, oregano, wine, water, tomato paste, seasoning, sugar and bay leaves. Cover and simmer for 20 minutes, or until mixture is succulent and thick. Cool, then remove bay leaves.

Rinse aubergine cases and pat dry using absorbent kitchen paper. Arrange in a 30 x 20-cm (12 x 8-in) baking dish and fill cases with meat mixture. Mix ingredients for sauce, pour around aubergines and bake, covered, at 180 °C (350 °F, gas 4) for 45 minutes, by which time cases should be soft. Sprinkle generously with crumbled Feta cheese to cover tops, and return to oven for another 15 minutes. Spoon sauce over each serving. Serves 4.

Stuffed Leg of Lamb

Glazed Leg of Lamb

4 garlic cloves, thinly sliced
1 thick slice wholemeal bread,
    crumbled
45 ml (3 tbsp) seedless raisins
2.5 ml ($^1/_2$ tsp) dried thyme
5 ml (1 tsp) dried marjoram
2.5 ml ($^1/_2$ tsp) salt
1 x 1.8-2 kg ($3^3/_4$-$4^1/_2$ lb) leg
    of lamb
flour
15 ml (1 tbsp) oil
2 onions, chopped
salt and ground black pepper
125 ml (4 fl oz) water
10 ml (2 tsp) brown vinegar

GLAZE
30 ml (2 tbsp) smooth apricot
    jam
25 ml (5 tsp) lemon juice
30 ml (2 tbsp) brown sugar
25 ml (5 tsp) Worcester sauce
30 ml (2 tbsp) tomato sauce

Mix garlic with bread, raisins,
herbs and salt. Make several

incisions in leg and lard with
crumb mixture, then dredge on
all sides with a little flour. Heat
oil in roasting pan and soften
onions. Add leg and brown
lightly on all sides. Remove from
heat, season, then add water and
vinegar. Bake, covered, at 170 °C
(325 °F, gas 3) for about 2 hours,
until nearly done.
    Heat ingredients for glaze.
Dribble half of it over the leg,
then pour remainder over
15 minutes later. Bake for a
further 15 minutes, then place
on serving platter and stand in
warm place for a short while
before carving. If necessary
simply add a little stock to pan to
make gravy, or thicken if
preferred.
Serves 6.

Stuffed Leg of Lamb

1 x 1.8 kg ($3^3/_4$ lb) boned leg
    of lamb
2 garlic cloves, crushed
2.5 ml ($^1/_2$ tsp) dried oregano
5 ml (1 tsp) salt
2.5 ml ($^1/_2$ tsp) dried thyme
2.5 ml ($^1/_2$ tsp) paprika
45 ml (3 tbsp) flour
500 ml (16 fl oz) water

STUFFING
20 ml (4 tsp) oil
5 ml (1 tsp) butter
2 onions, chopped
200 g (7 oz) mushrooms, wiped
    and sliced
1 green pepper, seeded and diced
45 g (1$^1/_2$ oz) toasted, flaked
    almonds
225 g (8 oz) cooked rice
10 ml (2 tsp) soy sauce

Make the stuffing by heating
butter and oil and frying half
the onion, all the mushrooms,
green pepper and almonds. Keep

stirring, and remove when nicely
browned. Add rice and soy sauce
and toss well.
    Open out leg of lamb and make
the surface area larger and flatter
by scoring it a bit. Sprinkle with
garlic, oregano and 2.5 ml
($^1/_2$ tsp) salt. Stuff with rice
mixture and tie securely.
    Mix thyme, paprika, 2.5 ml
($^1/_2$ tsp) salt and flour, rub all over
lamb and place on rack in roasting
pan, adding water and remaining
onion at the side. Roast at
170 °C (325 °F, gas 3) for 2 hours,
basting a few times with pan
juices, then cover loosely with foil
and leave in oven for another
hour, adding water or stock to
roasting pan as necessary. Leave
in warming oven for 10 minutes,
then make gravy from pan juices
before carving meat.
Serves 6-8.

Casserole of Lamb and Mushrooms

Casserole of Lamb and Mushrooms

Any lean lamb may be used in this casserole, but knuckles are my choice because they have a few bones, which add to the flavour, and very little fat, and become very tender with slow simmering.

30 ml (2 tbsp) oil
1 kg (2¹/₄ lb) lamb knuckles cut in 2.5-cm (1-in) slices
salt and ground black pepper
1 large onion, chopped
2 garlic cloves, crushed
300 g (11 oz) mushrooms, wiped and sliced
1 fresh rosemary sprig, chopped
30 ml (2 tbsp) flour
250 ml (8 fl oz) seasoned stock
100 ml (3¹/₂ fl oz) red wine
5 ml (1 tsp) Worcester sauce
30 ml (2 tbsp) tomato paste
1 bay leaf

Heat oil and brown lamb slices on both sides, then remove to baking dish and season. To fat in pan add onion, garlic, mushrooms and rosemary. Fry over low heat until soft and beginning to brown, then combine with meat in baking dish. Add a nut of butter to pan, if necessary, then stir in flour. Cook 1 minute, stirring, then slowly add stock and wine. When thickened add Worcester sauce, tomato paste, bay leaf and a good pinch of sugar. Stir well and then pour over meat and mushrooms. Cover and bake at 180 °C (350 °F, gas 4) for 1 hour.

Remove from oven and stir to mix meat with the gravy. Reduce heat to 170 °C (325 °F, gas 3) and continue baking, covered, until meat is very tender. Adjust seasoning, remove bay leaf, and ladle over portions of rice.
Serves 4.

Leg of Lamb in Beer

This is a super combination, resulting in a succulent, tasty joint – and it's perfect food when entertaining as it needs little attention.

1 x 2 kg (4¹/₂ lb) leg of lamb
2–3 garlic cloves, thinly sliced
1 x 10-cm (4-in) fresh rosemary sprig
salt and ground black pepper
15 ml (1 tbsp) prepared mustard
2 carrots, diced
2 onions, chopped
2 bay leaves
45 ml (3 tbsp) chopped parsley
345 ml (12 fl oz) beer
5 ml (1 tsp) brown sugar

Lard lamb with garlic and rosemary needles. Season, then spread mustard over top. Place in roasting pan and roast at 200 °C (400 °F, gas 6) for 30 minutes. Pour off any accumulated fat and add carrots, onions, bay leaves, parsley, beer and sugar.

Reduce heat to 170 °C (325 °F, gas 3) and continue roasting, basting occasionally. After 1¹/₂–2 hours add a little water or stock to ensure about 500 ml (16 fl oz) for gravy. After roasting for 2¹/₂ hours, the lamb should be tender and a good colour, and the gravy chunky and no longer tasting of beer.

Allow to rest for 20 minutes in the warming oven before carving. Don't thicken the gravy, but serve separately or pour over the joint. It is not necessary to serve mint sauce with lamb prepared in this way.
Serves 8.

Spicy Lamb Curry

This is based on a traditional Malay curry, not hot, but full of interesting flavours.

30 ml (2 tbsp) oil
2–3 large onions, sliced
3 garlic cloves, crushed
15 ml (1 tbsp) curry powder
10 ml (2 tsp) turmeric
10 ml (2 tsp) ground coriander
5 ml (1 tsp) ground cumin
1 cinnamon stick
1 knob root ginger, peeled and crushed in garlic press
4 cardamom pods, split
2 bay leaves
3 whole cloves
1–1.25 kg (2$^{1}/_{4}$–2$^{3}/_{4}$ lb) shoulder of lamb, sliced
3 tomatoes, skinned and chopped
10 ml (2 tsp) salt
5 ml (1 tsp) sugar
200 ml (6$^{1}/_{2}$ fl oz) hot water or stock

Heat oil in large saucepan and brown onions. Add garlic, curry powder, turmeric, coriander, cumin, cinnamon, ginger, cardamom pods, bay leaves and cloves and fry for a few minutes, stirring and taking care not to scorch. Remove most of the fat from the lamb but do not slice off the bone. Add to pan and when coated with curry mixture add tomatoes and remaining ingredients.

Cover and simmer very slowly, stirring occasionally, for about 1$^{1}/_{2}$ hours, or until tender. You shouldn't need to add more liquid, or have to thicken the rich gravy. Remove whole spices and serve with rice and sambals (see below).
Serves 4–5.

Note

Sambals are the little side dishes served with curries and range from diced paw-paw to poppadoms, but the simplest (and most popular) are: desiccated coconut, chutney, cucumber in yoghurt or soured cream, sliced bananas, and sweet pickles.

Lamb with Aubergines and Yoghurt

This hearty casserole is ripe with vegetables and has a full-bodied flavour. Because of its Greek influence, it goes well with a spinach, olive and avocado salad, and rice to mop up the gravy. It can be made in advance and reheated to allow the full flavour to develop.

1 kg (2¹/₄ lb) lamb knuckles, sliced
400 g (14 oz) aubergines
oil
2 large onions, chopped
2 large garlic cloves, crushed
400 g (14 oz) tomatoes, skinned and chopped
45 g (1¹/₂ fl oz) flour
375 ml (12 fl oz) hot stock
100 ml (3¹/₂ fl oz) white wine
45 g (1¹/₂ oz) parsley, chopped
5 ml (1 tsp) brown sugar
5 ml (1 tsp) dried oregano
170 ml (5¹/₂ fl oz) natural yoghurt
15 ml (1 tbsp) mayonnaise

The lamb knuckles should be cut into 2.5-cm (1-in) slices; don't buy hefty chunks in all sorts of untidy shapes. Trim, cube and degorge (page 135) aubergines.

Fry lamb slices well on both sides in a little oil, doing it in batches, and transferring to large baking dish when browned. To frying pan add a little more oil, and add onions and garlic. When lightly browned, add tomatoes, and simmer for a few minutes until soft. Sprinkle in flour and slowly stir in hot stock and wine. Stir until sauce becomes thick and chunky. Remove from heat and add aubergine cubes, parsley, sugar and oregano. Pour over lamb and mix well so that aubergines don't lie on top.

Cover and bake at 170 °C (325 °F, gas 3) for 1 hour 20 minutes, by which time lamb should be tender. Cool. Reheat, covered, at 170 °C (325 °F, gas 3) for about 30 minutes.

To finish off, mix yoghurt and mayonnaise and swirl in lightly, then return to oven for 5–10 minutes.
Serves 4.

Crumbed Lamb Chops with Herbs

Dipped in yoghurt and herbs, crumbed and then slowly baked until tender, this is a delicious way of preparing loin or thick rib lamb chops.

1 kg (2¼ lb) chops
200 ml (6½ fl oz) plain drinking yoghurt or buttermilk
5 ml (1 tsp) dried thyme
5 ml (1 tsp) dried marjoram
10 ml (2 tsp) garlic salt
10 ml (2 tsp) prepared mustard
175 g (6 oz) toasted crumbs

Trim excess fat from chops. Mix remaining ingredients, except crumbs. Coat chops with yoghurt mixture, then roll in crumbs, patting on firmly. Chill for at least 2 hours to set crumbs.
  To bake, preheat oven to 170 °C (325 °F, gas 3). Brush one large or two medium shallow baking dishes with oil and heat for 5 minutes in oven. Turn chops once in hot oil, then cover and bake for 45 minutes. Uncover and bake for a further 30 minutes or until browned and tender. A potato and onion casserole goes well with this dish.
Serves 6.

Spiced Lamb Casserole

Choose small, meaty knuckles for this satisfying casserole, and serve with rice.

45 ml (3 tbsp) oil
1.5 kg (3 lb) lamb knuckles, sliced
1 large onion, chopped
2 garlic cloves, crushed
5 ml (1 tsp) turmeric
5 ml (1 tsp) ground cinnamon
5 ml (1 tsp) peeled, grated root ginger
10 ml (2 tsp) ground coriander
2.5 ml (½ tsp) ground cumin
2 Granny Smith apples, peeled and diced
45 ml (3 tbsp) chutney
10 ml (2 tsp) brown sugar
5 ml (1 tsp) salt
125 ml (4 fl oz) white wine
250 ml (8 fl oz) stock
60 g (2 oz) seedless raisins

Heat oil in large, heavy frying pan and add knuckles. When well browned remove to baking dish. Turn heat to low, add a dash more oil if necessary and sauté onion. Add garlic and all the spices and toss for a minute, then add apples and remaining ingredients. Mix well, pour over lamb, cover and bake at 170 °C (325 °F, gas 3) for 2 hours. Adjust seasoning and thicken gravy if necessary.
Serves about 6.

Hint

Add interest and colour to plain boiled rice by forking in a handful of chopped parsley, 1 or 2 seeded, diced and lightly blanched red peppers, and a nut of butter to moisten.

Lamb Chop Casserole

This casserole of shoulder chops in a savoury sauce is so easy to prepare. The chops turn out tender, juicy and full of flavour.

6 x 175 g (6 oz) shoulder chops
30 ml (2 tbsp) oil
2 large onions, chopped
2 garlic cloves, crushed
1 green pepper, seeded and diced
45 ml (3 tbsp) flour
45 ml (3 tbsp) tomato sauce
15 ml (1 tbsp) Worcester sauce
15 ml (1 tbsp) light brown sugar
25 ml (5 tsp) brown vinegar
250 ml (8 fl oz) meat stock
2 bay leaves
salt and ground black pepper
5 ml (1 tsp) mixed dried herbs

Preheat oven to 200 °C (400 °F, gas 6). Arrange chops in large baking dish to fit in single layer, and put into oven for 15 minutes. While baking, make sauce by heating oil and frying onions, garlic and green pepper. When softened, remove from heat and stir in flour. When well mixed, add tomato sauce, Worcester sauce, sugar, vinegar, stock and bay leaves and stir to combine.

Remove chops from oven and sprinkle with salt, pepper and herbs. Pour sauce over and cover securely. Reduce temperature to 170 °C (325 °F, gas 3) and bake for about 1¹/₂ hours, or until tender. Serves 6.

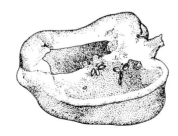

Lamb Stew with Squash

This unusual, spicy stew is baked, instead of simmered on the cooker, and requires little attention.

750 g (1³/₄ lb) chump chops (weight after trimming)
30 ml (2 tbsp) flour
5 ml (1 tsp) salt
10 ml (2 tsp) ground coriander
5 ml (1 tsp) turmeric
30 ml (2 tbsp) oil
2 onions, chopped
2 garlic cloves, crushed
125 ml (4 fl oz) stock or water
10 ml (2 tsp) brown vinegar
750 g (1³/₄ lb) squash (weight before peeling)
7.5 ml (1¹/₂ tsp) ground cinnamon
pinch of ground cloves
5 ml (1 tsp) ground ginger
15 ml (1 tbsp) brown sugar

Preheat oven to 170 °C (325 °F, gas 3). Having removed excess fat from chops, slice into fairly large pieces. Mix flour with salt, coriander and turmeric and dust meat on both sides. Heat oil in large frying pan and brown meat lightly over medium heat to prevent scorching. Remove to 30 x 20-cm (12 x 8-in) baking dish. Add a little more oil to frying pan if necessary and add onions and garlic. Cover the pan and allow to sweat gently. Add to lamb, pour stock over, sprinkle with vinegar, cover and bake for 45 minutes.

Peel squash and cut into smallish dice. Mix spices with sugar and shake cubes in this mixture until coated. Add to lamb, stir to mix, then return to oven and bake, covered, for 1 hour, stirring twice and adding a little more stock or water if necessary to ensure a rich gravy. Serves 4.

Herb-Crusted Lamb

Crusty, herby, lovely lamb.

1 x 2.5 kg (5¹/₂ lb) leg of lamb
3 garlic cloves, thinly sliced
1 small onion, grated
15 ml (1 tbsp) prepared mustard
15 ml (1 tbsp) soy sauce
90 g (3 oz) fresh wholemeal
  breadcrumbs
2.5 ml (¹/₂ tsp) dried thyme
2.5 ml (¹/₂ tsp) crushed dried
  rosemary
2.5 ml (¹/₂ tsp) finely grated
  lemon rind
salt and ground black pepper
10 ml (2 tsp) oil
1 onion, chopped

Wipe leg with vinegar-water,
remove outer membrane and
insert garlic in small slits all
over. Mix grated onion with
mustard and soy sauce. Using a
pastry brush, paint this mixture
all over the lamb, put it on a
rack in a baking dish, fat-side
up, and leave for 2 hours. Mix
crumbs with herbs, lemon rind
and seasoning. Moisten with oil
and set aside.

To roast lamb, preheat oven to
170 °C (325 °F, gas 3), add
chopped onion and 375 ml
(12 fl oz) water to roasting pan
and roast for 1¹/₂ hours. By this
time it should be nut-brown, so
cover loosely with a tent of foil,
shiny-side up. Roast for another
45–60 minutes, then remove.
Pour a little of the pan juices
into crumb mixture to make a
paste, then spread firmly all over
top of lamb. Return to oven and
roast a further 30–60 minutes,
basting occasionally. As it's a big
leg, a total of 3¹/₂ hours should
give you a pinkish middle with a
crisp exterior. Remember to
check level of juices in roasting
pan occasionally, adding hot
water or stock as necessary for
the gravy, and using the tent of
foil again towards the end if the
meat is browning too rapidly.
Remove lamb to serving dish
and keep warm. Pour juices into
a saucepan, and either reduce or
thicken.

Serve with roast potatoes or
Oven-baked spicy rice (page 101)
Serves about 10.

Note

**When pressed for time, the
following simple method is
useful and still very good. Mix
90 g (3 oz) brown breadcrumbs
with 2.5 ml (¹/₂ tsp) each dried
sage, thyme and marjoram,
1 small grated onion, 45 ml
(3 tbsp) chopped parsley and salt
and pepper. Moisten with 45 ml
(3 tbsp) melted butter or oil.
Spike lamb with garlic, but omit
all the other ingredients. Roast
on rack as above, then pat
crumb mixture all over exposed
surfaces 20 minutes before it's
done and baste several times
while browning.**

Yoghurt Sauce

**Serve a small portion of this
garlicky sauce with each
serving of Herb-crusted lamb.**

170 ml (5¹/₂ fl oz) thick natural
  yoghurt
2 small garlic cloves, crushed
15 ml (1 tbsp) chopped chives
5 ml (1 tsp) olive oil
pinch of salt
pinch of sugar
ground black pepper

Mix ingredients, cover and
stand at room temperature
for 2 hours.
Makes about 170 ml (5¹/₂ fl oz).

Roast Leg of Lamb with Fresh Herbs (left) and Savoury Lamb Stew (right)

Savoury Lamb Stew

A simple, homely casserole in which the lamb is slow-baked in a rich gravy.

4 x 175 g (6 oz) leg chops
2.5 ml (¹/₂ tsp) paprika
2.5 ml (¹/₂ tsp) dried thyme
2.5 ml (¹/₂ tsp) dried oregano
2.5 ml (¹/₂ tsp) curry powder
about 15 g (¹/₂ oz) flour
2.5 ml (¹/₂ tsp) salt
oil
1 large onion, chopped
2 garlic cloves, crushed
375 ml (12 fl oz) beef stock
2 medium tomatoes, skinned
   and chopped
45 ml (3 tbsp) chopped parsley
45 ml (3 tbsp) seedless raisins
5 ml (1 tsp) brown sugar
10 ml (2 tsp) Worcester sauce

Cut chops in half to make 8 neat pieces and remove any excess fat. Mix together the paprika, herbs, curry powder, 30 ml (2 tbsp) flour and 2.5 ml (¹/₂ tsp) salt and coat meat on both sides. Heat 30 ml (2 tbsp) oil in pan and brown chops lightly on both sides over medium heat, in 2 batches, to avoid stewing. Transfer to baking dish to fit closely. Add a little more oil to pan and fry onion and garlic. Sprinkle in 10 ml (2 tsp) flour, then add stock. Boil up, remove from heat, add tomatoes, and remaining ingredients. Mix well and pour over chops. At this stage you can set dish aside for a while if working ahead.

Bake, covered, at 170 °C (325 °F, gas 3), for 1¹/₂ hours, stirring once to mix meat and sauce. Serve with baked potatoes and green vegetables.
Serves 4.

Roast Leg of Lamb with Fresh Herbs

A traditional roast, lightly spiked with herbs, which is sure to become a family favourite.

1 x 2.5 kg (5¹/₂ lb) leg of lamb
2 x 5-cm (2-in) rosemary sprigs
4 x 5-cm (2-in) thyme sprigs
4 x 5-cm (2-in) marjoram sprigs
30 g (1 oz) fresh wholemeal
   breadcrumbs
3 garlic cloves, finely chopped
45 ml (3 tbsp) chopped parsley
¹/₂ onion, grated
10 ml (2 tsp) salt
5 ml (1 tsp) ground coriander
45 ml (3 tbsp) wholemeal flour
oil

Wipe lamb with vinegar and remove thin outer membrane. Chop rosemary needles, thyme leaves and marjoram leaves. Mix with breadcrumbs, garlic, parsley, onion and 5 ml (1 tsp) salt. Make deep slits all over lamb and stuff with little wads of crumb mixture.

Mix remaining salt with coriander and flour and rub all over leg. Dribble a little oil over top, and place leg on rack over roasting pan. Add a little water to pan to prevent scorching, and roast at 170 °C (325 °F, gas 3) for 3¹/₂ hours, adding water or stock to pan when necessary, and covering loosely with foil, shiny-side up, when browned sufficiently. Stand for 10 minutes in warming drawer before carving, while you make gravy from juices in roasting pan.
Serves 8–10.

Curried Chops

Marinated in a curry sauce, these chops may be barbecued or roasted in the oven.

6 x 125 g (4 oz) lamb loin chops
salt and ground black pepper

MARINADE
30 ml (2 tbsp) oil
1 large onion, chopped
2 garlic cloves, crushed
15 ml (1 tbsp) curry powder
5 ml (1 tsp) ground coriander
5 ml (1 tsp) turmeric
5 ml (1 tsp) peeled, grated
**   root ginger**
375 ml (12 fl oz) water
45 ml (3 tbsp) brown vinegar
30 ml (2 tbsp) smooth
**   apricot jam**
2 bay leaves

Trim chops and arrange in a non-metallic dish for marinating. Heat oil and soften onion and garlic. Lower heat and add curry powder, spices and ginger and fry gently for 2 minutes. Add water, vinegar, jam and bay leaves and simmer for 5 minutes. Pour over chops, cool and refrigerate, uncovered, for 2 days, turning several times. Grill over coals, or roast in oven.

   To roast, preheat oven to 170 °C (325 °F, gas 3). Place chops on rack in roasting pan. Add water to pan to prevent scorching, then roast for 45 minutes. Turn, season with salt and ground black pepper and baste. Roast for a further 45 minutes, or until very tender. Serve with Oven-baked rice (below) and the heated marinade.
Serves 6.

Oven-Baked Rice

300 g (11 oz) brown rice
785 ml (25 fl oz) water
5 ml (1 tsp) turmeric
2 cinnamon sticks
45 g (1¹/₂ oz) seedless raisins
5 ml (1 tsp) ground coriander
10 ml (2 tsp) oil
2.5 ml (¹/₂ tsp) salt
chopped parsley

Put all ingredients into a 23-cm (9-in) pie dish, cover and bake at 170 °C (325 °F, gas 3) for 1¹/₄ hours or until liquid is absorbed. Remove cinnamon and fork in a little chopped parsley for colour. Serves 6.

Marinated Roast Leg of Pork

Marinated Roast Leg of Pork

1 x 3 kg (6 lb) leg of pork
125 ml (4 fl oz) white wine
30 ml (2 tbsp) soy sauce
5 ml (1 tsp) ground ginger
30 ml (2 tbsp) brown sugar
3 garlic cloves, crushed
15 ml (1 tbsp) oil
12 fresh sage leaves
salt and ground black pepper
prepared mustard
1 onion, chopped

Remove rind from pork and score fat. Place in dish suitable for marinating – do not use copper or aluminium. Mix wine, soy sauce, ginger, sugar, garlic and oil. Pour over pork and leave in refrigerator overnight. Turn over in the morning. Just before roasting, dry leg well and make slits all over with a sharp knife. Insert tightly rolled sage leaves, season very lightly and spread top thinly with mustard. Reserve marinade.

Place on rack in roasting pan, fat side up. Pour some water into roasting pan and add onion. Roast at 170 °C (325 °F, gas 3) for 2¹/₂ hours. Pour over half the reserved marinade and cover loosely with foil, shiny-side up, as it should be beautifully browned. Roast for another hour, then pour over remaining marinade and add water or stock to roasting pan if necessary. Continue roasting until cooked through, about 4 hours total. Uncovered roasts always take longer than pot roasts, and pork must be cooked through.

Stand in warming drawer for about 15 minutes before carving, and thicken gravy if desired, or reduce by fast boiling. Braised cabbage and new potatoes make good accompaniments.
Serves about 12.

Pork with Orange

Seasoned with sage and mustard, simmered in wine and laced with orange, this oven-baked pot roast is succulent and delicious. The joint you buy is important as it must be a centre piece leg roast, that is, cut from the middle of the leg. This is a popular cut and easily available.

1 x 2 kg (4¹/₂ lb) leg of pork
1 large onion, chopped
5 ml (1 tsp) dry mustard
10 ml (2 tsp) dried sage
salt
paprika
125 ml (4 fl oz) white wine
250 ml (8 fl oz) water
30 ml (2 tbsp) orange marmalade
coarsely grated rind of 1 orange
2 bay leaves

Remove rind and all the fat from meat, then brown on all sides with onion in a heavy pan just smeared with oil. Place joint in baking dish and set pan aside. Mix mustard, sage and seasoning and sprinkle over meat.

Return pan with onion to low heat and add remaining ingredients. Heat, stirring to mix, then pour around pork. Cover, then bake at 180 °C (350 °F, gas 4) for 1¹/₂ hours. Turn, cover and cook until done – about 1¹/₂ hours more. Remove meat to serving platter and keep warm. Skim the gravy, then pour into saucepan and reduce over high heat, or thicken. Adjust seasoning. Serve with small boiled potatoes, stir-fried cabbage and carrots.
Serves 8.

Pineapple Pork Chops

These chops are a boon to the busy cook. There is no frying involved, they are simply marinated for a few hours and then baked until tender. The only last-minute attention is the reduction of the slightly fruity rich brown syrup.

6 x 125 g (4 oz) pork loin chops (weight after trimming)
1 large onion, coarsely grated
2 garlic cloves, crushed
10 fresh sage leaves, finely chopped, or 2.5 ml ($^1/_2$ tsp) dried
175 g (6 oz) canned unsweetened pineapple juice
20 ml (4 tsp) soy sauce
10 ml (2 tsp) honey
45 ml (3 tbsp) sultanas

The chops should be well trimmed before weighing.

Arrange to fit closely in glass baking dish. Sprinkle onion, garlic and sage over. Mix pineapple juice, soy sauce and honey. Pour over chops, cover and leave for about 3 hours, turning twice.

Add sultanas and bake, covered, at 170 °C (325 °F, gas 3) for about 1 hour 20 minutes or until tender. Remove chops to serving dish and keep warm. Pour juices into a small saucepan and boil over high heat until slightly reduced and a rich, caramel brown. Pour over chops. Especially good served with rice tossed with mushrooms and spring onions, and vegetables or a salad.
Serves 6.

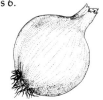

Pork Chops with Apple and Port

These chops are baked in a piquant sauce containing fruit, honey, cinnamon, lemon and port, which reduces to a spicy syrup. The flavour is quite bold, and rather unusual, and best accompanied by stir-fried cabbage and creamy mashed potatoes.

6 x 100 g ($3^1/_2$ oz) pork loin chops (weight after trimming)
oil
salt and ground black pepper
15 ml (1 tbsp) flour
100 ml ($3^1/_2$ fl oz) stock or water
60 ml (4 tbsp) port
2 Golden Delicious apples, peeled and finely chopped
45 ml (3 tbsp) sultanas
generous pinch of ground cinnamon
15 ml (1 tbsp) lemon juice
5 ml (1 tsp) honey

Trim rind and excess fat off chops. Heat a little oil in a heavy frying pan, and brown chops on both sides. Transfer to baking dish, to fit in a single layer, then season.

Add flour to fat in pan, and stir to absorb juices, then add stock and port and stir until smooth and thick. Remove from heat and add apples, sultanas, cinnamon, lemon juice and honey. Spread this mixture over tops of chops and cover securely before baking at 170 °C (325 °F, gas 3) for $1^1/_4$ hours, or until chops are done.
Serves 6.

Note

Unless otherwise stated, Golden Delicious apples are my preference when cooking. Apart from the appeal of their creamy yellow colour, they hold their shape when cooked and have a delicate flavour which enhances both sweet and savoury dishes.

Baked Pork Chops with Soy Sauce and Honey

Minimal preparation and no frying makes this one of the easiest ways of serving pork chops. They are simply soaked in a light marinade and then baked until tender. Good with new potatoes tossed in parsley butter, and a green salad.

900 g–1 kg (2–2¹/₄ lb) pork loin chops
2 large garlic cloves
25 ml (5 tsp) soy sauce
30 ml (2 tbsp) honey
45 ml (3 tbsp) dry white wine
2.5 ml (¹/₂ tsp) ground ginger
5 ml (1 tsp) dried sage

Remove rind and most of the fat from chops and arrange to fit in glass dish suitable for both marinating and baking. Crush

garlic directly over chops and rub in with back of knife. Mix remaining ingredients, pour over chops and marinate for about 4 hours at room temperature, or all day in the refrigerator. Turn chops occasionally while marinating.
  Remove dish 1 hour before baking and bake, covered, at 170 °C (325 °F, gas 3) for 1 hour. Remove cover, turn chops and bake uncovered for another 20 minutes or until tender and juices are slightly reduced and syrupy. Ladle a spoonful over each serving.
Serves about 6.

Lemon Pork Chops with Mustard Sauce

These chops, lightly flavoured with lemon and sage, are crumbed and baked and served with mustard sauce made in the old-fashioned way.

1 kg (2¹/₄ lb) pork chops
7.5 ml (1¹/₂ tsp) dried sage
150 g (5 oz) fine, toasted breadcrumbs
5 ml (1 tsp) salt
100 ml (3¹/₂ fl oz) yoghurt or buttermilk
45 ml (3 tbsp) mayonnaise
25 ml (5 tsp) lemon juice
2.5 ml (¹/₂ tsp) finely grated lemon rind

MUSTARD SAUCE
250 ml (8 fl oz) milk
1 egg yolk
10 ml (2 tsp) dry mustard
20 ml (4 tsp) flour
10 ml (2 tsp) brown sugar

15 ml (1 tbsp) brown vinegar
pinch of salt
small knob of butter

Remove rind and most of the fat from chops. Crush sage between fingers after measuring and mix with crumbs and salt. Mix yoghurt, mayonnaise, lemon juice and rind. Dip chops into yoghurt mixture, then into crumbs and chill for 2–3 hours.
  To bake, preheat oven to 170 °C (325 °F, gas 3). Lightly oil base of large baking dish, heat for a few minutes, then arrange chops in single layer, turning once. Cover and bake for 1 hour, then uncover and bake for 30 minutes more.
  For the sauce, put all ingredients, except butter, into the top of a double boiler, whisk well and then stir over simmering water until thick and smooth. Finally, stir in butter.
Serves about 6.

Roast Pork with Orange and Port

Gently seasoned with herbs, spices and orange rind, the gravy flavoured with orange juice and a dash of port, this is a simple but rather special way of treating a joint.

1 x 2 kg (4$^{1}/_{2}$ lb) leg of pork
7.5 ml (1$^{1}/_{2}$ tsp) salt
5 ml (1 tsp) paprika
5 ml (1 tsp) dry mustard
5 ml (1 tsp) ground ginger
5 ml (1 tsp) dried sage
5 ml (1 tsp) finely grated
  orange rind
375 ml (12 fl oz) water
1 onion, chopped
250 ml (8 fl oz) fresh orange
  juice
100 ml (3$^{1}/_{2}$ fl oz) port

Remove rind from leg and score underlying fat. (The rind may be salted and roasted separately.) Wipe leg with vinegar. Mix salt, paprika, mustard, ginger, sage and orange rind and rub into the leg. Place on rack in large roasting pan. Pour in the water and add the onion. Roast at 180 °C (350 °F, gas 4) for 1 hour, then reduce temperature to 170 °C (325 °F, gas 3) and roast for a further 1$^{1}/_{2}$ hours, adding more water to the roasting pan as necessary to prevent scorching. When nicely browned, cover the top loosely with foil, shiny-side up.

  Pour the orange juice and port over, and roast for another hour, basting twice. (Total cooking time about 3$^{1}/_{2}$ hours.) Remove to serving platter and leave in warming drawer for about 15 minutes before carving. The gravy should have reduced sufficiently, but may be thickened if desired.
Serves about 8.

Apple Pork Chops

Oven-baked chops with a
light gravy.

6 x 125 g (4 oz) pork loin chops
30 ml (2 tbsp) flour
2.5 ml (¹/₂ tsp) turmeric
2.5 ml (¹/₂ tsp) salt
generous pinch of ground
    cinnamon
20 ml (4 tsp) oil
onion rings
dried apple rings, soaked†
freshly chopped sage
brown sugar
200 ml (6¹/₂ fl oz) apple juice

Remove rind and excess fat
from chops and rub with a
mixture of flour, turmeric, salt
and cinnamon. Heat oil and
brown chops on both sides, then
arrange in a single layer in
baking dish to fit without
crowding.
    On each chop place two large
onion rings and two apple rings.

Sprinkle each chop with 2.5 ml
(¹/₂ tsp) freshly chopped sage
and a generous pinch of brown
sugar. Pour in apple juice at the
side, then cover and bake just
below centre of oven at 180 °C
(350 °F, gas 4) for about 1 hour
or until cooked through.
    Remove chops to warm
serving dish and tip juices into a
small saucepan. Reduce by rapid
boiling until syrupy – this takes
only a few minutes – then pour
over chops and serve.
Serves 6.

†Soak apple rings in water to
cover, until soft.

Pork Casserole with Mustard, Capers and Sage

This is a simple casserole with
a subtle flavour – a family
favourite, with a classy touch.

6 x 175 g (6 oz) pork loin chops
30 ml (2 tbsp) oil
salt and ground black pepper
1 onion, finely chopped
2 garlic cloves, crushed
45 ml (3 tbsp) flour
250 ml (8 fl oz) chicken stock
45 ml (3 tbsp) white wine
14 fresh sage leaves, finely
    chopped
5 ml (1 tsp) French mustard
10 ml (2 tsp) capers, rinsed and
    chopped
pinch of salt
pinch of sugar
30 ml (2 tbsp) double cream or
    thick soured cream

Cut off rind and trim chops of
most of the fat. Heat oil and
brown chops very lightly on
both sides. Arrange in baking
dish to fit closely, in single
layer. Season. To fat in pan add
onion and garlic. When
softened, add flour, and stir for
a minute, then slowly stir in
stock and wine. Allow to
thicken, then add sage, mustard,
capers, salt, sugar and cream or
soured cream. Mix well and pour
over chops.
    Cover and bake at 170 °C
(325 °F, gas 3) for 1 hour
10 minutes, or until chops are
tender and gravy is thick and
aromatic – the timing depends
on thickness of chops, size of
dish and position in oven. Good
with lemon-flavoured rice.
Serves 6.

Chinese-style Spare Ribs of Pork

Chinese-Style Spare Ribs of Pork

These ribs are first steamed until tender, marinated and then baked – which is not the usual way of dealing with them, but it does save hours of broiling, basting and drying out in the oven. They are neither overly sticky nor sweet, but do need to be eaten using fingers, with forks for the Chinese rice.

1.25–1.5 kg (2¹/₄–3 lb) spare ribs in one or two pieces
15 ml (1 tbsp) oil
1 onion, chopped
2 garlic cloves, crushed
45 ml (3 tbsp) soy sauce
100 ml (3¹/₂ fl oz) dry white wine
30 ml (2 tbsp) honey
1 knob root ginger, peeled and crushed
15 ml (1 tbsp) brown vinegar
10 ml (2 tsp) brown sugar

Steam ribs over simmering water for about 1¹/₂ hours or until tender. Meanwhile, make marinade by heating oil and frying onion and garlic until soft. Remove saucepan from heat and add soy sauce, wine, honey and ginger.

As soon as ribs are cool enough to handle, slice lengthways into long strips. Arrange in a single layer in a large glass baking dish and pour marinade over while they are still hot. Leave at room temperature for about 3 hours, turning occasionally.

Before baking, sprinkle with vinegar and sugar and then bake at 180 °C (350 °F, gas 4) for 30 minutes or until browned.

Place ribs on serving platter and surround with rice. Don't forget the finger bowls.
Serves 4.

Chinese Rice

2 leeks, thinly sliced
30 ml (2 tbsp) oil
200 g (7 oz) white, long-grain rice
500 ml (16 fl oz) heated chicken stock
25 ml (5 tsp) soy sauce
100 g (3¹/₂ oz) mung bean sprouts
45 g (1¹/₂ oz) almonds, toasted and chopped

Soften leeks in heated oil. Add rice and toss until coated with oil. Add stock and soy sauce, cover and simmer for 25 minutes or until cooked. Fork in sprouts and almonds.
Serves 4–6.

Fruity Pork Chops

800 g (1 lb 14 oz) pork loin chops
2–3 garlic cloves
125 ml (4 fl oz) pure apple juice
25 ml (5 tsp) soy sauce
25 ml (5 tsp) brown sugar
2.5 ml (¹/₂ tsp) dried rosemary
thin slices of orange and apple
brown sugar
ground cinnamon
butter

Arrange chops in baking dish. Crush garlic over chops. Mix apple juice, soy sauce, sugar and rosemary and pour over. Place 1 thin slice of orange and apple on each chop. Sprinkle a little sugar and cinnamon over apple, and dot with butter. Bake, uncovered, at 170 °C (325 °F, gas 3), for 1¹/₂ hours until tender, and liquid is slightly syrupy.
Serves 4–6.

Roast Pork with Apple Juice and Sage

Roast Pork with Apple Juice and Sage

1 x 2.5 kg (5¹/₂ lb) leg of pork
45 g (1¹/₂ oz) fresh wholemeal
  breadcrumbs
12–16 fresh sage leaves, finely
  chopped
5 ml (1 tsp) finely grated lemon
  rind
30 ml (2 tbsp) finely chopped
  parsley
30 ml (2 tbsp) chopped chives
15 ml (1 tbsp) oil
salt and ground black pepper
paprika and dry mustard
1 onion, chopped
500 ml (16 fl oz) apple juice
375 ml (12 fl oz) water or stock
2 Granny Smith apples, peeled
  and finely diced
30 ml (2 tbsp) honey

Remove rind from pork (salt
and roast it separately if
desired) and make deep incisions
all over top and sides. Mix
crumbs, sage, lemon rind,
parsley, chives and oil. Gather
the herby crumbs into little
wads, and push into the holes.
Season leg and place on rack in
large roasting pan. Dust top
with paprika and mustard.
  Put onion into roasting pan
and pour in 250 ml (8 fl oz) apple
juice and 250 ml (8 fl oz) water
or stock. Add apples and dribble
with honey. Roast just below
centre of oven at 200 °C (400 °F,
gas 6) for 45 minutes. Baste well,
then cover top loosely with foil,
shiny-side up. Pour remaining
apple juice and water into pan.
Reduce oven temperature to
170 °C (325 °F, gas 3) and roast
for about 3 hours more, basting
twice and adding more liquid if
necessary. The pork should be
cooked right through, and the
gravy reduced to a rich, thick
sauce. Check seasoning. Stand
pork in a warming oven for
about 15 minutes before carving.
Serves about 10.

Pork Chops with Cheese and Crumb Topping

500 g (18 oz) pork loin chops
1 onion, chopped
2.5 ml (¹/₂ tsp) salt
2.5 ml (¹/₂ tsp) ground black
  pepper
2.5 ml (¹/₂ tsp) dried sage
100 ml (3¹/₂ fl oz) chicken stock
100 ml (3¹/₂ fl oz) semi-sweet
  white wine
1 garlic clove, crushed
2 bay leaves
paprika

TOPPING
45 ml (3 tbsp) fresh brown
  breadcrumbs
30 ml (2 tbsp) finely chopped
  parsley
90 g (3 oz) Mozzarella cheese,
  grated
45 ml (3 tbsp) reserved pan juices
5 ml (1 tsp) prepared mustard

Brown trimmed chops on both
sides with onion. Sprinkle with
salt, pepper and sage. Add stock,
wine, garlic and bay leaves. Bring
to the boil, cover and simmer over
low heat for about 45 minutes
until tender. Mix remaining
ingredients, except paprika, and
spread over each chop. Sprinkle
with paprika. Place under
preheated grill until melted and
lightly browned. Thicken pan
gravy, if desired, and serve
separately.
Serves 4.

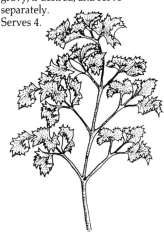

Ginger Glazed Ham

A change from ham and pineapple, this ham is brushed with a sweet apricot glaze and surrounded with spiced apricots. Serve with a tangy mustard sauce.

1 x 5 kg (11 lb) ham
beer
water
2 whole, peeled onions each stuck with 3 cloves
2 whole carrots
4 bay leaves
12 peppercorns
whole cloves

GLAZE
800 g (1 lb 14 oz) canned apricot halves
75 g (2¹/₂ oz) soft brown sugar
7.5 ml (1¹/₂ tsp) ground ginger
10 ml (2 tsp) smooth apricot jam

Soak ham overnight in cold water to cover. Next day, remove and wash well. Place in large saucepan and cover with beer and water – the beer makes it especially succulent. Add remaining ingredients, except cloves, then cover and simmer for 4–5 hours or until tender. As soon as it can be handled, remove skin and return ham to liquid to cool.

Score ham, insert cloves in squares and bake at 170 °C (325 °F, gas 3) for 45 minutes, basting with the glaze until crisp and golden brown.

For the glaze, drain syrup from apricots, measure out 125 ml (4 fl oz) and reserve the remainder. Place apricot syrup, sugar, ginger and jam in a small saucepan and melt over low heat, stirring.
Serves about 20.

Spiced Apricots

reserved apricot syrup from glaze
4 whole cloves
1 cinnamon stick
2.5 ml (¹/₂ tsp) ground mixed spice
10 ml (2 tsp) white wine vinegar
reserved apricots
maraschino cherries

Make up reserved apricot syrup to 250 ml (8 fl oz) with water, if necessary. Heat syrup, spices and vinegar in a large shallow saucepan. Add apricots, hollows down, and simmer very gently for 5 minutes. Remove from heat and cool apricots in syrup.

Place a cherry in each half and arrange around ham.

Mustard and Soured Cream Mayonnaise

Serve chilled, with cold ham.

250 ml (8 fl oz) thick mayonnaise
250 ml (8 fl oz) soured cream
30 ml (2 tbsp) French mustard
5 ml (1 tsp) lemon juice
45 ml (3 tbsp) chopped chives
pinch each of salt and sugar

Stir all ingredients together until well blended, then refrigerate, covered, for several hours before serving. Makes about 500 ml (16 fl oz).

Glazed Roast Pork

A beautiful, mahogany-coloured leg, larded with sage and marinated in soy sauce, honey and wine.

1 x 2 kg (4¹/₂ lb) leg of pork
1 thick slice wholemeal bread, crumbled
8–12 fresh sage leaves, chopped
2 garlic cloves, crushed
15 ml (1 tbsp) oil
salt
paprika

MARINADE
25 ml (5 tsp) soy sauce
30 ml (2 tbsp) honey
5 ml (1 tsp) ground ginger
250 ml (8 fl oz) dry white wine
1 large onion, chopped
2 bay leaves

Remove rind from leg as thinly as possible, cut small incisions on all surfaces. Mix bread, sage, garlic and oil and push little wads of the breadcrumb mixture into the incisions. Place pork, fat-side down, in glass dish for marinating. Mix ingredients for marinade and pour over. Arrange pork rind round sides. Refrigerate overnight, turning in the morning.

To roast, sprinkle each side of leg with salt and paprika. Place, fat-side up, on rack in roasting pan, and pour over one-third of the strained marinade. Roast at 170 °C (325 °F, gas 3) for 1 hour. Pour over another third of the marinade and roast for another hour. If browning too rapidly, cover loosely with a tent of foil, shiny-side up. Pour over remaining marinade and continue roasting until done – up to 4 hours in total. When deeply pricked, the juices should run clear. Serve hot with apple sauce, or cold with coleslaw. Serves about 8.

Pork Fillet in Sweet and Sour Sauce

This dish is quite different from the batter-dipped fried pork served with a sticky, sweet and sour sauce. Instead, strips of lean fillet are slow-simmered with vegetables and pineapple in a sauce subtly flavoured with sherry, sugar, soy sauce and vinegar.

675 g (1¹/₂ lb) pork fillet
oil for frying
1 large onion, chopped
1 green pepper, seeded and diced
2 celery sticks, chopped
425 g (15 oz) canned pineapple rings in natural juice
170 ml (5¹/₂ fl oz) water
30 ml (2 tbsp) light brown sugar
25 ml (5 tsp) soy sauce
25 ml (5 tsp) brown vinegar
45 ml (3 tbsp) sherry
15 ml (1 tbsp) cornflour

Remove any sinewy bits from fillet, slice into long strips, and then into thin slices across the grain. Heat 30 ml (2 tbsp) oil in large frying pan. Fry half the pork and set aside. Repeat. Add a little more oil to fat in pan if necessary and stir-fry onion, green pepper and celery. Return meat to pan. Drain pineapple and add juice and water to meat. Bring to the boil, then cover and simmer gently until pork is cooked and tender. Add pineapple rings, cut into small cubes. Stir together sugar, soy sauce, vinegar, sherry and cornflour until smooth. Add to pan, cover and simmer about 15 minutes to blend flavours. Adjust seasoning.
Serves 4–6.

Moussaka

My version of this popular Greek dish.

500 g (18 oz) aubergines
olive and vegetable oil for frying
1 large onion, chopped
2 garlic cloves, crushed
2.5 ml ($^1/_2$ tsp) dried oregano
500 g (18 oz) minced veal
25 ml (5 tsp) tomato paste
100 ml ($3^1/_2$ fl oz) dry white
   wine
45 ml (3 tbsp) chopped parsley
2.5 ml ($^1/_2$ tsp) ground cinnamon
salt and ground black pepper
5 ml (1 tsp) sugar
2 eggs, separated
45 g ($1^1/_2$ oz) butter
60 ml (4 tbsp) flour
400 ml (13 fl oz) milk
grated Cheddar cheese
5 ml (1 tsp) freshly grated
   nutmeg

Wash and trim ends off
aubergines. Slice into thin
rounds and dégorge (page 135).
Pat dry with absorbent kitchen
paper and fry on both sides in
mixture of olive and vegetable
oil. Keep the heat fairly low and
occasionally cover the pan and
the slices will brown and soften
without absorbing quite so much
oil. Do them in batches and
drain on absorbent kitchen
paper.
   In same pan sauté onion and
garlic. Sprinkle in oregano, then
add veal. Cook, stirring, until
browned and no longer lumpy.
Mix tomato paste, wine, parsley,
cinnamon, seasoning and sugar.
Pour over veal, stir well, cover
and simmer for 20 minutes.
Whisk egg whites until foamy.
Remove pan from heat and stir
in egg whites. The meat sauce
should be moist but not sloppy.
Make a thick white sauce with
butter, flour and milk. Stir in
60 g (2 oz) cheese and when
melted remove from heat. Add a
little cheese sauce to the beaten
egg yolks, then mix into
remaining sauce. Stir in nutmeg
and season. To assemble, cover
bottom of baking dish with half
the aubergine slices, top with
meat sauce, cover with
remaining aubergines, then pour
cheese sauce over top. Sprinkle
with extra cheese, then bake,
uncovered, at 180 °C (350 °F,
gas 4) for 35–40 minutes. Turn
off oven and leave for
15 minutes before serving.
Serves 5–6.

Veal Schnitzel with Tomato and Mozzarella

A wonderful way of serving schnitzels: first crumbed and fried, then baked in a bright tomato and vermouth sauce topped with melting Mozzarella. This dish may be assembled in advance. Serve with risotto or Saffron rice (page 114) and a crisp, garlicky salad.

6 x 75 g (2¹/₂ oz) veal schnitzels
1 egg
10 ml (2 tsp) water
60 g (2 oz) toasted breadcrumbs, finely crushed
salt and ground black pepper
30 ml (2 tbsp) grated Parmesan cheese
oil for frying
1 onion, chopped
1 garlic clove, crushed
400 g (14 oz) canned tomatoes, chopped
2.5 ml (¹/₂ tsp) dried basil
2 bay leaves
30 ml (2 tbsp) chopped parsley
45 ml (3 tbsp) dry vermouth
5 ml (1 tsp) sugar
200 g (7 oz) Mozzarella cheese, sliced
generous pinch of dried oregano

Slice each schnitzel into 2 equal pieces. Beat egg with water and mix crumbs with 2.5 ml (¹/₂ tsp) salt, a little pepper and Parmesan. Brush veal with egg, then dip into crumbs, coating both sides. Chill at least 1 hour to set crumbs.

Heat 30 ml (2 tbsp) oil in frying pan and brown veal very lightly, turning once. Do this in batches and add a little more oil when necessary. Arrange schnitzels to fit closely in a single layer in a large 30 x 23-cm (12 x 9-in) baking dish.

To make sauce, lightly sauté onion and garlic. Add tomatoes, plus juice, 2.5 ml (¹/₂ tsp) salt, basil, bay leaves, parsley, vermouth and sugar. Cover and simmer gently for 30 minutes. Remove bay leaves and spoon sauce over veal. Top with Mozzarella and dust with oregano. If preparing in advance, set aside at this point. Bake, uncovered, at 170 °C (325 °F, gas 3) for 40 minutes, then pour in a little water or stock at the side – the finished dish should be moist and juicy – and bake for 10 minutes longer. Serves 4.

Casserole of Veal in Mustard Cream Sauce

Slices of veal shin with marrow bones make a singularly succulent dish. Serve with saffron rice and a bold green bean and olive salad.

45 ml (3 tbsp) flour
2.5 ml (¹/₂ tsp) salt
7.5 ml (1¹/₂ tsp) dry mustard
750 g (1³/₄ lb) veal shin cut in 2.5-cm (1-in) slices
45 ml (3 tbsp) oil
1 onion, chopped
4 leeks, sliced
250 g (9 oz) tomatoes, skinned and chopped
100 ml (3¹/₂ fl oz) white wine
100 ml (3¹/₂ fl oz) chicken stock
2 bay leaves
5 ml (1 tsp) sugar
125 ml (4 fl oz) soured cream
25 ml (5 tsp) French mustard

Mix flour, salt and mustard. Nick edges of veal and coat with flour mixture. Heat oil in large frying pan and brown veal on both sides. Remove to baking dish in single layer. Add a little more oil to pan, if necessary, and soften onion and leeks. Add tomatoes, wine, stock, bay leaves, sugar and any left-over flour mixture. Boil up, then pour over veal. Cover and bake at 170 °C (325 °F, gas 3) for 1 hour. Turn carefully, stir gravy, and continue baking for a further 30 minutes until tender.

Mix soured cream with mustard, stir into casserole and return to oven until heated through. Adjust seasoning, and sprinkle with chopped parsley and basil, if available, before serving.
Serves 4.

Veal Goulash with Noodles

A richly coloured, Hungarian stew using simple ingredients.

30 ml (2 tbsp) oil
30 g (1 oz) butter
750 g (1³/₄ lb) veal, cubed
2 large onions, chopped
2 garlic cloves, crushed
1 red pepper, seeded and diced
10 ml (2 tsp) paprika
45 ml (3 tbsp) flour
300 ml (10 fl oz) chicken stock
125 ml (4 fl oz) tomato purée
100 ml (3¹/₂ fl oz) white wine
salt and ground black pepper
large pinch of sugar
2 bay leaves
250 g (9 oz) ribbon noodles
nut of butter
25 ml (5 tsp) poppy seeds
125 ml (4 fl oz) soured cream
chopped parsley

Heat oil and butter in a very large frying pan. Add meat and brown in batches to avoid stewing. Remove meat and set aside. Add a little more oil to pan if necessary and soften onions, garlic and pepper, sprinkle in paprika and flour. Keep heat low, as over-heated paprika becomes bitter. Return meat and stir in stock, tomato purée, wine, salt, pepper, sugar and bay leaves.

Stir to mix, then cover and simmer very gently, stirring occasionally, for about 1¹/₂ hours or until meat is very tender. Remove bay leaves and if sauce needs to be thickened, tilt lid of pan and simmer over low heat.

Cook noodles in plenty of salted water. Drain, then toss with butter and poppy seeds.

Swirl soured cream into meat mixture, turn out onto large, warmed platter, sprinkle with chopped parsley and surround with the noodles.
Serves 4 generously.

Osso Buco

This unpretentious Milanese dish consists of shin of veal in a robust gravy. It is important that each slice of veal has a thick marrow bone in the centre, that the fresh garnish, or gremolada, is used, and that the dish is served with Saffron rice (see right) or risotto.

45 ml (3 tbsp) flour
5 ml (1 tsp) salt
ground black pepper
1.25 kg (2³/₄ lb) veal shin cut in 5-cm (2-in) slices
45 ml (3 tbsp) oil
2 onions, chopped
2 garlic cloves, crushed
345 ml (11 fl oz) chicken stock
150 ml (5 fl oz) dry white wine
400 g (14 oz) canned tomatoes, chopped
2 bay leaves
2.5 ml (¹/₂ tsp) sugar
2.5 ml (¹/₂ tsp) dried rosemary

GREMOLADA
30 ml (2 tbsp) finely chopped parsley
1 garlic clove, crushed
5 ml (1 tsp) finely grated lemon rind

Mix flour, salt and pepper and use to coat veal slices. Heat oil and brown lightly on both sides in large frying pan or casserole. Towards end of frying period add onions and garlic and a little more oil if necessary. Continue frying for 1–2 minutes, then remove from heat and add 250 ml (8 fl oz) stock, wine, tomatoes plus the juice, bay leaves and sugar. Either bake in casserole, or transfer to large baking dish, arranging veal so that there is no chance of the marrow falling out. Cover securely and bake at 170 °C (325 °F, gas 3) for 1¹/₂ –2 hours, or until tender. If dish is well covered there should be no need to turn or baste slices. Remove from oven and cool.

Add rosemary and remaining chicken stock 45 minutes before required. Cover and reheat at the same temperature. Mix the ingredients for gremolada, sprinkle over the top and serve with Saffron rice, a green salad, and triangles of toast for the marrow.
Serves about 6.

Saffron Rice

2.5 ml (¹/₂ tsp) saffron threads
25 ml (5 tsp) hot water
15 g (¹/₂ oz) butter
15 ml (1 tbsp) oil
1 onion, finely chopped
200 g (7 oz) white long-grain rice
500 ml (16 fl oz) hot chicken stock
salt and ground black pepper
1–2 cinnamon sticks

Soak saffron in the hot water for at least 1 hour. Heat oil and butter, add onion and allow to soften. Add rice and toss until glistening, then slowly stir in hot stock. Add saffron plus water, seasoning and cinnamon. Bring to the boil, then cover and simmer over very low heat for about 25 minutes. Remove cinnamon sticks and serve.
Serves 4–6.

Saddle of Venison

This prime cut deserves special treatment.

about 250 g (9 oz) pork fat
2 garlic cloves, crushed
5 ml (1 tsp) mixed dried herbs
small saddle of venison
30 ml (2 tbsp) oil
1 large onion, chopped
salt and ground black pepper
125 ml (4 fl oz) water
15 ml (1 tbsp) chutney
smooth apricot jam

MARINADE
250 ml (8 fl oz) red wine
45 ml (3 tbsp) brown vinegar
45 ml (3 tbsp) water
2 lemon slices
1 carrot, sliced
8 peppercorns
1 bay leaf
5 ml (1 tsp) salt

Cut pork fat into cubes, reserving 2 thin strips. Roll cubes in garlic and dried herbs. Remove thin covering membrane from saddle and lard meat with pork fat. Place in glass or non-metallic dish.

Mix ingredients for marinade, pour over saddle and refrigerate for 48 hours, turning several times.

Heat oil in roasting pan with lid, and fry onion. Dry saddle, reserving marinade, and brown lightly. Season. Add water, chutney and 125 ml (4 fl oz) strained marinade. Place strips of pork fat on top, cover and roast at 170 °C (325 °F, gas 3) until done, allowing about 30 minutes per 450 g (1 lb) plus an extra 30 minutes. Remove, spread with a thin layer of jam and brown quickly under the grill. Thicken gravy, adding a little more water, wine or stock if necessary. Serve with Red wine jelly (see below).

Red Wine Jelly

250 ml (8 fl oz) dry red wine
5 ml (1 tsp) powdered gelatine
10 ml (2 tsp) sugar
4 blades of mace
5 ml (1 tsp) finely grated orange rind

Put ingredients into a saucepan, bring to the boil, stirring, and boil for at least 1 minute. Strain into small pots and leave to set. Makes 250 ml (8 fl oz).

Vegetable Biriani

Based on a dish from Northern India, this is an aromatic combination of rice, lentils, vegetables and spices.

200 g (7 oz) brown rice
100 g (3½ oz) brown lentils, picked over and rinsed
5 ml (1 tsp) salt
5 ml (1 tsp) turmeric
5 ml (1 tsp) ground coriander
2.5 ml (½ tsp) ground cumin
1 cinnamon stick
815 ml (26 fl oz) water
200 g (7 oz) aubergine
30 g (1 oz) butter
30 ml (2 tbsp) oil
2 leeks, sliced
1 large onion, chopped
2–4 garlic cloves, crushed
2.5 ml (½ tsp) masala paste (or more to taste)
1 red pepper, seeded and diced
4 juicy tomatoes, skinned and chopped
300 g (11 oz) courgettes, peeled and sliced
175 g (6 oz) green peas
pinch of salt
pinch of sugar
75 g (2½ oz) flaked almonds
30 g (1 oz) butter
90 g (3 oz) sultanas

Put rice, lentils, salt, spices and water into a saucepan. Bring to the boil, cover, lower heat and leave to cook gently for about 50 minutes, by which time liquid should be absorbed. Fluff up with a fork and remove cinnamon stick. Meanwhile, dégorge aubergine (page 135), and cube. Heat butter and oil in large frying pan and sauté leeks, onion, garlic and masala paste. When softened, add aubergine, red pepper, tomatoes, courgettes and peas. Cook for approximately 10 minutes, stirring occasionally, until courgettes are translucent. Remove from heat and add salt and sugar. In a large, deep, buttered dish, layer one-third of the rice, half the vegetable mixture, another third of the rice, remaining vegetable mixture, then remainder of the rice. Bake, covered, at 170 °C (325 °F, gas 3) for 30 minutes. Just before end of baking time, fry almonds in butter. When lightly browned, add sultanas, heat through and spoon over top of biriani.
Serves about 8.

Crêpes Ratatouille

Crêpes Ratatouille

In this dish, pancakes are wrapped round a savoury vegetable filling, covered with a white sauce, sprinkled with cheese, and then baked. This dish can be assembled successfully in advance.

BLENDER CRÊPES
125 g (4 oz) flour
generous pinch of salt
1 egg
250 ml (8 fl oz) milk
125 ml (4 fl oz) water
25 ml (5 tsp) oil
2.5 ml (¹/₂ tsp) dried oregano
  (optional)

FILLING
15 ml (1 tbsp) vegetable oil
15 ml (1 tbsp) olive oil
1 medium aubergine, cubed
1 green pepper, seeded and diced
1 onion, chopped
200 g (7 oz) courgettes, scrubbed
  and sliced

salt and ground black pepper
2 large tomatoes, skinned and
  chopped
2 garlic cloves, crushed
5 ml (1 tsp) dried basil
5 ml (1 tsp) sugar

SAUCE
knob of butter
45 ml (3 tbsp) flour
500 ml (16 fl oz) milk
salt and pepper
5 ml (1 tsp) prepared mustard

grated Cheddar or Gruyére
  cheese
30 ml (2 tbsp) grated Parmesan
  cheese

Put all ingredients for crêpes into a blender and blend well, stopping to scrape down sides once or twice. Stand for 1 hour, blend again, then make thin crêpes in an 18-cm (7-in) frying pan. As they are done, stack on large plate with a circle of greaseproof paper between each.
  For the filling, put oils,

aubergine, green pepper, onion, courgettes and seasoning into a large saucepan. Cover and stew slowly, stirring occasionally, for about 35 minutes or until soft. Add tomatoes, garlic, basil and sugar. Half-cover saucepan and cook until tomatoes are pulpy. If necessary, remove lid and boil rapidly to reduce excess liquid. Cool, then divide between crêpes, roll into cigar shapes and place side by side in buttered baking dish. The filling is enough for 8–10 crêpes.
  Make white sauce by melting butter, stirring in flour, then adding milk slowly, stirring constantly. When thick, add seasonings and pour over crêpes. Sprinkle generously with cheese, top with Parmesan and heat through at 170 °C (325 °F, gas 3) for about 40 minutes.
Serve 1–2 crêpes per person.

Chickpea Stew

30 g (1 oz) butter
30 ml (2 tbsp) oil
1 large onion, chopped
2 garlic cloves, crushed
2 carrots, diced
1 red pepper, seeded and diced
300 g (11 oz) brown mushrooms,
  sliced
300 g (11 oz) tomatoes, skinned
  and chopped
25 ml (5 tsp) tomato paste
45 g (1¹/₂ oz) parsley, chopped
2.5 ml (¹/₂ tsp) dried basil
2.5 ml (¹/₂ tsp) dried thyme
675 g (1¹/₂ lb) cooked chickpeas
125 ml (4 fl oz) vegetable stock

Heat butter and oil in large saucepan. Stir-fry onion, garlic, carrots, red pepper and mushrooms. Add remaining ingredients. Season, cover and simmer for 30 minutes. Thicken sauce with beurre manié.
Serves 6.

Wholemeal Pitta (page 215) with (left to right) Aubergine Salad, Tzatsiki (page 123), Hummus and Felafel

Hummus

350 g (12 oz) cooked chickpeas
45 ml (3 tbsp) lemon juice
3 garlic cloves
45 ml (3 tbsp) tahini
45 ml (3 tbsp) olive oil
salt
finely chopped parsley
olive oil

Drain chickpeas, reserving 100 ml (3¹/₂ fl oz) of cooking liquid. Using the grinding blade of a food processor, purée chickpeas, lemon juice, garlic, tahini and olive oil. With motor running, pour in reserved cooking liquid or 100 ml (3¹/₂ fl oz) water. The consistency should be that of thick mayonnaise. Add salt to taste, cover and chill. To serve, sprinkle with parsley and dribble with a little olive oil.

Aubergine Salad

1 medium aubergine
30 ml (2 tbsp) vegetable oil
30 ml (2 tbsp) olive oil
2 leeks, thinly sliced
1 green pepper, seeded and diced
1 garlic clove, crushed
2.5 ml (¹/₂ tsp) dried oregano
2.5 ml (¹/₂ tsp) dried basil
salt and ground black pepper
1 tomato, chopped
toasted pine nuts or walnuts
(optional)

Dégorge aubergine (page 135) and then cube. Heat oils in frying pan and add aubergine, leeks, green pepper, garlic, herbs and seasoning. Cover and stew gently until soft, then spoon into bowl and add tomato. Sprinkle with nuts, if desired, cover and leave to cool.
Serves 4.

Felafel

Serve these baked felafel with creamy tzatsiki (page 123).

500 g (18 oz) cooked chickpeas, drained
2.5 ml (¹/₂ tsp) salt
45 ml (3 tbsp) finely chopped parsley
2 garlic cloves, crushed
5 ml (1 tsp) ground cumin
5 ml (1 tsp) ground coriander
30 ml (2 tbsp) wholemeal flour
1 egg, beaten
oil for baking

Place chickpeas in food processor and, using the grinding blade, grind to a dry mealy mixture. Put into bowl and add salt, parsley, garlic and spices. Sprinkle in flour and bind with egg, then roll into 15 small balls. Preheat oven to 180 °C (350 °F, gas 4). Cover base of Swiss roll tin with a fairly generous layer of oil and heat in oven. Roll balls in the hot oil, then bake for 20 minutes. Using a spatula, turn them carefully. Raise heat to 220 °C (425 °F, gas 7) and bake for another 15 minutes or until crisp and brown. Makes 15.

Haricot Bean Salad

300 g (11 oz) cooked haricot beans
10 ml (2 tsp) lemon juice
30 ml (2 tbsp) olive oil
2.5 ml (¹/₂ tsp) dried oregano
1 tomato, diced
6 black olives, sliced
4 spring onions, chopped
salt and freshly ground pepper
crumbled Feta cheese

Toss to mix, cover and stand for at least 30 minutes.

Note

Serve these dishes with Wholemeal pitta (page 215) for a complete meal.

Mushroom and Lentil Moussaka with Soufflé Topping

As with all moussakas, this dish takes some time to put together, but it makes a most delicious and nourishing meal served with a crisp salad and chunks of hot garlic bread.

600 g (1 lb 5 oz) aubergines
oil for frying
200 g (7 oz) brown lentils, picked over and rinsed
500 ml (16 fl oz) salted water
30 ml (2 tbsp) olive oil
1 large onion, chopped
1 green pepper, seeded and diced
2 garlic cloves, crushed
300 g (11 oz) brown mushrooms, wiped and sliced
400 g (14 oz) tomatoes, skinned and chopped
10 ml (2 tsp) brown sugar
2.5 ml (¹/₂ tsp) ground cinnamon
1 bay leaf
2.5 ml (¹/₂ tsp) salt
30 g (1 oz) parsley, chopped

TOPPING
45 g (1¹/₂ oz) butter
45 ml (3 tbsp) flour
500 ml (16 fl oz) milk
2 eggs, separated
salt and pepper
2.5 ml (¹/₂ tsp) freshly grated nutmeg
175 g (6 oz) Cheddar cheese, grated

Cut stem ends off aubergines, slice into 5-mm (¹/₄-in) thick rings, then dégorge (page 135). Fry on both sides until lightly browned and soft. If fried on a fairly low heat in a heavy-based pan, and half-covered every now and then, the amount of oil absorbed will be considerably reduced.

Meanwhile, boil lentils in salted water for 50 minutes or until soft, and water is absorbed. In a large frying pan heat olive oil and soften onion, green pepper and garlic. Add mushrooms, and when softened add tomatoes, sugar, cinnamon, bay leaf, salt and parsley. Cover and simmer for 20 minutes, stirring occasionally. Remove bay leaf and stir in cooked lentils. The mixture should be moist and fairly thick.

Make topping by melting butter, then stirring in flour. Cook for 1 minute, remove from heat and slowly stir in milk (semi-skimmed may be used). Return to heat and cook, stirring, until thickened. Beat egg yolks, add a little hot sauce, then return yolk mixture to sauce and mix in, using balloon whisk. Season with salt, pepper and nutmeg. Stiffly whisk the egg whites and fold in.

To assemble, cover base of 30 x 20-cm (12 x 8-in) baking dish with half the aubergine slices, then spoon lentil mixture over. Cover with remaining aubergine slices, then pour topping over. Sprinkle with grated cheese and bake at 180 °C (350 °F, gas 4) for 30 minutes, then turn off oven and leave for another 15 minutes to settle. Serves 6.

Note
This dish reheats well: Bake initially for 30 minutes at 180 °C (350 °F, gas 4), and remove. Reheat at 170 °C (325 °F, gas 3) for 30 minutes.

Pot Beans

This is a hot and savoury version of fasoulia, the popular Greek dish. Economical, easy to prepare, and remarkably good served on brown rice with a green salad.

500 g (18 oz) haricot beans
100 ml (3¹/₂ fl oz) oil
2 large onions, sliced
5 ml (1 tsp) dried thyme
5 ml (1 tsp) dried oregano
125 g (4 oz) canned tomato paste
4 garlic cloves, crushed
2 bay leaves
15 ml (1 tbsp) honey
salt and ground black pepper
stock or water
1 bunch spinach, shredded
   (optional)
45 g (1¹/₂ oz) parsley, chopped
soy sauce
grated Cheddar cheese (optional)

Soak beans overnight, then drain and rinse. Heat oil in a large saucepan and add onions. When softened, add beans and toss over medium heat for 5 minutes. Add herbs, tomato paste, garlic, bay leaves, honey and seasoning. Add enough stock or water to cover, then cover saucepan and simmer gently for 1¹/₂ hours, or until beans are soft and liquid is thick and reduced. Add spinach, if using, and parsley. Cover and simmer for another 30 minutes. To serve, add soy sauce to taste, then spoon over servings of rice, and top with grated cheese. Serves 6–8.

Spicy Lentil Curry

A surprisingly delicious curry. Serve on rice with sambals (page 95) and a tomato and onion salad.

30 g (1 oz) butter
30 ml (2 tbsp) oil
2 large onions, sliced
1 green pepper, seeded and diced
2 garlic cloves, crushed
2 celery sticks, thinly sliced
3 carrots, coarsely grated
10 ml (2 tsp) curry powder
5 ml (1 tsp) ground cumin
5 ml (1 tsp) turmeric
5 ml (1 tsp) ground fennel
275 g (10 oz) brown lentils,
   picked over and rinsed
750 ml (1¹/₄ pints) water
1 bay leaf
30 g (1 oz) parsley, chopped
5 ml (1 tsp) salt
10 ml (2 tsp) brown sugar
170 ml (5¹/₂ fl oz) tomato purée
soured cream
snipped chives

Heat oil and butter and sauté onions, green pepper, garlic, celery and carrots. When softened, add spices and stir over low heat for a few minutes.

Add lentils, water, bay leaf, parsley, salt, sugar and tomato purée. Mix well and spoon into a large baking dish. Bake, covered, at 180 °C (350 °F, gas 4) for about 1 hour, or until lentils are soft, stirring once or twice. Remove from oven and streak in a few spoons of soured cream, sprinkle with chives and warm through for another 5 minutes before serving. Serves 6.

Casserole of Lentils and Rice with Pizza Topping

200 g (7 oz) brown lentils, picked over and rinsed
100 g (3¹/₂ oz) brown rice
30 ml (2 tbsp) oil
15 g (¹/₂ oz) butter
2 medium onions, finely chopped
2 green or red peppers, seeded and diced
30 g (1 oz) parsley, chopped
30 g (1 oz) fresh wholemeal breadcrumbs
2 eggs
125 ml (4 fl oz) buttermilk
salt and ground black pepper
3–4 firm tomatoes, thinly sliced
grated Mozzarella or Cheddar cheese
grated Parmesan cheese
2.5 ml (¹/₂ tsp) dried oregano
generous pinch of dried basil
30 ml (2 tbsp) olive oil

Simmer lentils in 500 ml (16 fl oz) salted water for about 50 minutes or until soft. In another saucepan cook brown rice in 300 ml (10 fl oz) salted water for about 45 minutes. Heat oil and butter and sauté onions and peppers. Spoon lentils and rice into a large bowl and add cooked onions and peppers, parsley and bread-crumbs. Beat eggs with butter-milk and add together with seasoning. Mix well, without mashing, and spoon into a deep, buttered 23-cm (9-in) pie dish.

Level top and cover with tomatoes. Cover tomatoes with plenty of grated Mozzarella or Cheddar, and add a sprinkling of Parmesan. Sprinkle herbs over cheese and dribble with oil. Bake at 180 °C (350 °F, gas 4) for about 25 minutes, until bubbling and cheese has melted. Serve with creamy mashed potatoes and a salad.
Serves 6.

Lentils and Aubergines in Barbecue Sauce

A thick, savoury stew, which is delicious served on pasta or brown rice, topped with crumbled Feta or grated Cheddar or Parmesan cheese. A lettuce and avocado salad tossed with French dressing is a good accompaniment, with crusty rolls an optional extra.

200 g (7 oz) brown lentils, picked over and rinsed
500 ml (16 fl oz) salted water
45 ml (3 tbsp) oil
300 g (11 oz) young aubergines, cubed
1 large onion, chopped
2 garlic cloves, crushed
1 small green or red pepper, seeded and diced
200 g (7 oz) courgettes, scrubbed and sliced
250 ml (8 fl oz) tomato purée
15 ml (1 tbsp) honey
25 ml (5 tsp) soy sauce
30 g (1 oz) parsley, chopped
250 ml (8 fl oz) water
5 ml (1 tsp) dried basil

Boil lentils gently in the water for about 50 minutes until soft. Meanwhile, heat oil in large pan and add aubergines, onion, garlic, pepper and courgettes. Toss over low heat for 5 minutes.

Add remaining ingredients, cover and simmer gently for 30 minutes. Add cooked lentils and, if necessary, another 125 ml (4 fl oz) water, or enough to make a good gravy. Simmer very gently for another 15 minutes. Adjust seasoning – it may need a pinch of salt, or a little sugar – then leave to stand to allow flavours to mellow. Reheat and serve as suggested.
Serves 4.

Lentil and Potato Pie

Brown lentils are a good source of protein, and if you like their distinctive, rather earthy flavour, you'll enjoy this pie, in which they're baked between layers of sliced potatoes and onions, and topped with cheese. This simple dish is one of our favourite vegetarian meals, accompanied by buttered cabbage.

275 g (10 oz) brown lentils, picked over and rinsed
800 g (1 lb 14 oz) potatoes, thinly sliced
2 large onions, thinly sliced
salt and ground black pepper
750 ml (1¼ pints) hot stock or 10 ml (2 tsp) Marmite in 750 ml (1¼ pints) hot water
grated Cheddar cheese
butter
paprika

Cover lentils with water and leave to soak for about 2 hours. Grease a deep 23-cm (9-in) pie dish and cover the base with half the potatoes and onions. Season lightly. Top with drained lentils, evenly spread. Cover with remaining onions and potatoes, and season lightly again. Pour over hot stock, cover with greased foil, shiny-side up, or with a lid, and bake at 180 °C (350 °F, gas 4) for 1 hour.

Remove cover and sprinkle thickly with cheese, dot with butter, and dust with paprika. Bake, uncovered, for a further 20 minutes, by which time potatoes and lentils should be soft, liquid absorbed, and cheese melted and bubbling.
Serves 6–8.

Spiced Chickpeas

A fragrant stew to serve on brown rice with bowls of coconut and chopped nuts, and a green salad.

45 ml (3 tbsp) oil
2 onions, chopped
2–3 garlic cloves, crushed
2.5 ml (½ tsp) ground cumin
2.5 ml (½ tsp) turmeric
2.5 ml (½ tsp) ground cinnamon
2.5 ml (½ tsp) ground ginger
5 ml (1 tsp) ground coriander
2 celery sticks, chopped
1 green pepper, seeded and diced
450 g (16 oz) cooked chickpeas, drained
45 g (1½ oz) parsley, chopped
400 g (14 oz) canned tomatoes, chopped, plus juice
2 bay leaves
250 ml (8 fl oz) water or vegetable stock
5 ml (1 tsp) salt or 10 ml (2 tsp) vegetable salt
5 ml (1 tsp) sugar

Heat oil in a large saucepan. Add onions, garlic, spices, celery and pepper. Cover and cook over very low heat until onions are soft. Add remaining ingredients, bring to the boil, then cover and simmer on low heat for about 30 minutes, stirring occasionally. Add a little water if necessary for a good gravy. Check seasoning and serve as suggested.
Serves 4–6.

Note

Chickpeas (or garbanzos) have been popular for centuries. Round, and cream-coloured, they are fairly bland in flavour and slightly nutty in texture, and require a long soaking and cooking period before being used in spreads, salads and stews.

Haricot Bean Salad

This happy combination of French and Greek flavours is an economical, substantial salad to serve with wholemeal bread.

500 g (18 oz) haricot beans
2 bouquets garnis
2 bay leaves
5 ml (1 tsp) salt
3–4 leeks, thinly sliced
1 green or red pepper, seeded and chopped
1 large celery stick, sliced
30 g (1 oz) parsley, chopped
large pinch of sugar
tomato, black olives and Feta cheese

DRESSING
100 ml (3^1/$_2$ fl oz) vegetable oil
45 ml (3 tbsp) olive oil
1 garlic clove, crushed
25 ml (5 tsp) lemon juice
2.5 ml (^{1}/$_2$ tsp) salt
5 ml (1 tsp) dried oregano

TZATSIKI
^{1}/$_2$ cucumber
250 ml (8 fl oz) plain drinking yoghurt
125 ml (4 fl oz) soured cream
10 ml (2 tsp) honey
1 garlic clove, crushed
salt and ground black pepper
8–10 mint leaves, finely chopped

Soak beans overnight. Next day drain, rinse, cover with fresh water, add bouquets garnis and bay leaves and boil until soft, adding salt towards the end of the cooking period.

Make dressing by mixing all ingredients, and leave to stand while beans are cooking.

Make tzatsiki several hours in advance and chill thoroughly. Peel and grate cucumber coarsely and squeeze very dry between pieces of absorbent kitchen paper. Mix with remaining ingredients, cover and chill.

Drain cooked beans and spoon into large bowl. Toss while hot with dressing, using a fork and taking care not to mash them. Add leeks, pepper, celery, parsley and sugar. Cover and stand for at least 2 hours, or chill overnight. To serve, adjust seasoning in bean salad, then spoon onto large serving platter. Surround with chunks of tomato and top with black olives. Sprinkle generously with crumbled Feta, and serve tzatsiki separately.
Serves 8.

Greek Vegetable Casserole with Beans and Feta

A delicious medley of Mediterranean-style vegetables. Served in a large earthenware casserole, topped with crumbled Feta and black olives, it's beautiful to look at and good to eat. Serve on brown rice, with a lettuce and avocado salad tossed in garlicky French dressing.

30 ml (2 tbsp) vegetable oil
30 ml (2 tbsp) olive oil
1 large onion, chopped
2 leeks, sliced
1 green pepper, seeded and diced
2 garlic cloves, crushed
250 g (9 oz) aubergine, rinsed
   and cubed
250 g (9 oz) courgettes, peeled
   and sliced
4 large, juicy tomatoes, skinned
   and chopped
300 g (11 oz) cooked soya or
   haricot beans
5 ml (1 tsp) salt
ground black pepper
5 ml (1 tsp) dried oregano
5 ml (1 tsp) dried basil
5 ml (1 tsp) sugar
250 ml (8 fl oz) stock or 5 ml
   (1 tsp) Marmite in 250 ml
   (8 fl oz) water
black olives
200–250 g (7–9 oz) Feta cheese,
   coarsely crumbled

Heat oils in large pan and sauté onion, leeks, pepper and garlic. When softened, add aubergine, courgettes and tomatoes. Cover and sweat for 5 minutes over low heat. Add drained beans, salt, pepper, herbs, sugar and stock. Stir to mix, then turn into a large baking dish. Bake, covered, at 150 °C (300 °F, gas 2) for 1 hour 15 minutes, stirring once or twice and adding a little more liquid if necessary.

About 10 minutes before serving, add a handful of sliced black olives and then sprinkle with Feta. Return to oven just to heat through.
Serves 4–6.

Cannelloni

An Italian dish, traditionally made with rectangles or tubes of pasta rolled around a filling, covered with a tomato sauce and cheese, and baked. Instead of pasta, I have used crêpes, stuffed with low-fat soft cheese, smothered in a mushroom or tomato sauce and melting Mozzarella. A good choice for an informal meal because the crêpes, filling and sauce can all be made in advance. Good with a lettuce, avocado and herb salad, and a hot garlic loaf.

BLENDER CRÊPES
125 g (4 oz) flour
generous pinch of salt
1 egg
250 ml (8 fl oz) milk
125 ml (4 fl oz) water
25 ml (5 tsp) oil

FILLING
500 g (18 oz) low-fat soft cheese
2 egg yolks
30 ml (2 tbsp) grated Parmesan cheese
1 garlic clove, crushed
5 ml (1 tsp) dried oregano
generous pinch of salt
ground black pepper
45 g (1¹/₂ oz) spring onions, chopped

MUSHROOM SAUCE
30 ml (2 tbsp) oil
5 ml (1 tsp) butter
300 g (11 oz) brown mushrooms, wiped and sliced
1 large onion, chopped
1 garlic clove, crushed
1 fresh rosemary sprig
45 ml (3 tbsp) flour
250 ml (8 fl oz) stock
250 ml (8 fl oz) milk
salt and ground black pepper
lemon juice

or

TOMATO SAUCE
30 ml (2 tbsp) oil
1 large onion, chopped
1 garlic clove, crushed
5 ml (1 tsp) dried basil
400 g (14 oz) ripe, juicy tomatoes, skinned and chopped
2 bay leaves
generous pinch of salt
5 ml (1 tsp) honey or 10 ml (2 tsp) brown sugar
30 g (1 oz) parsley, chopped
45 ml (3 tbsp) white wine

Mozzarella cheese for topping

To make crêpes, put all ingredients into blender and blend until smooth, stopping to scrape down sides with a spatula. Cover and stand for 1 hour, then blend briefly before making thin crêpes, stacking them between sheets of greaseproof paper as they're done.

Mix the filling ingredients together until smooth, using a wooden spoon. If working ahead, chill filling until required.

To make mushroom sauce, heat oil and butter and sauté mushrooms, onion, garlic and rosemary. When just beginning to soften and shrink, remove rosemary and add flour, then slowly stir in stock and milk. When thickened, remove from heat, season, and add a dash of lemon juice.

To make tomato sauce, heat oil and sauté onion, garlic and basil. Add tomatoes and remaining ingredients. Cover and simmer for approximately 30 minutes, stirring occasionally, until sauce is thick and syrupy. Remove bay leaves.

To assemble, divide cheese filling between crêpes, roll into cigar shapes, and place side by side in greased baking dish. Pour mushroom or tomato sauce over and top with sliced Mozzarella. Bake at 180 °C (350 °F, gas 4) for about 25–30 minutes, until bubbling.
Makes 8 small portions.

Vegetable Stir-Fry

45 ml (3 tbsp) oil
2–4 garlic cloves, crushed
300 g (11 oz) brown mushrooms,
   wiped and sliced
3–4 leeks, sliced
3 large celery sticks, sliced
salt and ground black pepper
¹/₂ cauliflower
¹/₂ cucumber, peeled and diced
4 young carrots, cut in julienne
150 g (5 oz) chopped pecan nuts

SAUCE
45 ml (3 tbsp) sherry or port
250 ml (8 fl oz) vegetable stock
25 ml (5 tsp) soy sauce
5 ml (1 tsp) peeled, grated root
   ginger
20 ml (4 tsp) cornflour

Heat 30 ml (2 tbsp) oil in large
pan or wok and add garlic,
mushrooms, leeks and celery.
Stir-fry for about 5 minutes,
then remove to baking dish, plus
any pan juices. Season lightly.

Break cauliflower into florets.
Add another 30 ml (2 tbsp) oil to
pan and add cucumber,
cauliflower and carrots. Reduce
heat and stir-fry, half covered,
until tender but crisp. The
mixture will reduce somewhat
and could take up to 15 minutes
with regular tossing. Add to
vegetables in baking dish.
   Whisk together ingredients for
sauce and stir into vegetable
mixture. Finally add pecan nuts,
tossing until ingredients are
thoroughly combined. Bake,
covered, at 180 °C (350 °F, gas 4)
for 20–30 minutes until
deliciously aromatic.
Serves 4–6.

Aubergines Stuffed with Rice and Walnuts

These crunchy, stuffed
aubergines may be assembled in
advance. Serve with a simple
green salad and a hot French
loaf.

4 x 125 g (4 oz) or 2 x 250 g (9 oz)
   aubergines
30 ml (2 tbsp) olive oil
4–6 spring onions, chopped
2 garlic cloves, crushed
100 g (3¹/₂ oz) walnuts, coarsely
   chopped
1 celery stick, chopped
2 medium tomatoes, skinned and
   chopped
salt and pepper
pinch of sugar
generous pinch of dried oregano
60 g (2 oz) cooked brown rice
15 ml (1 tbsp) mayonnaise
grated Mozzarella cheese

paprika
stock or water

Wash and trim off bud ends of
aubergines, then boil in
unsalted water for about 10
minutes until beginning to
soften. Halve lengthways and
when cool remove pulp, leaving
cases about 15 mm (³/₄ in) thick.
Cube flesh. Heat oil and sauté
spring onions, garlic, walnuts
and celery. When softened, add
tomatoes, seasonings, oregano
and aubergine cubes. Cover and
simmer for 5–10 minutes until
tomatoes are pulpy. Stir in rice
and mayonnaise.
   Mound this mixture into
reserved cases, arranged close
together in baking dish, and top
generously with grated cheese.
Sprinkle with paprika, and
carefully pour about 2.5 cm (1 in)
stock into dish. Bake, uncovered,
at 170 °C (325 °F, gas 3) for
45 minutes.
Serves 4.

Brown Rice with Lentils, Mushrooms and Almonds

Served with a creamy green salad, this vegetarian main dish is a real delight.

200 g (7 oz) brown lentils, picked
    over and rinsed
1 bay leaf
nut of butter
5 ml (1 tsp) ground cumin
pinch of salt
300 g (10 oz) brown rice
nut of butter
pinch of salt
5 ml (1 tsp) mixed dried herbs
30 g (1 oz) butter
30 ml (2 tbsp) oil
2 onions, sliced
1 red pepper, seeded and sliced
300–400 g (11–14 oz) brown
    mushrooms, wiped and sliced
2 celery sticks, chopped
30 g (1 oz) parsley, chopped
175 g (6 oz) mung bean sprouts
45 ml (3 tbsp) soy sauce
45 g (1¹/₂ oz) almonds, halved
    and toasted

Put lentils into saucepan with 500 ml (16 fl oz) water, bay leaf, butter, cumin and salt. Bring to boil, then cover and simmer gently for about 50 minutes until water is absorbed and lentils are soft. At the same time, cook the rice in another saucepan with 845 ml (27 fl oz) water, butter, salt and herbs and simmer, covered, over low heat for about 45 minutes. Toss lentils and rice together and spoon into large, buttered baking dish, discarding bay leaf. Cover and keep warm in low oven, or set aside to reheat gently at dinnertime.

To prepare the vegetables, heat butter and oil in a large frying pan and add onions and red pepper. When soft and browning, increase heat and add mushrooms, celery and parsley. Stir-fry for 5 minutes and then add sprouts and soy sauce. Reduce heat and cook for a further 2 minutes, tossing with a wooden spoon. Pour mixture over warmed rice and lentils, and scatter with almonds.
Serves 8–10.

Note
The soy sauce should season the dish sufficiently, so don't be tempted to add salt before tasting.

Green Beans with Mushrooms and Soured Cream

30 ml (2 tbsp) oil
1 large onion, finely chopped
5 ml (1 tsp) chopped fresh
   rosemary needles
1 garlic clove, crushed
400 g (14 oz) green beans, trimmed
   and sliced
125 ml (4 fl oz) stock or water
salt and ground black pepper
150 g (5 oz) brown mushrooms,
   wiped and sliced
30 ml (2 tbsp) sherry
75 ml (2¹/₂ fl oz) soured cream

Heat oil and sauté onion,
rosemary, garlic and beans. Toss
for a few minutes until coated with
oil, then add stock or water and
seasoning. Half-cover and simmer
until tender, stirring occasionally.
After about 15 minutes the liquid
should have been absorbed.
   Add mushrooms and sherry.
Cook for a further 2–3 minutes,
stirring, then spoon into serving
dish. Swirl in the soured cream and
place in low oven just to heat
through.
Serves 4–6.

Savoury Courgettes

Broccoli with Lemon Cream Sauce

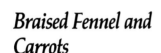

Savoury Courgettes

30 ml (2 tbsp) olive oil
1 onion or 2 leeks, sliced
2 garlic cloves, crushed
225 g (8 oz) tomatoes, skinned and chopped
400 g (14 oz) courgettes, peeled and sliced
1/2 green pepper, seeded and sliced
20 g (3/4 oz) parsley, chopped
100 ml (3 1/2 fl oz) dry white wine
2.5 ml (1/2 tsp) dried basil
2.5 ml (1/2 tsp) salt
pinch of sugar

Heat oil and lightly sauté onion (or leeks) and garlic. Add tomatoes, courgettes, green pepper and remaining ingredients. Stir to mix, then cover and simmer slowly for about 20 minutes, stirring occasionally. Serve hot, or else cool, cover, chill and serve as a salad. Serves 4–6.

Braised Fennel and Carrots

Fennel is the perfect partner for fish, and the carrots add colour.

1 large head fennel
250 g (9 oz) carrots
200 ml (7 fl oz) chicken stock
10 ml (2 tsp) lemon juice
salt and ground black pepper
30 g (1 oz) butter
pinch of sugar
snipped chives

Wash and trim fennel and cut into long, thin strips; cut carrots into thin matchsticks. Melt butter, add vegetables and stir until coated. Add remaining ingredients. Cover and cook very gently for about 30 minutes until tender. The liquid should all be absorbed. Serve sprinkled with snipped chives.
Serves 4–6.

Broccoli with Lemon Cream Sauce

500 g (18 oz) broccoli
paprika

SAUCE
125 ml (4 fl oz) soured cream
45 ml (3 tbsp) mayonnaise
15 ml (1 tbsp) fresh lemon juice
5 ml (1 tsp) French mustard
very generous pinch of finely grated lemon rind

Trim and slice broccoli lengthways. Poach in a little water until tender. To retain the bright colour, do not overcook. Chop coarsely, place in serving dish and keep warm.
Combine ingredients for sauce in a small saucepan, and heat gently while stirring. Do not allow to boil. When hot, pour over broccoli, dust with paprika and serve at once.
Serves 6.

Glazed Pickling Onions

500 g (18 oz) pickling onions
5 ml (1 tsp) salt
45 ml (3 tbsp) brown sugar
45 ml (3 tbsp) water
2 big nuts of butter
pinch of nutmeg

Pour boiling water over onions. Stand 10 minutes, then drain, nick off tops and bottoms, and slip off the skins. Cover with cold water, bring to the boil, add salt and cook for 3 minutes. Drain. You can do all this in advance.
To finish off, melt remaining ingredients in a large frying pan. Add onions. Cover and cook over medium heat, for 10–15 minutes, shaking pan occasionally until liquid has evaporated and onions are evenly browned.
Serves 6.

Brussels Sprouts with Mustard Sauce

The sweet and sour mustard sauce which coats these sprouts makes this dish particularly suitable for serving with pork or ham.

500 g (18 oz) young Brussels
 sprouts

EASY MUSTARD SAUCE
250 ml (8 fl oz) milk
1 egg yolk
10 ml (2 tsp) dry mustard
20 ml (4 tsp) flour
10 ml (2 tsp) brown sugar
15 ml (1 tbsp) brown vinegar
generous pinch of salt
small nut of butter

Trim sprouts and boil in a little salted water until just tender.
 The sauce may be made ahead and gently reheated when required. Put all the ingredients, except butter, into a small saucepan. Whisk to mix, then bring to the boil, stirring. Allow to bubble for a few minutes to thicken and cook flour, then remove from heat and stir in butter.
 To serve, spoon hot sprouts into serving dish, pour hot sauce over, and toss gently until mixed.
Serves 6.

Hint
For sprouts with a difference, remove outer leaves from 400 g (14 oz) sprouts, cut a cross in the stem end of each, and rinse. Put 150 ml (5 fl oz) chicken stock, a pinch of ground mace and 15 ml (1 tbsp) runny honey into saucepan. Add sprouts and boil until just tender. Season with salt and pepper, add 10 ml (2 tsp) lemon juice and 15 g (¹/₂ oz) butter, and serve.
Serves 4.

Stir-Fried Chinese Cabbage

This is definitely the aristocrat of the cabbage family. Leafy, tender and mild in flavour, Chinese cabbage should never be overcooked, and braising or stir-frying are the best cooking methods. It is also very good in a salad.

30 ml (2 tbsp) oil
4 spring onions, chopped
2 celery sticks, thinly sliced
1 green pepper, seeded and diced
small knob of root ginger,
 peeled and grated
¹/₂ head of Chinese cabbage,
 shredded
150 g (5 oz) lentil sprouts
25 ml (5 tsp) soy sauce
large pinch of sugar
toasted flaked almonds

Heat oil in large frying pan or wok and add spring onions, celery, green pepper and ginger. When vegetables have softened, add cabbage. Toss in sprouts. Mix well, cover and steam over low heat until cabbage is just wilted, but still a good colour. Stir in soy sauce and sugar and serve at once with a scattering of almonds.
Serves 4–5.

Hint
There are several different varieties of soy sauce, and some are saltier than others. When using soy sauce in cooking, do not add salt, as the soy sauce usually seasons the dish sufficiently – if necessary, adjust at the end of the cooking period.

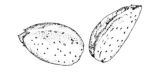

Oven-Baked Carrots

The following two recipes are convenient ways of preparing carrots because they can be baked at the same time as any meat dish or casserole requiring a low oven temperature.

Carrots in sherry

300 g (11 oz) young carrots
45 ml (3 tbsp) sherry
15 ml (1 tbsp) honey
45 ml (3 tbsp) finely chopped
    parsley
2.5 ml (¹/₂ tsp) salt
30 g (1 oz) butter

Peel and slice carrots lengthways into thin strips and arrange in a pie dish, more or less in a single layer. Pour in sherry and honey, sprinkle with parsley and salt and dot with butter. Cover and bake at 170 °C (325 °F, gas 3) for about 1 hour 10 minutes.
Serves 4.

Orange Carrots

500 g (18 oz) carrots
125 ml (4 fl oz) fresh orange
    juice
30 ml (2 tbsp) honey
45 ml (3 tbsp) finely chopped
    parsley
2.5 ml (¹/₂ tsp) finely grated
    orange rind
2.5 ml (¹/₂ tsp) salt
butter

Scrape and slice carrots lengthways into thin strips. Arrange in a large pie dish, and pour orange juice and honey over. Sprinkle with parsley, orange rind and salt and dot with butter. Cover and bake at 170 °C (325 °F, gas 3) for about 1 hour or until just cooked.
Serves 5–6.

Braised Chicory

Also known as Belgian endive, this delicate vegetable has long whitish leaves and very pale green tips, and should not be confused with curly endive. Cooked very simply, as follows, it is especially good with fish or chicken.

400 g (14 oz) chicory
30 ml (2 tbsp) oil
15 g (¹/₂ oz) butter
2 leeks, thinly sliced
10 ml (2 tsp) lemon juice
125 ml (4 fl oz) chicken stock
2.5 ml (¹/₂ tsp) salt
2 garlic cloves, crushed
30 g (1 oz) parsley, chopped
2.5 ml (¹/₂ tsp) sugar
grated Cheddar cheese (optional)

Remove any discoloured outer leaves from chicory, and cut off a thin slice from the corky base. Wash carefully. Heat oil and butter in wide, shallow pan.

Cover bottom with a layer of leeks. Halve heads of chicory lengthways if large and arrange on top of leeks in a single layer. Sprinkle with lemon juice and add stock, salt, garlic, parsley and sugar. Cover securely and simmer gently for 30 minutes or until soft. Sprinkle with cheese, if desired, and melt under the grill before serving.
Serves 6.

Orange Sweet Potato Casserole

Sweet potatoes are now found in many supermarkets as well as in Indian or oriental stores. The simplest way of preparing them is to bake them in their skins and serve them with butter. The following recipe, with orange as the predominant flavour, is particularly suitable for serving with ham, pork or turkey.

750 g (1³/₄ lb) sweet potatoes
cold water
salt
200 ml (6¹/₂ fl oz) fresh orange
   juice
30 ml (2 tbsp) honey
2.5 ml (¹/₂ tsp) finely grated
   orange rind
45 ml (3 tbsp) sherry
10 ml (2 tsp) brown sugar
2.5 ml (¹/₂ tsp) ground cinnamon
butter

Scrub potatoes, cover with cold water, add salt and parboil for about 20 minutes – they should be half-cooked. Peel, slice into medium-thick fingers and arrange in a single layer to cover the base of a buttered 23-cm (9-in) pie dish. Mix orange juice, honey, rind and sherry. Bring to the boil and pour over potatoes. Sprinkle with sugar and cinnamon, dot with slivers of butter and bake, uncovered, at 180 °C (350 °F, gas 4) for 45 minutes to 1 hour, until soft and lightly browned on top. Serves 6.

Baked Fried Potatoes

Chips the easy way, with no splattering, deep-frying or fuss.

potatoes, peeled, washed and
   dried
oil
salt

Cut potatoes into long, thin slices. Cover bottom of baking sheet with a generous layer of oil. Place in 170 °C, (325 °F, gas 3) oven to heat, then arrange chips in single layer, tossing to coat evenly. Bake on bottom shelf until lightly browned and cooked through. Drain on absorbent kitchen paper, sprinkle with salt, and serve.

Spiced Red Cabbage

Good with duck, venison and pork. Red cabbage tastes even better if prepared in advance, and reheated.

1 kg (2¹/₄ lb) red cabbage, finely
   shredded
2 onions, chopped
45 ml (3 tbsp) oil
2 large cooking apples, peeled
   and cubed
10 ml (2 tsp) salt
ground black pepper
125 ml (4 fl oz) water
125 ml (4 fl oz) red wine
5 ml (1 tsp) ground mixed spice
100 g (3¹/₂ oz) seedless raisins
30 ml (2 tbsp) brown sugar
nut of butter

Soak cabbage in salted water to cover for 1 hour, then drain and rinse. In a large saucepan, lightly fry onions in oil, then add cabbage and cover and simmer for 10 minutes. Add apples and remaining ingredients, except butter. Cover and simmer gently for 1 hour, adding a dash more water or wine if necessary. Cool and reheat gently when required, adding butter just before serving. Serves 8.

Hint
Add interest to green cabbage as follows: Bring a little salted water to the boil and add 500 g (18 oz) shredded cabbage, 4 thinly sliced leeks and 2 crushed garlic cloves. Boil for a few minutes until tender-crisp. Drain and spoon into top of large double boiler. Mix 150 ml (5 fl oz) soured cream, 5 ml (1 tsp) paprika, 2.5 ml (¹/₂ tsp) Worcester sauce and 10 ml (2 tsp) French mustard. Stir into cabbage, cover and cook over simmering water for 20 minutes. Serves 8.

Cauliflower Puff

This cauliflower dish can be prepared well in advance and requires only last-minute attention in whipping up the egg whites for the topping.

1 medium head cauliflower
lemon juice
45 g (1¹/₂ oz) butter
45 ml (3 tbsp) flour
400 ml (13 fl oz) milk
salt and pepper
5 ml (1 tsp) prepared mustard
45 g (1¹/₂ oz) Cheddar cheese,
   grated
2 egg whites, stiffly whisked
grated Parmesan cheese
paprika

Break cauliflower into florets, removing any really thick stalks. Sprinkle with lemon juice and poach in lightly salted water until soft. Do not overcook. Drain well, then place in buttered pie dish – the florets should just cover the base.

Melt butter and stir in flour. Stir for 1 minute, then remove saucepan from heat and slowly add milk. Return to heat, stir until thick, then remove and add salt, pepper, mustard and Cheddar cheese. Stir to melt, then cool.

When ready to serve, fold stiffly whisked egg whites into cheese sauce and spoon evenly over cauliflower. Sprinkle with Parmesan and paprika and bake at 200 °C (400 °F, gas 6) for 12 minutes until puffy and golden brown.
Serves 6.

Greek-Style Squash

A simple medley of vegetables that is particularly good with roast lamb.

1 x 750 g (1³/₄ lb) winter squash
30 ml (2 tbsp) oil
2 onions, chopped
2 tomatoes, skinned and chopped
2 garlic cloves, crushed
2.5 ml (¹/₂ tsp) ground cinnamon
2.5 ml (¹/₂ tsp) dried oregano
30 g (1 oz) parsley, chopped
100–125 ml (3¹/₂–4 fl oz) chicken
　stock
10 ml (2 tsp) honey
salt and ground black pepper

Peel squash. Cut flesh into long strips, discard seeds and pith and cut into small dice – you should have about 500 g (18 oz).
　Heat oil in large saucepan and soften onions. Add tomatoes, garlic, cinnamon, oregano, parsley and squash. Toss to mix, then add stock – the amount

depends on the juiciness of the tomatoes. Add honey and seasoning. Cover and simmer until squash is tender, stirring occasionally.
Serves 5–6.

Note

Origanum vulgare is closely related to marjoram, but is more pungent in flavour, especially when dried. It is used extensively in Greek and Italian cooking, and is without equal for flavouring lamb and tomato dishes, pizzas and pasta. The name is derived from the Greek words for mountain, and joy, because of the way in which the herb proliferates on the hillsides of certain Greek islands.

Stuffed Squash

Pattypans are rather quaint young relatives of custard marrow. Serve them whole, or add interest by scooping out the insides, then filling them with a simple stuffing before popping the lids back on.

6 x 60–75 g (2–2¹/₂ oz) pattypan
　squash
30 g (1 oz) Cheddar cheese,
　grated
2 spring onions, chopped
10 ml (2 tsp) finely chopped
　parsley
generous pinch of ground mace
salt and ground black pepper
nut of butter

Wash and boil squash in a little salted water for about 12–15 minutes until just tender, but not too soft. Cool, slice off pointed tops and carefully scoop out most of the pulp. Chop, then mix with cheese, spring onions

and remaining ingredients. Fill shells and replace caps. Arrange in small baking dish brushed with oil, and heat through at 170 °C (325 °F, gas 3) for about 15 minutes.
Serves 6.

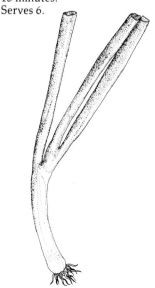

Ratatouille with Olives

2 medium aubergines, diced
2 large courgettes or 6 small
   ones, peeled and sliced
45 ml (3 tbsp) olive oil
1 large onion, sliced
3 tomatoes, skinned and chopped
1 large red pepper, seeded and
   diced
1 garlic clove, crushed
2.5 ml (^{1}/$_2$ tsp) dried basil
salt and ground black pepper
pinch of sugar
75 g (2^1/$_2$ oz) black olives,
   stoned and sliced

Dégorge (see box) aubergines
and courgettes. Heat the olive oil
in a large, heavy saucepan and
fry onion until soft but not
browned. Turn heat to very low
and toss in the aubergines,
courgettes, tomatoes, red pepper,
garlic, basil and salt and pepper.
   Simmer very gently, half-
covered, for about 45 minutes,
stirring occasionally. Vegetables
should be soft, but not mushy,
with very little liquid. Add sugar
and olives, and adjust seasoning.
Stir to mix and serve with grilled
steak or a roast. Cool if serving
as a first course. I like to top the
cold ratatouille with a little
soured cream and snipped chives,
although this is taking a great
liberty with a traditional
Provençal dish. Serves 4–6.

TO DÉGORGE AUBERGINES,
COURGETTES AND
CUCUMBERS

Remove stem and calyx and
slice or dice vegetable. Score
the surface of the flesh,
sprinkle with salt and leave
on a tilted plate or in a
colander for about
30 minutes, so that the liquid
can run off. Rinse off excess
salt and dry thoroughly with
absorbent kitchen paper
before proceeding with the
recipe.

TO SKIN TOMATOES
Pour boiling water over,
stand for 5 minutes, then
rinse under cold water. Skins
should slip off easily. Nick
out stem end before using.

Mince and Pasta Casserole

First cousin to lasagne, but without Mozzarella or Ricotta cheese or the traditional Bolognese sauce. Although I prefer this ratio of noodles to minced beef, as the result is never stodgy, 300 g (11 oz) noodles may be used if you wish to make the dish go further.

250 g (9 oz) medium ribbon
   noodles

CHEESE SAUCE
45 g (1¹/₂ oz) butter
45 g (1¹/₂ oz) flour
750 ml (1¹/₄ pints) milk
5 ml (1 tsp) dry mustard
100 g (3¹/₂ oz) Cheddar cheese,
   grated
salt and pepper

MEAT SAUCE
30 ml (2 tbsp) oil
1 large onion, chopped
1 large celery stick, sliced
2 garlic cloves, crushed
500 g (18 oz) lean minced beef
400 g (14 oz) canned tomato soup
5 ml (1 tsp) dried oregano
2.5 ml (¹/₂ tsp) dried basil
30 g (1 oz) parsley, chopped
grated Parmesan cheese

Boil noodles in plenty of salted water. Drain and toss with a little oil to keep the strands separate.

Make the cheese sauce by melting the butter and stirring in the flour. Remove from heat and gradually stir in the milk, preferably heated. Return to heat and stir until thick, then whisk in mustard, cheese and seasoning.

For the meat sauce, heat oil and soften onion, celery and garlic. Add meat and toss until no longer red. Add tomato soup, herbs, parsley and 250 ml (8 fl oz) of the cheese sauce. Mix well and season.

Grease a 30 x 20-cm (12 x 8-in) baking dish. Cover the base with half the noodles. Spoon over half the meat mixture, top with the remaining noodles, then with the remaining meat mixture. Pour the remaining cheese sauce over to cover completely. Sprinkle over a little grated Parmesan cheese. Bake, uncovered, at 170 °C (325 °F, gas 3) for 50 minutes.
Serves 8–10.

Mediterranean Vegetable Sauce for Pasta

Regard this as a basic recipe as other vegetables, such as mushrooms or courgettes, may be added or substituted. The following is a good, simple version, which cooks into a delicious, thick stew. Ladle it over pasta and top each serving with soured cream mixed with chives, then sprinkle with crumbled Feta.

30 ml (2 tbsp) vegetable oil
30 ml (2 tbsp) olive oil
4 large leeks, thinly sliced
3 garlic cloves, crushed
1 green pepper, seeded and diced
2 celery sticks, sliced
2 medium aubergines, rinsed and diced
400 g (14 oz) tomatoes, skinned and chopped

25 ml (5 tsp) tomato paste
5 ml (1 tsp) dried basil
30 g (1 oz) parsley, chopped
salt and ground black pepper
5 ml (1 tsp) sugar
125 ml (4 fl oz) stock or water
sliced black olives (optional)

Heat oils in a very large, heavy frying pan. Add leeks and garlic. Reduce heat to low and simmer, covered, until soft. Add green pepper, celery, aubergines, tomatoes, tomato paste, basil, parsley, seasoning, sugar and stock. Cover and simmer for about 45 minutes, stirring occasionally and adding more liquid as required for the gravy – up to 250 ml (8 fl oz). The mixture should not be dry or too watery – bear in mind that it should be thick enough to coat the pasta. Adjust seasoning and, if desired, add a few sliced black olives just before serving.
Serves 4.

Noodles with Spinach, Mushrooms and Cheese

500 g (18 oz) frozen spinach, thawed
250 g (9 oz) medium ribbon noodles
30 ml (2 tbsp) oil
300 g (11 oz) brown mushrooms, wiped and sliced
1 onion, chopped
5 ml (1 tsp) chopped fresh rosemary needles
25 ml (5 tsp) soy sauce
250 g (9 oz) low-fat soft cheese
4 large spring onions, chopped
2 eggs
250 ml (8 fl oz) buttermilk
salt and ground black pepper
2 tomatoes, thinly sliced
2 garlic cloves, crushed
dried oregano
Mozzarella cheese
45 ml (3 tbsp) grated Parmesan cheese

Drain spinach in a colander, pressing out all moisture with a wooden spoon. Boil noodles, drain and toss with a little oil.

Heat the oil and sauté mushrooms, onion and rosemary. When onions are browned, remove from heat and add soy sauce.

In a large bowl mix the spinach, cheese and spring onions (add some of the green tops). Beat eggs with buttermilk, salt and pepper and add. Stir in the mushroom mixture and noodles. Spoon into a greased, 28 x 23-cm (11 x 9-in) baking dish. Cover top with tomatoes and sprinkle over garlic and oregano. Top with a thick layer of thinly sliced Mozzarella, and finally sprinkle with Parmesan. Bake at 170 °C (325 °F, gas 3) for 45 minutes then turn off oven and leave for about 10 minutes to settle before serving. This dish does not reheat successfully.
Serves 6.

Mince, Mushroom and Pasta Casserole

A comforting, informal supper dish, using a modest amount of pasta to ensure that it remains succulent and moist. Team with a crisp salad and a hot garlic loaf.

375 g (13 oz) small egg noodles
45 g (1½ oz) butter
60 g (2 oz) flour
750 ml (1¼ pints) milk
salt and pepper
30 ml (2 tbsp) oil
2 onions, chopped
2 garlic cloves, crushed
1 green pepper, seeded and diced
300 g (11 oz) mushrooms, wiped and sliced
500 g (18 oz) mince
5 ml (1 tsp) dried oregano
400 g (14 oz) canned mushroom soup
30 ml (2 tbsp) soy sauce
grated Mozzarella and Parmesan cheese

Boil noodles in plenty of salted water, drain, then toss with a little oil and set aside.

Make a thick white sauce with butter, flour and milk. Season, cover and set aside.

Heat oil in a large frying pan and add onions, garlic, green pepper and mushrooms. When softened, add mince and oregano. Toss until meat turns brown, then spoon contents of pan into a large bowl. Stir in soup, 250 ml (8 fl oz) of the white sauce, soy sauce, a little salt and pepper, and the noodles.

Spoon into a large, lightly oiled baking dish. Cover and bake at 170 °C (325 °F, gas 3) for 30 minutes. Remove from oven and pour over the remaining 500 ml (16 fl oz) white sauce. Sprinkle generously with grated cheeses and return to oven for about 25 minutes until hot and bubbling.
Serves 8.

Pasta with Mushroom Sauce

I find this recipe a real life-saver – all you need are a few basic ingredients and 20 minutes in hand to produce a delicious meal for 4–6 people. Protein is added by tossing the spaghetti with some chopped nuts, and topping each serving with Parmesan, Cheddar or, for a change, Feta cheese.

300 g (11 oz) spaghetti, fettucine, tagliatelle or noodles
30 g (1 oz) butter
30 ml (2 tbsp) oil
4 leeks, thinly sliced
2 celery sticks, chopped
1 green pepper, seeded and diced
500 g (18 oz) brown mushrooms, wiped and sliced
1 fresh rosemary sprig, chopped
2 garlic cloves, crushed
45 ml (3 tbsp) flour
375 ml (12 fl oz) hot stock
45 ml (3 tbsp) soy sauce
45 ml (3 tbsp) sherry
45 ml (3 tbsp) soured cream

While pasta is cooking in plenty of boiling salted water, heat butter and oil in a large saucepan and add leeks, celery and green pepper. When beginning to soften, add mushrooms, rosemary and garlic. Toss over medium heat until smelling really good, then sprinkle in the flour and stir to mix. Slowly add stock, soy sauce and sherry. Stir well and then allow to thicken slowly, half-covered. Just before serving, swirl in the soured cream and spoon onto hot drained pasta.
Serves 4–6.

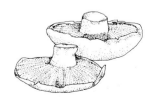

Spinach Pesto

Pesto is surely one of the greatest of Italian sauces. It is very rich and highly flavoured, so a little goes a long way – 30 ml (2 tbsp) on top of a serving of pasta is sufficient. A departure from the traditional recipe is the use of Cheddar cheese instead of Parmesan. If you prefer the latter, use less. I have also used walnuts instead of pine nuts. A processor is essential for this recipe.

2 bunches of young spinach
   leaves
75 g (2¹/₂ oz) walnuts
4 garlic cloves
60 g (2 oz) fresh basil leaves
125 g (4 oz) Cheddar cheese,
   grated
salt and ground black pepper
250 ml (8 fl oz) vegetable oil
45 ml (3 tbsp) olive oil

Trim and wash spinach – you'll need 500 g (18 oz) leaves, weighed after preparation. Cook in the water adhering to the leaves until soft. Drain well, pressing out moisture with a wooden spoon. Using the grinding blade, process the walnuts, garlic and basil until finely chopped. Add the cooked spinach, cheese and seasoning. Process again, and then add the olive and vegetable oils in a slow steady stream. You should end up with a thick, creamy green mixture. Spoon into storage jars, run a thin film of oil over the top and refrigerate. It will keep for several days.

   Before serving, stir well and stand at room temperature for 30 minutes. Make sure that the pasta and the plates are very hot because the sauce is not heated.

Note
My interpretation of traditional Pesto can be found on page 31.

Easy Pizza with Wholemeal Crust

There are surely more varieties of pizza than there are roads in Rome – not only with regard to the topping, but also the base. Traditionally, it's a yeast dough which I, personally, find very often dry. The following is a quick alternative.

CRUST
125 g (4 oz) wholemeal flour
125 g (4 oz) plain flour
2.5 ml ($^1/_2$ tsp) salt
5 ml (1 tsp) baking powder
75 ml ($2^1/_2$ fl oz) oil
100 ml ($3^1/_2$ fl oz) skimmed milk
10 ml (2 tsp) lemon juice

TOPPING
100 ml ($3^1/_2$ fl oz) tomato sauce
10 ml (2 tsp) Worcester sauce
2.5 ml ($^1/_2$ tsp) each dried
   oregano and thyme
2 tomatoes, sliced
1 onion, coarsely grated
2 garlic cloves, crushed
grated Cheddar and Parmesan
   cheese
anchovies, black olives, cooked
   mushrooms (optional)
olive oil
2.5 ml ($^1/_2$ tsp) garlic salt

To make the crust, mix flours, salt and baking powder. Add oil, milk and lemon juice. Quickly mix to a ball – use an electric beater if possible – and press evenly onto the base of a lightly oiled 33 x 20-cm (13 x 8-in) Swiss roll tin, or a pizza pan.

Mix tomato sauce, Worcester sauce and herbs and spread over the dough, right to the edges. Cover with tomatoes, onion and garlic. Sprinkle thickly with Cheddar cheese and dust with Parmesan. If using, soak anchovies in milk. Top pizza with anchovies, olives and mushrooms, if desired. Dribble the top with a little olive oil, sprinkle with garlic salt and bake at 200 °C (400 °F, gas 6) for about 30 minutes, until bubbly and cooked. Cut into fingers and serve very hot.
Serves about 8.

Hint

Traditionally, soft, white Italian Mozzarella should be used instead of Cheddar cheese. It is the perfect pizza cheese, melting to a golden-brown blanket. Use sliced rather than grated.

Stuffed Peppers

These peppers make a lovely light lunch or, served in smaller portions, a starter.

3 very large or 6 medium green
   peppers
15 ml (1 tbsp) oil
15 g ($^1/_2$ oz) butter
1 onion, chopped
2 garlic cloves, crushed
100 g (3$^1/_2$ oz) long-grain rice
2.5 ml ($^1/_2$ tsp) each ground
   turmeric, cumin and fennel
   seed
5 ml (1 tsp) ground coriander
250 g (9 oz) tomatoes, skinned
   and chopped
250 ml (8 fl oz) chicken stock
1 bay leaf
salt and ground black pepper
pinch of sugar
200 g (7 oz) canned shrimps,
   drained and rinsed
30 ml (2 tbsp) desiccated coconut
soured cream and paprika

Halve large peppers or slice tops off medium ones. Remove seeds and white ribs and drop into a large saucepan of boiling water, pressing down gently to submerge. Boil for 5 minutes, then drain.

Heat oil and butter and soften onion and garlic. Add rice and spices and toss over low heat for 1 minute. Add tomatoes, stock, bay leaf, salt, pepper and sugar. Cover and simmer gently for about 25 minutes until rice is cooked. Remove bay leaf and add shrimps and coconut, tossing with a fork until mixed.

Arrange peppers, hollows up, close together in shallow baking dish. Spoon in rice mixture, pour 250 ml (8 fl oz) water round, then cover and bake at 170 °C (325 °F, gas 3) for 30–40 minutes, until soft. Top each pepper with 10 ml (2 tsp) soured cream, dust with paprika and return to oven, uncovered, for 10 minutes. Serves 3 or 6.

Stir-Fry with Mushrooms and Sprouts

oil for frying
4 leeks, thinly sliced
1 small onion, chopped
2 celery sticks, sliced
2 medium carrots, cut in julienne
2 garlic cloves, crushed
300 g (11 oz) mushrooms, wiped
   and sliced
200 g (7 oz) shredded cabbage
$^1/_2$ cucumber, peeled and cubed
150 g (5 oz) lentil sprouts
45 ml (3 tbsp) soy sauce
200 ml (6$^1/_2$ fl oz) chicken stock
20 ml (4 tsp) cornflour
pinch of sugar
toasted almonds

In a large frying pan or wok heat 45 ml (3 tbsp) oil and stir-fry leeks, onion, celery, carrots and garlic. After about 5 minutes on medium heat, transfer to a large, warmed dish and place in preheated 170 °C (325 °F, gas 3) oven.

To pan add a little more oil and add mushrooms, cabbage and cucumber. Sauté until softened, stirring, then add the sprouts, soy sauce and stock mixed with cornflour and sugar. Cover and simmer for a few minutes, then mix into the other vegetables in the oven dish. Return to oven for about 10 minutes, then serve on rice and top with plenty of toasted almonds. It should not be necessary to add salt.
Serves 4–6.

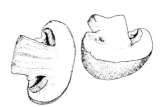

Vegetable Paella

45 ml (3 tbsp) vegetable oil
45 ml (3 tbsp) olive oil
2 large leeks, sliced
1 onion, chopped
3 garlic cloves, crushed
1 green pepper, seeded and diced
300 g (11 oz) brown rice
300 g (11 oz) mushrooms, wiped
 and sliced
250 g (9 oz) aubergine, diced †
5 ml (1 tsp) each dried oregano,
 basil and turmeric
400 g (14 oz) tomatoes, skinned
 and chopped
350 g (12 oz) green beans, chopped,
 or 350 g (12 oz) peas
30 g (1 oz) parsley, chopped
salt and ground black pepper
pinch of sugar
500 ml (16 fl oz) chicken, vegetable
 or Marmite stock
125 ml (4 fl oz) white wine
250 g (9 oz) Feta or Cheddar cheese

Using a large saucepan or wok,
heat oils and add leeks, onion, garlic
and pepper. When softened, add
rice and toss until coated with oil.
Reduce heat and add mushrooms,
aubergine, herbs and turmeric.
Toss for a minute or two, then add
tomatoes, the beans or peas,
parsley, seasoning, sugar, stock
and wine.

Mix well, then turn into a large
baking dish. Cover and bake at
180 °C (350 °F, gas 4) for
35 minutes. Stir lightly with a fork,
then continue baking for another
20–25 minutes until vegetables are
cooked and the liquid absorbed.
The mixture should be moist but
not at all watery. Turn off oven
heat and cover top with diced Feta
or grated Cheddar, and return to
oven for 5–10 minutes to heat
through. Serves 6.

† Large aubergines need to be
dégorged before use. See page 135
for instructions.

Lentil Salad

**This is a favourite summer salad.
Surround with wedges of hard-
boiled eggs, and serve with
cheese and wholemeal bread for
a nourishing, complete meal.**

300 g (11 oz) brown lentils,
 rinsed and picked over
750 ml (1¼ pints) water
2.5 ml (½ tsp) salt
2 bay leaves
2.5 ml (½ tsp) turmeric
100 ml (3½ fl oz) French
 dressing (page 47)
3–4 spring onions, chopped
2 large carrots, grated
2–3 celery sticks, chopped
45 ml (3 tbsp) chopped parsley
100 g (3½ oz) mung bean
 sprouts (or sprouts of choice)
25 ml (5 tsp) soy sauce

Put lentils into saucepan with
water, salt, bay leaves and
turmeric. Bring to the boil, then
cover and simmer gently until
soft and liquid has been absorbed.
Tip into a large bowl and discard
bay leaveš. Fork in the dressing,
taking care not to mash the
lentils. Add spring onions,
carrots, celery, parsley, sprouts
and soy sauce. Toss lightly to
mix, and then set aside, covered,
for about 2 hours – or chill for
longer. Serve as suggested – or
brighten up the lentils by
dribbling over a little plain
yoghurt and topping with
chopped mint, or substitute
soured cream and sprinkle with
nuts.
Serves 6.

Spinach Pancakes

or Crêpes Florentine. This dish can be prepared in advance and baked when required. The pancake batter and the cheese sauce are both made in a blender.

CRÊPES
125 g (4 oz) flour
generous pinch of salt
1 egg and 1 egg yolk
250 ml (8 fl oz) milk
125 ml (4 fl oz) water
25 ml (5 tsp) oil

FILLING
500 g (18 oz) frozen spinach, thawed
generous pinch of salt
generous pinch of freshly grated nutmeg

SAUCE
600 ml (19 fl oz) milk
45 ml (3 tbsp) flour
125 g (4 oz) Gruyère cheese, grated
2.5 ml ($^1/_2$ tsp) each dry mustard and salt
45 g (1$^1/_2$ oz) butter, softened
grated Parmesan cheese
paprika

Put ingredients for crêpes into blender, blend well and stand for at least 30 minutes. The consistency should be creamy and medium-thick, and the batter will be enough for 10 crêpes, 18–20 cm (7–8 in) in diameter. Stack, after cooking, with sheets of greaseproof paper between each crêpe.

For the filling, cook spinach, drain very well in colander and press out all moisture. Season with salt and nutmeg.

For sauce, put 500 ml (16 fl oz) milk, flour, Gruyère cheese, mustard, salt and butter into blender, blend well and then pour into saucepan and cook over low heat, stirring, until thick and cheese has melted. Stir 125 ml (4 fl oz) of this sauce into the spinach purée. Fill each crêpe with a large spoonful of the purée and roll into cigar shapes. Place side by side, close together in a shallow, buttered baking dish. Thin the remaining cheese sauce with remaining milk and pour over crêpes. Sprinkle generously with Parmesan (or Cheddar or Gruyère if preferred) and dust with paprika. Bake at 180 °C (350 °F, gas 4) for 30 minutes. Serves 10 as a starter or 5 as a main course.

Italian Quiche

Baked in a 30-cm (12-in) pizza pan, this is a huge and hearty quiche with a wholemeal crust and a ratatouille-style filling.

PROCESSOR PASTRY
125 g (4 oz) wholemeal flour
60 g (2 oz) plain flour
2.5 ml (½ tsp) salt
125 g (4 oz) butter, diced
10 ml (2 tsp) lemon juice
30–45 ml (2–3 tbsp) cold water

FILLING
45 ml (3 tbsp) oil
2 leeks, chopped
1 small onion, chopped
1 green pepper, seeded and diced
2 garlic cloves, crushed
250 g (9 oz) courgettes, peeled
    and diced
250 g (9 oz) aubergines, diced
2.5 ml (½ tsp) salt
ground black pepper
45 ml (3 tbsp) chopped parsley
2.5 ml (½ tsp) dried oregano
generous pinch of dried basil
125 g (4 oz) cream cheese
375 ml (12 fl oz) milk
3 eggs
1 large tomato, thinly sliced
100 g (3½ oz) Cheddar cheese,
    grated
30 ml (2 tbsp) grated Parmesan
    cheese

To make the pastry, use the grinding blade to mix the flours, salt and butter until finely blended. With the motor running, add lemon juice and water. Stop as soon as it forms a ball, turn out onto floured board and roll out, using a floured rolling pin. Using fingers, press into pizza pan, flute edges, prick well and chill.

For the filling, heat oil in a large pan and sauté leeks, onion, pepper and garlic. When translucent, add courgettes and aubergines, then season with salt and pepper. Cover and cook over low heat, stirring occasionally until soft. Spoon into a bowl. Add parsley and dried herbs. Cool.

Bake chilled crust at 200 °C (400 °F, gas 6) for 12 minutes. Brush about 15 ml (1 tbsp) flour over base. Spoon in vegetable filling. Beat cream cheese, milk, eggs and large pinch of salt. Arrange tomato over vegetables, pour custard over, sprinkle with cheeses and bake at 180 °C (350 °F, gas 4) for 30–35 minutes. Turn off oven and leave for 20 minutes. Serve with a salad. Serves 8.

Asparagus and Spring Onion Quiche

CRUST
175 g (6 oz) flour
2.5 ml (¹/₂ tsp) salt
2.5 ml (¹/₂ tsp) baking
powder
100 ml (3¹/₂ fl oz) oil
45 ml (3 tbsp) iced water
squeeze of lemon juice
10 ml (2 tsp) cornflour

FILLING
450 g (1 lb) canned asparagus
spears, well drained
6 spring onions, chopped
250 g (9 oz) low-fat soft cheese
2.5 ml (¹/₂ tsp) dried tarragon
2.5 ml (¹/₂ tsp) salt
ground black pepper
3 eggs
125 ml (4 fl oz) milk
125 ml (4 fl oz) single cream
30 ml (2 tbsp) chopped parsley
paprika and grated Gruyère

To make the crust, sift flour, salt and baking powder. Add oil, water and lemon juice. Mix lightly with a fork, shape into a ball and roll out thinly between two sheets of greaseproof paper. Line a deep, 23-cm (9-in) flan tin, prick well and bake at 200 °C (400 °F, gas 6) for 15 minutes. Remove and dust base with cornflour. Cool.

If asparagus stems are thick, slice in half lengthways and arrange on base of crust, together with spring onions. Beat cheese with tarragon, salt and pepper. Beat in eggs, one at a time, followed by the milk, cream and parsley. Pour carefully onto crust, dust with paprika and sprinkle with Gruyère. Reduce oven temperature to 180 °C (350 °F, gas 4) and heat a baking tray in it for a few minutes. Place flan tin on the hot tray and bake for 45 minutes or until set.
Serves 6–8.

Stuffed Baked Potatoes

4 large baking potatoes
30 g (1 oz) butter, melted
about 150 ml (5 fl oz) milk,
heated
125 g (4 oz) Cheddar, grated
salt and ground black pepper
2.5 ml (¹/₂ tsp) prepared mustard
30 ml (2 tbsp) chopped parsley
paprika

Scrub potatoes, rub skins with oil and bake at 200 °C (400 °F, gas 6) for about 1 hour until soft. Either slice in half lengthways and serve half per person, or slice off just the tops. Scoop flesh into a bowl, leaving a firm shell. Mash with the melted butter and milk, then add remaining ingredients, except paprika. Pile into shells, brush lightly with milk and dust with paprika. Reheat at 180 °C (350 °F, gas 4). Serves 4–8.

Tuna-Stuffed Potatoes

4 large baking potatoes
200 g (7 oz) canned tuna in
brine, drained and shredded
10 ml (2 tsp) capers, rinsed and
chopped
5 ml (1 tsp) lemon juice
45 ml (3 tbsp) mayonnaise
salt and ground black pepper
about 75 ml (2¹/₂ fl oz) milk,
heated
Cheddar cheese, grated
butter

Pre-heat oven to 200 °C (400 °F, gas 6). Prepare potatoes and bake as in previous recipe. Reduce oven temperature to 180 °C (350 °F, gas 4). Scoop flesh into a bowl, leaving shells intact. Mash potato and add remaining ingredients except cheese and butter. Pile into shells and top with cheese and a knob of butter. Return to oven until cheese has melted.
Serves 4–8.

Phyllo Parcels

500 g (18 oz) frozen phyllo
  pastry, thawed in refrigerator
  for 24 hours

CHICKEN, CHEESE AND SPINACH
FILLING
4 chicken breasts (500 g (18 oz)
  with bone)
salted water
1 onion, chopped
few parsley sprigs
1 bay leaf
1 whole carrot
30 g (1 oz) butter
500 g (18 oz) frozen spinach,
  thawed
2 leeks, finely chopped
250 g (9 oz) low-fat soft cheese
45 ml (3 tbsp) grated Parmesan
5 ml (1 tsp) chopped fresh
  rosemary needles
salt and ground black pepper

EGG AND LEMON SAUCE
30 g (1 oz) butter
45 ml (3 tbsp) flour

500 ml (16 fl oz) hot, seasoned
  chicken stock
2 egg yolks
25 ml (5 tsp) lemon juice
generous pinch of finely grated
  lemon rind
pinch of sugar

Poach breasts in plenty of salted
water together with onion,
parsley, bay leaf and carrot.
When done, remove skin and
bone and chop into small dice.
Strain and reserve stock for
sauce. Melt butter and add
spinach and leeks. Cook over
low heat until all moisture has
evaporated. Combine chicken,
spinach, low-fat and Parmesan
cheeses, rosemary and seasoning
and work into a smooth mixture.
  Remove 3 sheets of phyllo –
they should measure about
42 x 37 cm (17 x 15 in). Brush top
sheet with oil, garlic oil or
melted butter. Place a mound of
filling in the centre and then
draw up the corners to form a
parcel, twisting the top to seal.

Brush outside of parcel with oil
or butter and sprinkle lightly
with water. Make 7 more parcels
in the same way, place on 2
large, oiled baking sheets and
bake at 200 °C (400 °F, gas 6) for
20 minutes until golden brown.
  While they are baking, make
the sauce. Melt butter, stir in
flour. When straw-coloured,
remove from stove and slowly
add stock. Return to heat and
stir until thickened. Beat egg
yolks with lemon juice and rind,
stir in a little of the hot sauce,
then return to heat and stir until
cooked and creamy. Adjust
seasoning and add pinch sugar.
Serve with chicken parcels, rice,
and a salad.
Makes 8 parcels.

Note
**Tissue-thin, feathery phyllo
pastry requires special
treatment. Refer to page 220 for
full instructions.**

Sprout, Feta and Almond Filling

As a delicious alternative, try
this vegetarian mixture when
making phyllo parcels.

175 g (6 oz) mung bean sprouts
200 g (7 oz) Feta cheese, rinsed
  and diced
45 g (1¹/₂ oz) chopped toasted
  almonds
2 egg yolks
25 ml (5 tsp) soy sauce
2 celery sticks, finely chopped
6 spring onions, chopped
4 small courgettes, peeled and
  coarsely grated
pinch of sugar

Combine ingredients and make
and bake 6 parcels as in previous
recipe. Serve with a creamy
cabbage salad.
Makes 6 parcels.

Mushroom Roulade

Mushroom Roulade

A soufflé-type roll with a filling
– this is a sophisticated starter
or light main course which
really is not all that difficult to
make. Perhaps the most difficult
part is achieving a really smooth
panada, but it is possible to
cheat a little and start it off in a
blender.

ROULADE
60 g (2 oz) butter, softened
60 g (2 oz) plain flour
500 ml (16 fl oz) milk
2.5 ml (¹/₂ tsp) salt
5 ml (1 tsp) dry mustard
5 ml (1 tsp) sugar
4 eggs, separated

FILLING
30 ml (2 tbsp) oil
**300 g (11 oz) button mush-
rooms, wiped and chopped**
1–2 garlic cloves, crushed
**5 ml (1 tsp) chopped fresh
rosemary**

250 g (9 oz) low-fat soft cheese
4–6 spring onions, chopped
**15 ml (1 tbsp) finely chopped
parsley**
salt and ground black pepper
pinch of sugar

TOPPING
250 ml (8 fl oz) soured cream
chopped chives

Put butter, flour and milk into
blender, and blend until well
mixed. Pour into a heavy-based
saucepan and bring to the boil,
using a balloon whisk to bring
mixture to a very thick and
smooth consistency. Allow
1–2 minutes for flour to cook.
Remove and add salt, mustard
and sugar and beat well.
   Beat egg yolks, mix in a little of
the hot sauce, then stir into rest
of sauce. Beat well, then fold in
the stiffly whisked egg whites. Be
gentle but thorough. Oil a
33 x 20-cm (13 x 8-in) Swiss roll
tin, line with greaseproof paper,
allowing an overhang at the ends,

brush with oil again and dust
with flour, shaking off excess.
Pour in soufflé mixture,
spreading evenly, and bake just
below centre of oven at 170 °C
(325 °F, gas 3) for 1 hour, or until
risen, firm and golden brown.
Loosen edges with a knife, invert
onto a large sheet of greaseproof
paper, remove backing paper and
roll up. Cool.
   To make the filling, heat oil
and briskly fry mushrooms,
garlic and rosemary until all liquid
has evaporated – mixture must
be dry. Tip into a bowl and
leave until cold, then add
remaining ingredients, combining
thoroughly. Unroll roulade,
spread with filling, and re-roll.
When required, reheat in low
oven, and serve in thick slices
with the soured cream and chive
topping.
Serves 8 generously.

Smoked Salmon Roulade

A delicious alternative.

250 g (9 oz) cream cheese
**125 g (4 oz) smoked salmon,
chopped**
**generous pinch of finely grated
lemon rind**
2 spring onions, chopped
ground black pepper
30 ml (2 tbsp) soured cream
pinch of sugar

TOPPING
250 ml (8 fl oz) soured cream
chopped chives

Following the instructions in the
previous recipe, make the
roulade.
   Combine ingredients, spread
over baked roll, roll up and serve
at room temperature with the
soured cream and chive topping.
Serves 8 generously.

Spinach and Brown Mushroom Quiche

A substantial, large, cheesy quiche, which reheats well.

PASTRY
100 g (3¹/₂ oz) plain flour
100 g (3¹/₂ oz) wholemeal flour
pinch of salt
125 g (4 oz) butter
75 ml (2¹/₂ fl oz) iced water
squeeze of lemon juice
1 egg, separated

FILLING
500 g (18 oz) frozen spinach,
    thawed
generous pinch of salt
2.5 ml (¹/₂ tsp) dried dill
30 ml (2 tbsp) oil
30 g (1 oz) butter
300 g (11 oz) brown mushrooms,
    wiped and roughly chopped
2 leeks, sliced
1 small onion, chopped
1 fresh rosemary sprig

salt and ground black pepper
250 ml (8 fl oz) milk
2 eggs plus reserved yolk
125 ml (4 fl oz) soured cream
5 ml (1 tsp) French mustard
100 g (3¹/₂ oz) Gruyère or
    Cheddar cheese, grated
2.5 ml (¹/₂ tsp) dried oregano

To make pastry, mix flours and salt. Rub in butter until crumbly, then bind with water and lemon juice. Form into a ball and chill for about 30 minutes, then roll out and line a deep 28-cm (11-in) diameter quiche tin. Prick well and bake at 200 °C (400 °F, gas 6), just below centre of oven, for 20 minutes. Brush with lightly beaten egg white (reserve yolk for filling) and return to oven for 5 minutes.

For filling, drain spinach well, pressing out all moisture, then season with salt and dill. Heat oil and butter and sauté mushrooms, leeks, onion and rosemary. When semi-cooked, remove rosemary and season the

mixture lightly. Beat milk with eggs and egg yolk, soured cream, mustard, salt and pepper. Spread drained spinach over crust and spoon mushroom mixture over. Pour egg mixture over, sprinkle with cheese and oregano and bake at 170 °C (325 °F, gas 3) for 45 minutes or until set.
Serves 8.

Variation

SPINACH AND CHEESE QUICHE
250 g (9 oz) frozen spinach,
    thawed and well drained
250 g (9 oz) low-fat soft cheese
2.5 ml (¹/₂ tsp) salt
generous pinch of freshly grated
    nutmeg
2 eggs, beaten
125 ml (4 fl oz) soured cream
1 small onion, grated
45 ml (3 tbsp) chopped parsley
15 ml (1 tbsp) grated Parmesan
    cheese

Combine spinach, cottage cheese, salt and nutmeg. Add eggs, soured cream, onion and parsley. Pour into crust and sprinkle with Parmesan. Bake at 180 °C (350 °F, gas 4) for 30 minutes. Serve warm, rather than hot.
Serves 8.

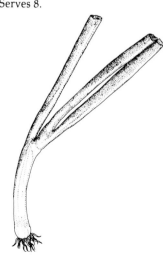

Chilled White Mushroom and Cheese Tart

For a light lunch, an unusual starter, or as part of a cold buffet, this quiche is a winner. I have used a bland crumb crust which does not interfere with the delicate filling, and a garnish of sliced avocado dusted with milled black pepper ensures that no-one mistakes it for cheesecake – which it closely resembles in appearance. Use a deep 20-cm (8-in) pie dish, make it several hours in advance, and keep refrigerated.

CRUST
125 g (4 oz) crushed savoury
    biscuits
100 g (3¹/₂ oz) butter, melted

FILLING
30 ml (2 tbsp) oil
6 spring onions, chopped
300 g (11 oz) white button
    mushrooms, wiped and sliced
1 garlic clove, crushed
2 fresh rosemary sprigs
salt and ground black pepper
250 g (9 oz) low-fat soft cheese
2 eggs, separated
20 ml (4 tsp) powdered gelatine
200 ml (6¹/₂ fl oz) chicken stock
125 ml (4 fl oz) whipping cream,
    whipped
few drops of Worcester sauce
pinch of sugar

Mix ingredients for crust and press onto base of greased pie dish. Chill.

Heat oil in large frying pan and add spring onions, mushrooms, garlic and rosemary. Toss over high heat for 3 minutes until starting to shrink and soften. Remove and set aside, and season when cold, so that juices are not extracted.

Beat cheese and yolks together until smooth. Soften gelatine in the stock, dissolve over low heat and gradually whisk into cheese mixture. Add mushroom mixture to cheese mixture, discarding rosemary. Chill until starting to thicken – this takes a while. Whisk egg whites with a pinch of salt and fold in together with cream, Worcester sauce and sugar. Pour onto crust and chill until set. Garnish just before serving.
Serves 8.

Oranges with Sabayon Grand Marnier

Just the thing with which to round off a heavy dinner. Those who want fresh fruit can simply have a serving of orange slices; others can smother them with the sybaritic sabayon. This is often made with sherry, sometimes with rum, but Grand Marnier is good here because it complements the oranges. Brandy or whisky, however, would also be suitable.

oranges
caster sugar

SABAYON
6 egg yolks
125 g (4 oz) caster sugar
10 ml (2 tsp) cornflour
90 ml (3 fl oz) Grand Marnier
200 ml (6¹/₂ fl oz) whipping
   cream, whipped

Peel and thinly slice as many oranges as you'll need. Remove pith and pips. Layer on flat glass dish, sprinkle with just a little caster sugar and pour over any juice that escaped on the cutting board. Cover and chill all day to allow the juices to 'draw'. Don't be tempted to make a sugar syrup – the beauty of this dessert lies in the fresh, raw orange, with the rich, sweet sauce. However, if desired, the slices may be sprinkled with very finely shredded peel, cooked until soft in a light syrup.

   To make the sabayon, put egg yolks, sugar and cornflour in top of double boiler and whisk, using a balloon whisk, over gently simmering water. When very thick and light add Grand Marnier. Now stir over the simmering water with a wooden spoon until the custard is thick. It must thicken, or it will separate on standing, but it must not cook, or it will curdle. Pour into a bowl, cover once cooled, and chill thoroughly.

   Just before serving, fold in cream gently but thoroughly, then pour into a large and pretty container, like a coloured glass goblet. The sabayon should not be poured, but ladled over each serving. Quantities can easily be halved.

Makes about 625 ml (1 pint) of sauce.

Pavlova with Fruit and Cream

Pavlova with Fruit and Cream

Pavlova is an Australian speciality, also claimed by New Zealand. Crisp outside, soft underneath, topped with fruit and cream. Traditionally it should be made in a pie dish, but I prefer a free-standing circle.

MERINGUE
3 egg whites
pinch of salt
200 g (7 oz) caster sugar
10 ml (2 tsp) cider vinegar
10 ml (2 tsp) cornflour

FILLING
800 g (1 lb 14 oz) canned peach slices
pulp of 6 fresh passion fruit
2 firm bananas, sliced and tossed in lemon juice
250 ml (8 fl oz) whipping cream
15 ml (1 tbsp) icing sugar
few drops of vanilla extract

For the meringue whisk egg whites with a pinch of salt until foamy, using an electric beater. Gradually whisk in the caster sugar, a spoonful at a time. Whisk until stiff. Using a metal spoon, fold in the vinegar and cornflour lightly but thoroughly. Spoon meringue onto baking sheet brushed with oil and dusted with cornflour – make a circle with a fairly thick base and a raised edge. Bake at 140 °C (275 °F, gas 1) for 1 hour. Do not open the oven door at all during the baking period. After an hour, turn off the heat and leave until absolutely cold, preferably overnight. Remove carefully, peeling off the foil slowly, and put on serving plate.

The filling can be prepared ahead and piled in just before serving. Drain peaches well, add passion fruit and bananas, cover and set aside. Whip cream with icing sugar and vanilla extract and chill. To serve, fold fruit into cream and fill shell. Serves 8.

Chocolate-Swirled Rum Crèmes

A tot of rum and circles of melted chocolate make this rich, custard-based dessert both decorative and delicious.

10 ml (2 tsp) powdered gelatine
45 ml (3 tbsp) cold water
375 ml (12 fl oz) milk
1 vanilla pod
2 eggs, separated
45 g (1¹/₂ oz) caster sugar
pinch of salt
5 ml (1 tsp) cornflour
30 ml (2 tbsp) dark rum
125 ml (4 fl oz) whipping cream, whipped

TOPPING
45 g (1¹/₂ oz) milk chocolate
25 ml (5 tsp) water

Soften gelatine in cold water. Scald milk with vanilla. Mix yolks with sugar, salt and cornflour. Pour on a little hot milk, stir to mix, then return to saucepan and heat, stirring, until mixture coats the back of a wooden spoon. Remove from heat and stir in gelatine. Pour into a bowl and add rum. Cool and then chill briefly, or stir over ice until beginning to thicken. Whisk egg whites until stiff but not dry and fold in together with cream. Pour into one large glass bowl, or 6–8 small bowls or glasses, and chill for 15 minutes.

Place chocolate and water in saucepan over hot water. Stir until very smooth and runny. Drop a large teaspoonful onto the top of each half-set crème and swirl in lightly (not deeply) in concentric circles, using the point of a skewer. Return to fridge and set firm.
Serves 6–8.

Coffee Vacherin with Cream and Fruit

Crisp, coffee-flavoured meringue rounds, sandwiched with whipped cream and pears or lychees – a sinfully sweet and irresistible dessert. The meringue rounds may be made days in advance and stored in an airtight container. Add the cream filling 4 hours before serving, and refrigerate. This softens the meringue slightly and makes for easier cutting.

2 egg whites
175 g (6 oz) caster sugar
10 ml (2 tsp) instant coffee powder
10 ml (2 tsp) water

FILLING
250 ml (8 fl oz) whipping cream
20 ml (4 tsp) icing sugar
5 ml (1 tsp) instant coffee powder

5 ml (1 tsp) Tia Maria
400 g (14 oz) canned pears or lychees

Whisk egg whites until stiff. Gradually add half the sugar, beating well, then beat in coffee powder dissolved in the water. Beat until very stiff, then fold in the remaining caster sugar, using a metal spoon. Lightly oil a large baking sheet, dust with cornflour, and shake off the excess. Spoon on meringue to form two 20-cm (8-in) circles. Bake at 110 °C (225 °F, gas ¹/₄) for 1 hour 30 minutes, then turn off oven and leave until cold. Lift off sheet, and store, or fill.

Whip cream with icing sugar. Dissolve coffee in liqueur, add to cream, and whip until stiff. Drain fruit thoroughly, dry well using absorbent kitchen paper, and then chop into small pieces. Fold into cream. Sandwich meringue rounds with half the cream and pile the remainder on top. Chill. Serves 8.

Variation

ALMOND MERINGUE
Try this as an alternative to the Coffee Vacherin: Whisk 4 egg whites until foamy. Gradually add 100 g (3¹/₂ oz) caster sugar, while whisking. When very stiff, fold in another 100 g (3¹/₂ oz) caster sugar, using a metal spoon. Lastly fold in 90 g (3 oz) ground almonds, then proceed as above.

Sabayon Malibu

Serve with fruit salad – include a can of mangoes for a tropical touch.

4 egg yolks
90 g (3 oz) caster sugar
5 ml (1 tsp) cornflour
75 ml (2¹/₂ fl oz) Malibu
150 ml (5 fl oz) whipping cream, whipped

Using a balloon whisk, whisk egg yolks, sugar and cornflour in a small saucepan over gently simmering water. When thickened, stir in Malibu and continue stirring, using a wooden spoon, until mixture thickens again. Do not overheat, but the yolks must be cooked. Remove from heat, pour into a small bowl, cool, cover and chill. Fold in cream just before serving. Makes about 400 ml (13 fl oz).

Chocolate Liqueur Mousse

As this mousse is very rich, serve small quantities in individual glasses.

**100 g (3¹/₂ oz) plain chocolate
3 eggs, separated
25 ml (5 tsp) Crème de Cacao
5 ml (1 tsp) instant coffee powder
250 ml (8 fl oz) whipping cream, whipped**

Break up chocolate and melt in top of small double boiler, having first smeared inside of container with a little melted butter. Don't stir more than is necessary to soften it completely.

Using an electric whisk, beat egg yolks, liqueur and coffee powder. Add melted chocolate and beat well. Whisk egg whites with a pinch of salt until stiff but not dry and using a metal spoon,

fold in together with whipped cream. Keep folding until thoroughly combined, then pour into 6 glasses and chill for at least 4 hours. Serve plain, or decorate with chocolate curls, made by drawing a vegetable peeler down the long side of a warm slab of chocolate.
Serves 6.

Variation

IRISH COFFEE CHOCOLATE MOUSSE
Substitute 30 ml (2 tbsp) Irish whisky for the Crème de Cacao and add a few drops of vanilla with the cream.

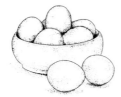

Chocolate Mousse Pie

This is a simple, honest-to-goodness chocolate pie, which takes on a sophisticated flavour if decorated with rum-flavoured whipped cream.

CRUST
**10 ml (2 tsp) cocoa powder
100 g (3¹/₂ oz) butter, melted
125 g (4 oz) sweet biscuit crumbs**

FILLING
**250 ml (8 fl oz) milk
45 g (1¹/₂ oz) plain chocolate
15 ml (1 tbsp) cocoa powder
2 eggs, separated
90 g (3 oz) caster sugar
10 ml (2 tsp) powdered gelatine
45 ml (3 tbsp) cold water
few drops of vanilla extract
125 ml (4 fl oz) whipping cream, whipped**

Dissolve cocoa powder in butter and mix with crumbs. Press into the base of a greased 20-cm (8-in)

pie dish. Chill while making filling.

Scald milk, chocolate (broken into pieces) and cocoa powder, stirring to melt chocolate. Beat yolks with sugar, stir in a little hot milk mixture, then return to saucepan and cook over low heat, stirring, until thickened. Do not boil. Remove from heat. Soften gelatine in cold water then stir into custard. When dissolved, add vanilla and pour into bowl to cool. Chill until beginning to thicken. Stiffly whisk egg whites with a pinch of salt, then fold in together with whipped cream. Pour into crust and chill until set.
Serves 6.

Hint

For the finest vanilla flavour, sink a vanilla pod into a jar of sugar or caster sugar and keep on hand to use in desserts and cakes, instead of using sugar plus vanilla extract.

Chocolate Pots

Chocolate Pots

200 g (7 oz) plain chocolate,
 broken in pieces
45 ml (3 tbsp) water
6 eggs, separated
5 ml (1 tsp) finely grated orange
 rind
45 ml (3 tbsp) Curaçao

In the top of a double boiler melt
chocolate in water. When
melted, turn heat to very low
and beat in egg yolks, one at a
time, using a wooden spoon. Stir
well after each addition and
when thick and smooth, remove
from heat. Stir in orange rind
and Curaçao.
 Leave to cool slightly. Whisk
egg whites with a pinch of salt
until stiff, but not dry. Fold into
chocolate mixture until well
blended, then pour into 8 little
pots. Set in refrigerator for at
least 4 hours. Serve plain, or
with a twirl of cream and a little
grated chocolate. Serves 8.

Chocolate Pudding

100 g (3½ oz) plain chocolate,
 broken in pieces
5 ml (1 tsp) instant coffee
 powder
10 ml (2 tsp) water
15 g (½ oz) butter
10 ml (2 tsp) powdered gelatine,
 softened in 25 ml (5 tsp) cold
 water
few drops of vanilla extract
400 g (14 oz) canned evaporated
 milk, chilled and whipped
10 ml (2 tsp) lemon juice
45 ml (3 tbsp) icing sugar

Slowly melt chocolate, coffee,
water and butter in top of
double boiler. When smooth
remove from heat and stir in
gelatine until dissolved. Add
vanilla, allow to cool slightly.
Whip lemon juice and icing sugar
into evaporated milk until very
stiff. Beat in chocolate mixture
slowly then refrigerate.
Serves 8–10.

Fraises Brûlée

or Burnt Strawberries – a
delicious combination of berries
and orange liqueur, topped with
cream and crusted with sugar.
Assembled in minutes, chilled
for 4 hours and then flashed
under the grill just before
serving, it's a joy for the busy
cook. An 18-cm (7-in) heatproof
pie dish is essential.

300–350 g (11–12 oz) ripe
 strawberries
45 ml (3 tbsp) Curaçao
200 ml (6½ fl oz) whipping
 cream
2.5 ml (½ tsp) finely grated
 orange rind
45 ml (3 tbsp) light brown sugar

Wash, hull and halve strawberries and arrange to cover the
base of the pie dish. Sprinkle
with Curaçao. Whip cream with
orange rind until stiff, then
spread over the fruit. Sprinkle

the sugar evenly over the top.
Leave in coldest part of the
refrigerator for 4 hours.
 Preheat grill for several
minutes and place dish under
heat for about 1 minute. As soon
as sugar melts and darkens,
remove and serve. Serves 4–5.

Variation

GRAPE BRÛLÉE
Fill an 18-cm (7-in) heatproof
dish with a mixture of 1 sweet
melon, cut into small dice, 250 g
(9 oz) halved and de-pipped
grapes, one piece finely chopped
preserved ginger and 45 g
(1½ oz) chopped hazelnuts.
Dribble with 30 ml (2 tbsp)
ginger syrup. Stiffly whip 250 ml
(8 fl oz) cream with 2.5 ml
(½ tsp) ground cinnamon and
pour over fruit. Put in coldest
part of refrigerator for 6 hours.
To serve, sprinkle 45 g (1½ oz)
light brown sugar evenly over
cream and place under preheated grill to melt sugar. Serve
at once.

Fruit Salad Special with Coffee Cream Topping

Fruit Salad Special with Coffee Cream Topping

A simple but elegant fruit salad. The ingredients are rather special, so is the topping, and the colour combination is superb. The effect will be lost if served in one big bowl so use 6 little glass dishes instead.

2 large bananas
1 large, firm avocado
24 strawberries
30 ml (2 tbsp) lemon juice
30 ml (2 tbsp) caster sugar
toasted flaked almonds

CREAM TOPPING
250 ml (8 fl oz) whipping cream
25 ml (5 tsp) icing sugar
10 ml (2 tsp) Kahlúa
5 ml (1 tsp) instant coffee powder

Slice bananas thinly, cut avocado into small dice and slice strawberries. Divide the fruit between the dishes, and to each dish add 5 ml (1 tsp) lemon juice and 5 ml (1 tsp) caster sugar. Toss gently, then cover and chill.

Whip ingredients for cream topping together until soft peaks form. Do not over-beat. Cover and chill. Just before serving, pour a blanket of the coffee cream over each fruit salad, and sprinkle with the almonds. Serves 6.

Kiwi Fruit and Strawberries with Curaçao

A bright, refreshing dessert to serve at the end of a good dinner. For best effect, layer the red and green fruit in a large glass bowl, or in champagne glasses. Serve garnished with a sprig of mint, dribbled with a spoonful of soured cream, or topped with a small scoop of vanilla ice cream.

3 kiwi fruit
12–24 strawberries

SYRUP
125 ml (4 fl oz) water
45 ml (3 tbsp) caster sugar
5 ml (1 tsp) finely grated orange rind
45 ml (3 tbsp) Curaçao

First make the syrup. Put water, sugar and rind into a small saucepan and boil rapidly for 2–3 minutes. Remove and add Curaçao.

Peel kiwi fruit and wash and hull strawberries. Slice both fruits into very thin rounds. Layer into bowl or glasses and strain 25 ml (5 tsp) of the syrup over each serving. Cover and chill for several hours. Serves 6.

Note

One is inclined to regard New Zealand as the home of kiwi fruit, but in fact it was originally imported from China, and known as the Chinese Gooseberry. Egg-shaped, with emerald green flesh, the flavour is a subtle combination of strawberry, orange, watermelon and banana and is wonderfully versatile, combining well with meat, fish and poultry. It is great for highlighting desserts and can also be made into jam.

Orange Liqueur Ice Cream

Orange Liqueur Ice Cream

Serve fresh and pure; with chocolate sauce; or with Mandarin Orange Sauce Flambé.

4 eggs, separated
90 g (3 oz) caster sugar
5 ml (1 tsp) very finely grated orange rind
75 ml (2^1/$_2$ fl oz) orange-flavoured liqueur
250 ml (8 fl oz) double cream †
few drops of vanilla extract

Using an electric beater, whisk egg yolks, sugar, orange rind and liqueur at high speed for several minutes. Whisk egg whites stiffly with a pinch of salt. When egg yolk mixture is thick and custardy, fold in whipped cream and egg whites. Finally add vanilla. Fold gently until well combined, then freeze quickly. Serves 6–8.

Mandarin Orange Sauce Flambé

300 g (11 oz) canned mandarin oranges, drained
200 ml (6^1/$_2$ fl oz) fresh orange juice
45 ml (3 tbsp) mixed peel
25 ml (5 tsp) honey
45 ml (3 tbsp) seedless raisins
45 ml (3 tbsp) chopped walnuts
25 ml (5 tsp) brandy

Mix all ingredients, except brandy, in a small bowl, cover and refrigerate up to 48 hours. To serve, heat thoroughly in small saucepan. Flame with the warmed brandy and serve at once.
Makes about 375 ml (12 fl oz).

Hint

Use pale, clear honey in baked desserts – the darker the honey, the stronger the flavour.

Rich Coffee Ice Cream

This recipe was inspired by an ice cream I ate from a cone on a street corner near the Arab Market in Israel. It was quite superb and the colour of mud and I would gladly have traded all my shekels for the recipe.

45 ml (3 tbsp) instant coffee powder
100 ml (3^1/$_2$ fl oz) hot water
100 g (3^1/$_2$ oz) caster sugar
3 eggs, separated
250 ml (8 fl oz) double cream †
few drops of vanilla extract

In a large, deep mixing bowl dissolve the coffee powder in the hot water. Cool slightly, then add caster sugar and egg yolks. Using an electric beater, whisk very well at high speed for several minutes until the mixture becomes somewhat paler – or muddy – and slightly thickened. Whisk the egg whites with a pinch of salt until stiff. Whip cream and vanilla. Fold cream and egg whites into coffee mixture. Be gentle but very thorough – never beat it. Freeze quickly, in individual freezer ramekins, or in a 1.5-litre (2^3/$_4$-pint) container.

If using individual ramekins, decorate each with whipped cream and grated chocolate or chopped toasted nuts. If using a mould, line it first with plastic wrap, then unmould ice cream when firm. Garnish and then return to freezer until required. Alternatively, it may be dribbled with chocolate sauce.
Serves about 8.

†**For this and all ice creams, it is particularly important to use a good, thick, double cream.**

Cold Christmas Pudding

Ice Cream Christmas Pudding

250 ml (8 fl oz) water
60 g (2 oz) seedless raisins
45 ml (1¹/₂ oz) mixed peel
12 cherries, chopped
30 ml (2 tbsp) chopped preserved ginger
2.5 ml (¹/₂ tsp) ground nutmeg
5 ml (1 tsp) ground cinnamon
60 g (2 oz) nuts, chopped
175 g (6 oz) very fine Nice biscuit crumbs
25 ml (5 tsp) brandy
25 ml (5 tsp) rum
2 litres (3¹/₂ pints) vanilla ice cream
200–250 ml (6¹/₂–8 fl oz) double cream
icing sugar
rum

Put water, raisins, peel, cherries, ginger and ices into a saucepan. Bring to the boil, then cover and simmer for 10 minutes. Drain if necessary, then add nuts, biscuit crumbs, brandy and rum. Mix well and cool.

Line a bombe mould with 1.5 litres (2³/₄ pints) of the ice cream. Use the back of a spoon dipped in water and work quickly. Spoon the fruit mixture into the hollow in the middle. Cover with the remaining ice cream and freeze for 24 hours.

Unmould onto a freezer-proof serving plate – run base of mould under running tap, loosen round the top with a blunt knife or spatula, and ease out.

Whip cream stiffly with a little icing sugar, and a large tot of rum. Cover entire surface of the bombe with the cream, either smoothly, flicked up with a spatula, or prettily piped. Return to freezer until required. Remove, decorate with holly and stand for about 5 minutes before serving.
Serves about 12.

Cold Christmas Pudding

This is a superb alternative to hot plum pudding.

250 g (9 oz) mixed dried fruit
250 ml (8 fl oz) water
125 g (4 oz) stoned dates, chopped
125 g (4 oz) walnuts, chopped
90 g (3 oz) glacé cherries, chopped
1 packet lemon jelly
250 ml (8 fl oz) hot water
125 ml (4 fl oz) white port
¹/₂ packet Marie biscuits
5 ml (1 tsp) ground mixed spice

Boil mixed dried fruit in 250 ml (8 fl oz) water for 5 minutes. Drain and add dates, nuts and cherries. Dissolve jelly in 250 ml (8 fl oz) hot water. Add port. To fruit mixture add finely crushed biscuits and mixed spice. Finally add jelly. Stir well, pour into rinsed mould in the traditional dome shape, and chill. Unmould and decorate with holly. Serve with whipped cream flavoured with brandy or rum.
Serves 8–10.

Chocolate Liqueur Ice Cream

An extravagant and creamy ice cream, which is made in minutes. The simple sauce contains a modest amount of chocolate, no cream and no extra sugar, as the ice cream is sweet and rich.

45 ml (3 tbsp) Crème de Cacao
10 ml (2 tsp) instant coffee powder
few drops of vanilla extract
250 ml (8 fl oz) double cream
4 egg whites
generous pinch of salt
175 g (6 oz) canned evaporated milk, chilled overnight
5 ml (1 tsp) lemon juice
400 g (14 oz) canned condensed milk

To make the ice cream, pour the liqueur into a cup. Add coffee powder and vanilla, and stir well to dissolve the coffee. Whip cream until fairly stiff. Whisk egg whites with salt until stiff. Whip evaporated milk until very stiff, adding lemon juice while whipping. Pour condensed milk into a large bowl. Stir in the liqueur mixture – do not beat. When thoroughly combined, scoop the evaporated milk, egg whites and cream on the top. Using a spatula, fold up and over until smoothly mixed. Pour into a large container and freeze as quickly as possible.
Makes about 1.5 litres
(2³/₄ pints).

Chocolate Sauce

45 g (1¹/₂ oz) each plain and milk chocolate or 100 g (3¹/₂ oz) plain chocolate
400 ml (13 fl oz) evaporated milk
20 ml (4 tsp) cocoa powder
nut of butter
few drops of vanilla extract

Break up chocolate and put into small saucepan with evaporated milk, cocoa powder and butter. Heat, stirring to melt chocolate and then simmer for a few minutes, still stirring, until thickish and dark. Remove and stir in vanilla. If left to stand, put a piece of greaseproof paper on top to prevent a skin from forming. Reheat over hot water when required.
Makes about 400 ml (13 fl oz).

Irish Coffee Ice Cream

Custard Ice Cream

I almost didn't include this recipe in the book, because it defies all the rules that go into the making of a good, smooth, creamy ice cream. It sets so hard you can cut it with a knife, it's a cheesy yellow in colour, and really not the slightest bit elegant, but everybody loves it. There are two important points to remember: it should be frozen quickly to ensure a smooth texture, and it must be allowed to soften before serving. It is superb served with fresh fruit salad.

750 ml (1¼ pints) milk
3 eggs
60 g (2 oz) caster sugar
400 g (14 oz) canned condensed milk
few drops of vanilla extract

Scald milk. Beat eggs and sugar, and add a little of the hot milk.

Stir to mix, then add to rest of milk and cook slowly, stirring, until it coats the back of a wooden spoon. Remove from heat and stir in condensed milk and vanilla. Pour into a 2-litre (3½-pint) container, cool and freeze.
Serves 8–10.

Irish Coffee Ice Cream

175 g (6 oz) canned evaporated milk, chilled overnight
few drops of lemon juice
100 g (3½ oz) sifted icing sugar
15 ml (1 tbsp) instant coffee powder
40 ml (8 tsp) Irish whisky
250 ml (8 fl oz) double cream
3 egg whites, stiffly whisked

Chill bowl and beaters before whisking evaporated milk and lemon juice until stiff. Gradually beat in icing sugar. Dissolve coffee powder in whisky and beat into milk mixture. When very stiff, fold in whipped cream and egg whites gently but thoroughly. Pour into container and freeze quickly, folding over once or twice before it freezes firm, to prevent any chance of separating.
Serve plain, or on a pool of light, hot Chocolate sauce (page 158). Serves about 8.

Strawberry Ice Cream

250 g (9 oz) ripe strawberries
90 g (3 oz) caster sugar
15 ml (1 tbsp) light honey
250 ml (8 fl oz) double cream
few drops of vanilla extract
175 g (6 oz) canned evaporated milk, chilled for 12 hours
5 ml (1 tsp) lemon juice
3 egg whites
pinch of salt

Wash, hull and slice strawberries into small pieces. Sprinkle with sugar and honey. Cover and leave to stand for 1 hour, then purée until smooth. Pour into a large bowl. Whip cream with vanilla and fold in. Whip evaporated milk with lemon juice until stiff and fold in. Whisk egg whites with salt until stiff and fold in. Pour into 2-litre (3½-pint) container and freeze quickly.

Irish Coffee Pie

As the name implies, this is a mixture of whisky, coffee and cream. Combined with a rich egg custard and set in a nutty crust, it makes a lovely dessert.

CRUST
2.5 ml (¹/₂ tsp) instant coffee powder
100 g (3¹/₂ oz) butter, melted
125 g (4 oz) sweet biscuit crumbs
45 g (1¹/₂ oz) walnuts or pecan nuts, coarsely chopped

FILLING
375 ml (12 fl oz) milk
3 eggs, separated
60 g (2 oz) caster sugar
pinch of salt
10 ml (2 tsp) powdered gelatine
45 ml (3 tbsp) whisky
10 ml (2 tsp) instant coffee powder
few drops of vanilla extract
125 ml (4 fl oz) whipping cream, whipped

whipped cream and chocolate scrolls to decorate

To make the crust, dissolve coffee powder in melted butter and then combine with remaining ingredients. Press onto base of greased 20-cm (8-in) pie dish, and chill.

Scald milk. Beat yolks with sugar and pinch of salt. Pour on scalded milk and then return to saucepan and stir until it thickens, without boiling. Remove from heat. Soften gelatine in the whisky and stir into custard. Add coffee powder, and when dissolved, add vanilla and set aside until cold and beginning to thicken – this can be hurried by standing the bowl in iced water. Whisk egg whites until stiff but not dry, then fold in together with whipped cream.

Pour into crust and chill until set. Decorate with whipped cream and chocolate scrolls. Serves 8.

Lemon Soufflé

A delicately flavoured, creamy textured, custard-based soufflé made with everyday ingredients. It may be set either in a straight-sided dish tied with a paper collar, or more simply in little bowls, in which case reduce the amount of gelatine by 2.5 ml (¹/₂ tsp).

6 egg yolks
175 g (6 oz) caster sugar
500 ml (16 fl oz) milk
finely grated rind of 2 large lemons
15 ml (1 tbsp) powdered gelatine
100 ml (3¹/₂ fl oz) fresh lemon juice
250 ml (8 fl oz) whipping cream
few drops of vanilla extract
7–8 egg whites
whipped cream and finely grated lemon rind to decorate

Using an electric whisk and a deep bowl, beat yolks with caster sugar until pale and thick. Add milk and lemon rind. Beat to mix, then turn into top of double boiler and cook as for custard over simmering water, until mixture coats the back of a wooden spoon. Soften gelatine in the lemon juice. Pour cooked custard into a large bowl, add gelatine, stir until dissolved, then leave to cool, stirring occasionally – or hurry it up by placing the bowl in a dish of iced water and stirring until cold and beginning to thicken.

Whip cream with vanilla and fold in. Stiffly whisk egg whites with a pinch of salt and fold in. Pour into prepared dish, or little dishes (or glasses) and set in refrigerator. Before serving, decorate with a lattice of whipped cream and a sprinkling of finely grated lemon rind. Serves 10–12.

Loganberry Yoghurt Pie

A useful, basic recipe, which can be varied by using differently flavoured fruit juices and yoghurt – pineapple makes a delicious alternative, as does strawberry. These puddings are pleasingly large, and very easy to make. Be sure to use the thick, eating yoghurt, not the fluid, drinking kind.

CRUST
175 g (6 oz) sweet biscuit crumbs
100 g (3¹/₂ oz) butter, melted

FILLING
15 ml (1 tbsp) powdered gelatine
400 g (14 oz) canned loganberries in natural juice
500 ml (16 fl oz) raspberry yoghurt
200 ml (6¹/₂ fl oz) whipping cream
45 ml (3 tbsp) icing sugar
2 egg whites
pinch of salt
whipped cream to decorate

Make crust by mixing crumbs and butter, press onto base of greased 23-cm (9-in) pie dish and chill.

Drain juice from canned fruit and make up to 250 ml (8 fl oz) with water. Reserve loganberries. Soften gelatine in juice, then dissolve over low heat, taking care not to let the juice boil. Pour yoghurt into a large bowl. Slowly add fruit juice with dissolved gelatine, stirring all the time. Whip together cream and icing sugar and whisk egg whites stiffly with the pinch of salt. Fold these into the fruity mixture, pour into crust and chill until set. Before serving, decorate with whipped cream and reserved loganberries.
Serves 10.

Variations
PINEAPPLE YOGHURT PIE
Use a gingernut crust and substitute pineapple juice and yoghurt for the loganberry.

APRICOT YOGHURT PIE
Use apricot yoghurt and juice and increase the amount of icing sugar to 60 g (2 oz).

Chiffon Pie Grand Marnier

A crunchy nut crust holds a creamy orange filling spiked with liqueur.

CRUST
125 g (4 oz) sweet biscuit crumbs
75 g (2^1/$_2$ oz) butter, melted
10 ml (2 tsp) runny honey
45 g (1^1/$_2$ oz) walnuts, chopped
2.5 ml (^{1}/$_2$ tsp) finely grated
   orange rind

FILLING
3 eggs, separated
5 ml (1 tsp) cornflour
90 g (3 oz) caster sugar
2.5 ml (^{1}/$_2$ tsp) finely grated
   orange rind
125 ml (4 fl oz) fresh orange
   juice
10 ml (2 tsp) powdered gelatine
25 ml (5 tsp) cold water
45 ml (3 tbsp) Grand Marnier
125 ml (4 fl oz) whipping cream,
   whipped

Mix ingredients for crust and press onto base of greased pie dish, 20–23 cm (8–9 in) in diameter and 3 cm (1^1/$_4$ in) deep (to take the filling) and chill.

Beat egg yolks, cornflour, caster sugar, orange rind and juice. Soak gelatine in cold water. Cook yolk mixture in small saucepan or double boiler, stirring constantly until it thickens like custard. Remove from heat and add Grand Marnier. Add softened gelatine and stir until dissolved, then set aside to cool and thicken. If you're in a hurry, stir it over ice, or chill it – but very briefly – because it must not start to set.

Whisk egg whites with a pinch of salt and fold in together with the cream. Pour into chilled crust and set in refrigerator. Serve plain, or garnish with cream and nuts.
Serves 8–10.

Orange Syllabub

Apple Chiffon Pie

A delicious and simple pudding, for which Golden Delicious apples are essential.

CRUST
100 g (3¹/₂ oz) gingernut biscuit crumbs
100 g (3¹/₂ oz) Marie biscuit crumbs
100 g (3¹/₂ oz) butter, melted

FILLING
750 g (1³/₄ lb) Golden Delicious apples, peeled and sliced
1 cinnamon stick
nut of butter
150 ml (5 fl oz) water
45 ml (3 tbsp) honey or 25 ml (5 tsp) each honey and sugar
15 ml (1 tbsp) powdered gelatine
few drops of vanilla extract
125 ml (4 fl oz) whipping cream, whipped
ground cinnamon

To make crust, mix crumbs and butter and press into greased 20-cm (8-in) pie plate and chill.

Put apples, cinnamon, butter, 100 ml (3¹/₂ fl oz) water and honey into saucepan. Cover and simmer gently for about 10 minutes or until soft. Remove from heat. Soak gelatine in 45 ml (3 tbsp) water, add to hot apple mixture and stir until dissolved. Cool for 10 minutes, then remove cinnamon stick and spoon into blender (plus all the juices) and add vanilla. Blend until smooth, then pour into a bowl to cool. Fold in cream. Pour into crust, sprinkle generously with cinnamon and chill for 8–12 hours before serving. Serves 8–10.

Orange Syllabub

Syllabub is a dessert you can make before you've even put on your apron. Normally it is made with brandy, wine or sherry, but in the following recipe I have given it a fresh new flavour.

25 ml (5 tsp) orange-flavoured liqueur
45 ml (3 tbsp) fresh orange juice
30 ml (2 tbsp) caster sugar
generous pinch of very finely grated orange rind
250 ml (8 fl oz) whipping cream

Mix liqueur, juice, sugar and rind in a deep container. Stir to dissolve the sugar, then cover and chill for 2–3 hours. Pour the cream into the same container and whip everything together until stiff, then spoon into 4–6 wine glasses and chill for another 2 hours at least. Serve with unfilled brandy snaps. Serves 4–6.

Lemon Cheese Cream

This dessert tastes like cheesecake and looks like ice cream, but leaves them both standing when it comes to speed of preparation.

250 g (9 oz) low-fat soft cheese
45 ml (3 tbsp) caster sugar
2.5 ml (¹/₂ tsp) very finely grated lemon rind
2.5 ml (¹/₂ tsp) powdered gelatine
45 ml (3 tbsp) lemon juice
150 ml (5 fl oz) whipping cream
4 egg whites, stiffly whisked

Whip together cheese, sugar and lemon rind until smooth. Soften gelatine in lemon juice and dissolve over hot water. Beat slowly into cheese mixture. Fold in whipped cream and then egg whites. Pour into 8 wine glasses and chill for a few hours. Garnish with cream and a maraschino cherry. Serves 8.

Whisky Oranges

Whisky Oranges

4 medium to large navel oranges
100 g (3¹/₂ oz) caster sugar
250 ml (8 fl oz) water
shredded peel of 1 orange
25 ml (5 tsp) whisky

Peel oranges, removing all pith,
and slice into very thin rings.
Place in shallow pie dish, adding
the juices from the cutting board.
  Put sugar, water and shredded
peel into a small saucepan. The
peel should be free of any white
pith and cut into very thin julienne.
Bring to the boil, stirring, then
cover and simmer gently for
30 minutes. Remove and cool for
10 minutes. Add whisky. Pour
warm syrup over oranges and
scatter the cooked peel evenly
over the top. Cover and chill for
2–3 days. Serve plain, or with ice
cream or cream. Serves 4–6.

Tipsy Peaches

100 g (3¹/₂ oz) caster sugar
375 ml (12 fl oz) water
2 cinnamon sticks
10 ml (2 tsp) lemon juice
4 large fresh peaches
orange- or coconut-flavoured
  liqueur

Slowly bring sugar, water,
cinnamon and lemon juice to the
boil in a large frying pan, and
simmer for 5 minutes. Plunge
peaches first into boiling water
and then into cold water and slip
off skins. Halve and remove
stones. Place, hollow-side down,
in the boiling syrup, then cover
and poach until tender. Cool in
syrup, then slice and divide
between 6 smallish dessert
dishes. Into each dish pour 30 ml
(2 tbsp) of the poaching liquid
and 15 ml (1 tbsp) liqueur. Cover
and chill for several hours,
preferably overnight.
Serves 6.

Pears in White Wine

10 firm pears
500 ml (16 fl oz) semi-sweet
  white wine
250 ml (8 fl oz) water
45 ml (3 tbsp) orange marmalade
90 g (3 oz) caster sugar
coarsely grated rind of 1 orange
45 ml (3 tbsp) honey
soured cream or fresh cream to
  serve

Peel pears smoothly, leaving stalks
on. Bring the remaining
ingredients, except the cream, to
the boil in a deepish saucepan in
which the pears will all fit,
preferably on their sides. Add
pears to boiling syrup, cover and
poach gently for about 20 minutes
until soft, turning occasionally and
carefully. Remove pears to serving
dish, standing upright, then
reduce syrup in saucepan to
500 ml (16 fl oz) by fast boiling.
  Strain syrup over pears, cool,
cover with a tent of foil and chill
thoroughly. Serve with some of
the syrup poured over each pear
and a bowl of thick, soured cream,
or lightly whipped fresh cream.
Serves 10.

Variation

PEARS IN FRUIT JUICE AND PORT
Peel, core and halve 750 g (1³/₄ lb)
firm pears. Arrange in large frying
pan. Mix 250 ml (8 fl oz) grape
juice with 45 ml (3 tbsp) runny
honey. Pour over pears. Add
1 cinnamon stick and 2 whole
cloves. Cover and simmer until
soft, basting occasionally. Remove
pears to serving dish, rounded
sides up. Pour juices into small
saucepan. Remove spices, stir in
45 ml (3 tbsp) port mixed with
10 ml (2 tsp) cornflour and bring
to the boil. Pour over pears,
basting as they cool. Cover, chill
thoroughly, and serve with thick
cream.

Strawberry Cream

Pears in Whisky Cream Sauce

Fresh pears are poached in a light sugar syrup, which is then blended with cream, laced with whisky and thickened by adding a whole puréed pear. This refreshing dessert tastes just as good as it looks.

100 g (3¹/₂ oz) sugar
500 ml (16 fl oz) water
2 cinnamon sticks
4 whole cloves
4 large slightly under-ripe firm pears
250 ml (8 fl oz) cream
45 ml (3 tbsp) whisky
toasted flaked almonds

Put sugar, water, cinnamon and cloves into large saucepan and bring to the boil, stirring to dissolve sugar. Peel, halve and core pears and place, rounded side up, in syrup. Cover and poach until soft. Remove pears to serving dish (choose one with sides, to hold the sauce) and reserve two pear halves. Strain poaching liquid, return to saucepan and then reduce by boiling rapidly, uncovered, for about 10 minutes, until it measures 250 ml (8 fl oz) and becomes syrupy. Slowly stir in cream. Remove from heat and add whisky. Chop reserved pears and add. Cool slightly and then purée in blender until smooth.

Pour slowly over pears and leave to cool, then chill for a few hours. Scatter with almonds just before serving. Serves 6.

Strawberry Cream

The simplest way of serving strawberries and cream short of putting the one in a bowl and the other in a jug.

500 g (18 oz) strawberries
175 g (6 oz) caster sugar
20 ml (4 tsp) powdered gelatine
45 ml (3 tbsp) water
2 egg whites
400 ml (13 fl oz) whipping cream, whipped
whipped cream and strawberries to decorate

Hull, wash and slice strawberries, sprinkle with caster sugar and stand for about 30 minutes to draw the juices. Purée in blender until smooth, then pour into a bowl. Soften gelatine in water, dissolve over low heat, then stir into strawberry purée. Set aside until beginning to thicken. Stiffly whisk egg whites with a pinch of salt and fold in together with cream. Pour into a mould and chill until set. Unmould and decorate with extra whipped cream and strawberries. Serves 8–12.

Note

You may prefer to set the mixture in individual moulds, or, instead of unmoulding, you could tie a band of waxed paper round the rim of a straight-sided dish to form a collar, for the 'risen soufflé' look.

Pear Tart Praline

Pear Tart Praline

There are three steps to this pudding: the pears, the praline and the pastry. The pears are poached with wine and cinnamon; the cream layer flavoured with almonds and caramelized sugar, and the short pastry spiked with spices. The only requirements, then, are a little patience, and a 20-cm (8-in) flan ring.

PRALINE
100 g (3¹/₂ oz) sugar
75 g (2¹/₂ oz) whole, unblanched almonds

PASTRY
90 g (3 oz) butter, softened
30 ml (2 tbsp) icing sugar
1 egg yolk
125 g (4 oz) plain flour
5 ml (1 tsp) ground cinnamon
generous pinch of nutmeg
pinch of salt

FILLING
500 g (18 oz) firm pears
125 ml (4 fl oz) semi-sweet white wine
1 cinnamon stick
15 ml (1 tbsp) lemon juice
100 ml (3¹/₂ fl oz) water
45 ml (3 tbsp) sugar
250 ml (8 fl oz) whipping cream

Make praline by heating sugar and almonds slowly in a small, heavy saucepan. Allow the sugar to melt and caramelize with the almonds, while stirring slowly. When melted and brown, pour onto buttered cake tin or small biscuit tray and leave until cold. Remove (it should lift off in one piece) and grind until fine, or crush in a strong plastic bag with a rolling pin. Set aside.

To make the pastry, cream butter and icing sugar. Beat in egg yolk. Sift dry ingredients and add. Mix well, form into a ball, wrap in waxed paper and chill for about 1 hour until firm. Put the flan ring on a baking

sheet and press the pastry into it. Do not let it get warm – if it does, put into freezer for 5 minutes before baking. Prick sides and bottom well, and bake at 200 °C (400 °F, gas 6) for 15 minutes. Don't worry if it should puff up a bit, it will subside when cooled. When cold, remove ring and carefully transfer pastry shell to flat serving dish.

Poach the pears while the pastry is chilling. Peel, halve and core pears. Put wine, cinnamon, lemon juice, water and sugar into saucepan. Bring to the boil, then add pears. Poach gently until soft, then cool in liquid.

To assemble, whip cream until stiff. Fold in about 90 g (3 oz) of the praline and spoon into pie crust. Arrange drained pears on top – 8 halves should just fit. Sprinkle thickly with more praline.
Serves 6 generously.

Athol Brose

This potent little number from the Highlands of Scotland combines oats and honey and whisky in amazing proportions, and the result is about as heady as a neat drink

45 ml (3 tbsp) porridge oats
45 ml (3 tbsp) thin honey
45 ml (3 tbsp) Scotch whisky
250 ml (8 fl oz) whipping cream, stiffly whipped

Spread porridge oats on baking sheet and toast lightly under grill, then rub until fine between your palms. Stir honey and whisky into cream, then fold in 20 ml (4 tsp) oats. Spoon into small glasses, sprinkle with remaining oats and chill.
Serves 4.

Old-fashioned Trifle

To my mind, one should never trifle with trifle. It's a simple pudding, basically just cake, sherry and custard, with a flurry of trimmings. A good trifle needs neither the addition of jelly nor canned fruit to turn it into one of the most satisfying endings to a special meal.

1 x 18-cm (7-in) sponge layer
strawberry jam
100–125 ml (3^{1}/$_{2}$–4 fl oz) sherry
finely chopped glacé fruit
a handful of chopped nuts
a little preserved ginger
   (optional)
whipped cream, cherries and
   angelica to decorate

CUSTARD
750 ml (1^{1}/$_{4}$ pints) milk
3 eggs
1 egg yolk
25 ml (5 tsp) cornflour
60 g (2 oz) caster sugar

pinch of salt
few drops of vanilla extract
small nut of butter

Cut sponge in half, horizontally, and spread liberally with jam. Break it up and use to cover the bottom of the bowl. Sprinkle with sherry and strew with glacé fruit, nuts and ginger if using. Allow to stand while you make the custard.

Scald milk. Beat eggs, egg yolk, cornflour, sugar and salt. Pour on the hot milk, stirring, then return to saucepan and cook over low heat until it coats the back of a wooden spoon. Remove from heat and add vanilla and butter. Cool slightly, then pour over cake, cutting in gently. When cold, cover and chill. Before serving, decorate boldly and brightly on a thick layer of whipped cream.
Serves about 8.

Rum and Ricotta Creams

A most useful dessert for the hostess-in-a-hurry; quick to prepare, with a memorable flavour. Ricotta is a low-fat, Italian cheese with a very light texture. Nevertheless, this is a rich mixture, so it should be set in smallish glasses. Make these creams at least 6 hours ahead of serving, but preferably a day in advance.

500 g (18 oz) Ricotta cheese
125 g (4 oz) caster sugar
2 eggs, separated
10 ml (2 tsp) instant coffee
   powder
45 ml (3 tbsp) dark rum
few drops of vanilla extract
200 ml (6^{1}/$_{2}$ fl oz) whipping
   cream, whipped

Beat Ricotta, sugar and yolks until very light. Dissolve coffee

in rum, then stir into cheese mixture. Add vanilla. Whisk egg whites with a pinch of salt until stiff and fold in gently together with cream until thoroughly blended. Spoon into 10 glasses and chill.

Serve plain, or topped with whipped cream and a chocolate scroll.
Serves 10.

Fruit Salad with Nuts, Yoghurt and Honey

Fruit Salad with Nuts, Yoghurt and Honey

It's all in the title: a nutritious, fairly low-calorie dessert, always enjoyed by wholefood enthusiasts and those on a diet. The addition of avocado in a fruit salad is possibly a bit surprising, but it really does add a special touch. This fruit salad is most effective if served in a shallow glass dish rather than a deep bowl.

2 small Golden Delicious apples
2 ripe pears
2 bananas
$^1/_2$ pineapple
1 large avocado
25 ml (5 tsp) fresh lemon juice
45 g (1$^1/_2$ oz) nuts of choice, chopped and toasted
250 ml (8 fl oz) plain drinking yoghurt

25 ml (5 tsp) runny honey
generous pinch of finely grated orange rind
chopped nuts and/or grated orange rind to decorate

Peel and cube apples and pears. Slice bananas thinly, cube pineapple and dice avocado. Put into bowl and toss with lemon juice. Mix in nuts. Beat yoghurt, honey and orange rind. Pour over fruit, allowing it to dribble down. Cover and chill for 2–4 hours. For decoration, sprinkle with a few more nuts and/or a little grated orange rind.
Serves about 6.

White Chocolate Mousse

Chocolate mousses are amongst the richest of puddings, and this one is no exception, except that it does contain only 2 eggs, no extra yolks, and soured cream instead of fresh. Nevertheless, the result is still melt-in-the-mouth and the flavour elusive, with a trace of toffee liqueur.

100 g (3$^1/_2$ oz) white chocolate, broken up
30 ml (2 tbsp) milk
small nut of butter
25 ml (5 tsp) Old English Toffee Cream liqueur
few drops of vanilla extract
2 eggs, separated
45 ml (3 tbsp) caster sugar
10 ml (2 tsp) powdered gelatine
45 ml (3 tbsp) water
200 ml (6$^1/_2$ fl oz) soured cream
pinch of salt

Put chocolate in top of small double boiler with milk and butter. Melt over simmering water and when smooth, remove from heat and stir in liqueur and vanilla. Set aside.

Whisk egg yolks with sugar until pale and thick. Soak gelatine in water and dissolve over low heat, then stir into yolk mixture. Whisk to blend, then add the slightly cooled chocolate mixture and whisk again. Stir in soured cream. Whisk the egg whites with the pinch of salt, until stiff, then fold in.

Pour into small bowls or glasses, cover, and chill for about 6 hours to allow flavours to blend. Serve plain or whip a little cream with a dash of the liqueur and pipe a small swirl on the top of each. Serve icy cold.
Serves 6.

Peaches in Red Wine

This is the sort of dessert that deserves to be photographed: large, fresh peaches smothered in a thick, slightly spicy red wine sauce. Make it at the height of summer when peaches are really ripe and juicy, and buy the biggest you can find.

750 g (1³/₄ lb) large fresh peaches
375 ml (12 fl oz) good red wine
90 g (3 oz) caster sugar
30 ml (2 tbsp) honey
1 large cinnamon stick
4 small whole cloves
10 ml (2 tsp) cornflour

Plunge peaches into boiling water and remove skin. Halve, remove stones, and arrange in a heavy frying pan to fit quite snugly. Heat wine, sugar and honey in a small saucepan. Stir to dissolve sugar, then pour over peaches. Add cinnamon and cloves. Bring to the boil, then cover and poach gently for about 20 minutes, basting each peach several times. When soft, remove peaches with slotted spoon to serving dish – a large pie dish would be just right. Arrange hollow-sides down and cool. Remove spices from syrup and leave to cool.

Dissolve cornflour with a little of the cooled wine syrup, stir into the rest in the pan, and then boil up again until thickish. Spoon syrup over each peach, coating several times. When cold, cover and chill up to 12 hours. Serve with a bowl of thick cream.
Serves 6–8.

Toffee Liqueur Creams

This is a truly dreamy dessert: Liqueur-flavoured custard set in pretty glasses, topped with liqueur-flavoured cream.

2 eggs, separated
45 ml (3 tbsp) caster sugar
375 ml (12 fl oz) milk
1 vanilla pod
10 ml (2 tsp) powdered gelatine
75 ml (2¹/₂ fl oz) Old English Toffee Cream liqueur
100 ml (3¹/₂ fl oz) whipping cream

Whisk yolks with sugar. Scald milk with vanilla. Pour onto beaten eggs, then return to saucepan and cook as for custard. Remove from heat. Soften gelatine in 45 ml (3 tbsp) liqueur, then whisk into custard until dissolved. Pour into a bowl and allow to cool. Whisk egg whites with a pinch of salt until stiff. When custard begins to thicken, fold in egg whites gently, but thoroughly, until combined. Pour into 6 glasses, leaving room for the cream, and set in refrigerator.

Whip cream with remaining liqueur until as stiff as it will go, then pour in an even layer over top of set puddings. Return to refrigerator until required. This dessert may be prepared up to a day in advance.
Serves 6.

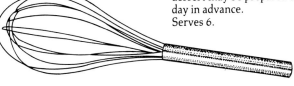

Sherry Bavarian Crème

This is a delicious but pale-coloured pudding, so serve it prettily in a big glass bowl and decorated like a trifle, or in individual glasses topped with chocolate curls.

25 ml (5 tsp) powdered gelatine
100 ml (3¹/₂ fl oz) cold water
4 egg yolks
90 g (3 oz) caster sugar
pinch of salt
500 ml (16 fl oz) milk
150 ml (5 fl oz) sweet or medium cream sherry
7–8 egg whites
250 ml (8 fl oz) whipping cream, whipped

Soften gelatine in cold water. Beat egg yolks with sugar and salt. Scald the milk. Pour hot milk onto egg mixture, stirring to dissolve the sugar, then pour back into saucepan. Add softened gelatine and then stir over low heat until it thickens like custard – do not boil. Remove from heat and stir in sherry, then pour into a bowl and leave until cold and beginning to thicken, stirring occasionally. Or chill briefly. Whisk egg whites stiffly with a pinch of salt and fold in together with cream. Pour into bowl, or glasses, and set in refrigerator. Serves 10–12.

Variation

IRISH COFFEE BAVARIAN CRÈME
A delicious variation may be made by substituting the following ingredients: 10 ml (2 tsp) gelatine; 45 ml (3 tbsp) cold water; 2 eggs, separated; pinch of salt; 60 g (2 oz) sugar; 400 ml (13 fl oz) milk; 10 ml (2 tsp) instant coffee powder; 30 ml (2 tbsp) Irish whisky; 200 ml (6¹/₂ fl oz) cream. Serves 6.

Stuffed Oranges

A fresh and fruity pudding.

8 medium, sweet oranges
300 g (11 oz) canned mandarins, drained
1 piece preserved ginger, finely chopped
45 ml (3 tbsp) orange-flavoured liqueur
whipped cream and walnuts to decorate

As this fruit salad is served in the orange shells, choose round, unblemished ones. Cut off the tops and with a grapefruit knife scoop out the insides. Be careful not to puncture the skins. Remove seeds and membranes and chop the flesh, catching the juices. Spoon into a bowl and add mandarins, ginger and liqueur. Cover and chill for a few hours. Leave shells upside down to drain.

To serve, fill shells with fruit. If desired, flavour the whipped cream with a little finely grated orange rind or liqueur to taste, or leave plain. Pipe generously on top of each orange to cover completely, top with a walnut, and serve.
Serves 8.

Variation

ORANGE SOUFFLÉ
Use to fill the orange shells
500 ml (16 fl oz) fresh orange juice; 15 ml (1 tbsp) gelatine; 4 eggs, separated; 10 ml (2 tsp) finely grated orange rind; 60 g (2 oz) caster sugar; 250 ml (8 fl oz) cream, whipped. Soak gelatine in 100 ml (3¹/₂ fl oz) of the juice. Heat remaining juice with rind. Beat yolks and sugar, pour in strained hot juice, then return to heat and cook as for custard. Remove, stir in gelatine, pour into bowl and cool. Fold in egg whites, stiffly whisked with a pinch of salt, and the cream. Set in refrigerator. Serves 8.

Cheese Creams with Mango Purée

Rich yet refreshing, and a beautiful colour: citrus-flavoured creams scooped onto a smooth sauce with a hint of liqueur. An elegant dessert which is surprisingly easy to prepare; serve icy cold on your prettiest plates.

7.5 ml (1¹/₂ tsp) powdered gelatine
30 ml (2 tbsp) cold water
250 g (9 oz) cream cheese
60 g (2 oz) caster sugar
few drops of vanilla extract
1 egg, separated
generous pinch of finely grated lemon rind or 2.5 ml (¹/₂ tsp) finely grated orange rind
100 ml (3¹/₂ fl oz) whipping cream, whipped
400 g (14 oz) canned mango slices in syrup
45 ml (3 tbsp) Malibu
fresh mint sprigs to decorate

Soften gelatine in water and dissolve over low heat. Beat cream cheese, sugar, vanilla, egg yolk and rind until smooth. Slowly whisk in the dissolved gelatine. Whisk egg white with a small pinch of salt and fold in together with cream. Chill. Drain mango slices and place in blender with 45 ml (3 tbsp) of the syrup. Add liqueur and blend until smooth. Pour into a jug and chill.

To serve, dribble a small pool of the sauce onto each plate. Place 1–2 scoops of the softly set cheese mixture on top – use an ice cream scoop or 2 dessert spoons to shape. Decorate with sprigs of mint.
Serves 6.

Variation
When sweet melons are in season, substitute the following sauce for the mango purée:

SWEET MELON AND RUM SAUCE
Using a blender, purée enough ripe sweet melon to give you 375 ml (12 fl oz) purée. Stir in 7.5–10 ml (1¹/₂–2 tsp) dark rum. If desired, add a little caster sugar, but if sweet melon is juicy and ripe, this should not be necessary. Pour into a jug and chill before using as a base for the cheese creams.

Strawberry Cheesecake

This recipe, using a mere handful of strawberries, makes a really big cheesecake. Topped with fresh berries and whipped cream, it makes a bright and beautiful ending to a meal.

CRUST
125 g (4 oz) Nice biscuit crumbs
60 g (2 oz) ground almonds (optional)
10 ml (2 tsp) icing sugar
75 g (2¹/₂ oz) butter, melted

FILLING
250 g (9 oz) strawberries, washed and hulled
45 ml (3 tbsp) milk
90 g (3 oz) caster sugar
250 g (9 oz) low-fat soft cheese
2 eggs, separated
few drops of vanilla extract
15 ml (1 tbsp) powdered gelatine
45 ml (3 tbsp) cold water
pinch of salt
125 ml (4 fl oz) whipping cream, whipped

To make the crust, mix ingredients and press onto base of greased 23-cm (9-in) pie dish and chill.

Slice strawberries and purée in blender with milk and 30 ml (2 tbsp) caster sugar. Beat together cheese, 75 g (2¹/₂ oz) caster sugar, egg yolks and vanilla. Soften gelatine in water and dissolve over low heat. Beat into cheese mixture together with the purée. Whisk egg whites stiffly with a pinch of salt and fold in together with cream. Pour into chilled crust and return to refrigerator until set. Garnish as suggested before serving.
Serves about 10.

Hint

Soft margarine is best for greasing dishes for chilled desserts as it does not set as hard as butter.

Vanilla Cheesecake

A simple cheesecake, unfailingly popular, and possibly the one I make most often.

CRUST
100 g (3^1/$_2$ oz) Nice biscuits
75–100 g (2^1/$_2$–3^1/$_2$ oz) butter, melted

FILLING
250 g (9 oz) low-fat soft cheese (or cream cheese)
90 g (3 oz) caster sugar
2 eggs, separated
10 ml (2 tsp) powdered gelatine
45 ml (3 tbsp) cold water
several drops of vanilla extract
pinch of salt
125 ml (4 fl oz) whipping cream, whipped

Crush biscuits. Instead of using a processor, which can reduce them to fine dust, I prefer putting the biscuits into a plastic bag and rolling until crumbly with a rolling pin. Toss with melted butter and press onto the base of a greased 20-cm (8-in) pie dish. Chill while making filling.

Using an electric beater, whisk the cheese, sugar and egg yolks until smooth. Soften gelatine in cold water and dissolve over low heat. Slowly beat into cheese mixture – if you dribble it directly onto the beaters it won't form little strings. Add vanilla. Whisk egg whites stiffly with the pinch of salt and fold in. Finally fold in the cream.

Pour onto crust and set in refrigerator. Serve plain or decorated with a lattice of whipped cream.
Serves 8.

Fruity Cheesecake

Laced with sherry and rich with fruit and nuts, this cheesecake is rather like a cold and creamy Christmas pudding.

CRUST
125 g (4 oz) sweet biscuit crumbs
100 g (3^1/$_2$ oz) butter, melted

FILLING
150 g (5 oz) mixed dried fruit
6 glacé cherries, chopped
45 ml (3 tbsp) chopped walnuts
30 ml (2 tbsp) finely chopped preserved ginger
30 ml (2 tbsp) honey
45 ml (3 tbsp) sweet sherry
10 ml (2 tsp) powdered gelatine
30 ml (2 tbsp) water
45 ml (3 tbsp) light brown sugar
250 g (9 oz) low-fat soft cheese
150 ml (5 fl oz) soured cream
2 egg whites
pinch of salt
ground cinnamon

Mix crumbs and butter and press onto the base of greased 20-cm (8-in) pie dish. Chill.

To make the filling, put dried fruit, cherries, walnuts, ginger, honey and sherry into the top of a double boiler, cover and steam gently over simmering water for 10 minutes. Remove and pour into a bowl. Soak gelatine in the water. Add to hot fruit mixture and stir until dissolved. Stir in brown sugar. When dissolved, stir in cheese and soured cream. When thoroughly combined, leave to cool, but do not allow it to set. Whisk egg whites with the pinch of salt until stiff and fold in. Pour into chilled crust, sprinkle with cinnamon and set in refrigerator.
Serves 8–10.

Chocolate Rum and Raisin Cheesecake

CRUST
125 g (4 oz) sweet biscuit crumbs
75 g (2¹/₂ oz) butter, melted
2.5 ml (¹/₂ tsp) ground cinnamon

FILLING
45 g (1¹/₂ oz) seedless raisins
30 ml (2 tbsp) dark rum
2 eggs, separated
90 g (3 oz) caster sugar
250 g (9 oz) low-fat soft cheese
45 g (1¹/₂ oz) plain chocolate
5 ml (1 tsp) instant coffee
  powder
75 ml (2¹/₂ fl oz) water
10 ml (2 tsp) powdered gelatine
125 ml (4 fl oz) whipping cream,
  whipped
few drops of vanilla extract
chocolate curls to decorate

First soak raisins in rum for at
least 4 hours.
  Mix ingredients for crust and

press onto the base of a greased
20-cm (8-in) pie dish. Chill.
  Beat egg yolks, sugar and
cheese until smooth. Break up
chocolate and put into small
container with coffee and 30 ml
(2 tbsp) water. Melt over low
heat, mix until smooth, then cool
slightly before beating slowly
into cheese mixture. Soak
gelatine for a few minutes in
45 ml (3 tbsp) water, then
dissolve over low heat. Slowly
add to cheese mixture, beating
all the time. Reserve a little
whipped cream for garnishing
and fold remainder into the
chocolate mixture. Whisk egg
whites with a pinch of salt, and
fold in. Finally fold in vanilla and
raisins, plus any rum not
absorbed, gently but thoroughly.
Pour into crust and chill well.
Decorate with a few rosettes of
whipped cream topped with
chocolate curls. Serves 8.

Cheesecake with Strawberry Topping

CRUST
150 g (5 oz) Nice biscuits,
  crushed
100 g (3¹/₂ oz) butter, melted

FILLING
250 g (9 oz) low-fat soft cheese
400 g (14 oz) canned condensed
  milk
45 ml (3 tbsp) lemon juice
250 ml (8 fl oz) soured cream
15 ml (1 tbsp) powdered gelatine
30 ml (2 tbsp) water

TOPPING
400 g (14 oz) canned
  strawberries
15 ml (1 tbsp) custard powder

For the crust, mix crumbs and
butter and press into a greased
23-cm (9-in) pie dish. Chill.
  Mix cheese and condensed
milk. Slowly stir in lemon juice,

then add soured cream. Soften
gelatine in water and dissolve
over low heat. Add slowly to
cheese mixture, stirring well,
then pour into crust and chill
until set.
  Drain can of strawberries,
reserving syrup. Mix a little of
the syrup with the custard
powder, and pour the remainder
into a small saucepan. Add
custard powder mixture and boil
up until thickened. Remove from
heat, add strawberries and beat
with a wooden spoon until pulpy.
Allow to cool completely before
spooning over the set filling.
Return to refrigerator until firm
enough to slice.
Serves 8.

Orange Liqueur Cheesecake (left) and Baked Orange Cheesecake (right)

Orange Liqueur Cheesecake

This cheesecake contains only one egg and no fresh cream so is slightly lower in calories than most.

CRUST
125 g (4 oz) biscuit crumbs
2.5 ml (¹/₂ tsp) finely grated orange rind
75 g (2¹/₂ oz) butter, melted

FILLING
10 ml (2 tsp) powdered gelatine
45 ml (3 tbsp) cold water
250 g (9 oz) low-fat soft cheese
90 g (3 oz) caster sugar
2.5 ml (¹/₂ tsp) finely grated orange rind
1 egg, separated
25 ml (5 tsp) orange-flavoured liqueur
200 ml (6¹/₂ fl oz) soured cream
pinch of salt

Mix ingredients for crust and press onto base of greased 20-cm (8-in) pie dish. Chill.

Soak gelatine in cold water. Beat cheese with sugar and orange rind and egg yolk until smooth. Dissolve gelatine over low heat and then beat into cheese mixture in a slow stream. Stir in liqueur and soured cream. Stiffly whisk egg white with a pinch of salt, then fold in. Pour into crust and chill for a full day if possible. Decorate with a gentle sprinkling of orange rind and a little whipped cream or canned, well-drained mandarin segments.
Serves 8.

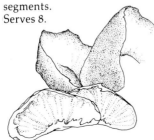

Baked Orange Cheesecake

CRUST
125 g (4 oz) sweet biscuit crumbs
75 g (2¹/₂ oz) butter, melted
5 ml (1 tsp) honey
45 g (1¹/₂ oz) pecan nuts, chopped (optional)

FILLING
250 g (9 oz) low-fat soft cheese
2 eggs, separated
90 g (3 oz) caster sugar
few drops of vanilla extract
10 ml (2 tsp) cornflour
125 ml (4 fl oz) single cream
2.5 ml (¹/₂ tsp) finely grated orange rind

TOPPING
200 ml (6¹/₂ fl oz) soured cream
few drops of vanilla extract
10 ml (2 tsp) light brown sugar
2.5 ml (¹/₂ tsp) finely grated orange rind
ground cinnamon

Mix ingredients for crust. Press onto base of greased 20-cm (8-in) pie dish with fairly high sides. Bake at 170 °C (325 °F, gas 3) for 10 minutes, then cool.

For the filling, beat together all the ingredients, except the egg whites, until smooth. Whisk egg whites, fold in, then pour onto crust. Place dish on a baking sheet and bake for 40 minutes or until just set.

Mix ingredients for topping, except cinnamon, pour evenly over cheesecake and dust lightly with cinnamon. Bake for another 10 minutes, turn off heat then open oven door and leave until cold. Serves 8.

Note

The filling can also be baked in ramekins and served as little soufflés. Spoon cheese mixture into 8–10 greased ramekins. Sprinkle with cinnamon, arrange on baking sheet and bake for about 40 minutes or until well risen and firm.

Brandy Tart with Ginger and Pecans

Closely related to the traditional old favourite, but with a delicious new flavour.

250 g (9 oz) stoned dates, chopped
5 ml (1 tsp) bicarbonate of soda
250 ml (8 fl oz) boiling water
2 knobs preserved ginger, finely chopped
45 g (1¹/₂ oz) butter
175 g (6 oz) caster sugar
1 egg, beaten
175 g (6 oz) flour
2.5 ml (¹/₂ tsp) baking powder
generous pinch of salt
60 g (2 oz) pecan nuts, chopped
few drops of vanilla extract

SYRUP
160 g (5¹/₂ oz) light brown sugar
250 ml (8 fl oz) water
pinch of salt
small nut of butter
125 ml (4 fl oz) brandy

Put dates and bicarbonate of soda into a bowl. Pour boiling water over. Add ginger. Cool completely, stirring now and then. Cream butter and caster sugar. Add egg and whisk until very light. Sift dry ingredients and stir into creamed mixture alternately with cooled date mixture, beginning and ending with flour. Add nuts and vanilla. Bake at 170 °C (325 °F, gas 3) in a buttered 23-cm (9-in) pie dish just below centre of oven for 1 hour, until risen and dark brown.

Meanwhile, boil brown sugar and water for 5 minutes. Add remaining syrup ingredients, stir well, then pour slowly over the hot tart. Serve at room temperature with whipped cream.

Serves 8–10.

Raisin Pecan Pie

This is a spicy, rich pie full of raisins and nuts and laced with brandy. Serve warm or at room temperature with whipped cream.

CRUMB CRUST
125 g (4 oz) digestive biscuits, crushed
2.5 ml ($^1/_2$ tsp) ground cinnamon
90 g (3 oz) butter, melted

FILLING
2.5 ml ($^1/_2$ tsp) ground nutmeg
2.5 ml ($^1/_2$ tsp) ground cinnamon
125 g (4 oz) seedless raisins
90 g (3 oz) pecan nuts, chopped
90 g (3 oz) soft brown sugar
45 ml (3 tbsp) honey
10 ml (2 tsp) cornflour
400 g (14 oz) canned evaporated milk
2 eggs
45 ml (3 tbsp) brandy
pinch of salt

Mix ingredients for crust and press onto base of greased 20-cm (8-in) pie dish.

To make the filling, toss together nutmeg, cinnamon, raisins and nuts and set aside. Whisk remaining ingredients together until well mixed. Add to raisin mixture and combine thoroughly. Pour evenly into crust and sprinkle lightly with a little extra ground cinnamon. Bake at 170 °C (325 °F, gas 3) for 30 minutes or until set.
Serves 8.

Baked Bananas

Fried bananas flamed with rum are a delicious old favourite, but do involve some last-minute attention. Done this way, however, you can assemble them before dinner and bake them during the main course – they'll come out soft, sweet and flavoured with rum. Serve with vanilla ice cream.

4 large, ripe but firm bananas
75 ml (2$^1/_2$ fl oz) fresh orange juice
45 ml (3 tbsp) light rum
10 ml (2 tsp) pale honey
20 ml (4 tsp) brown sugar
a little ground cinnamon
few nuts of butter

Peel bananas, halve lengthways and then halve again, so that each banana is cut into four. Put into shallow baking dish in single layer, close together.

Pour over orange juice and rum, dribble with honey, and sprinkle with sugar and cinnamon. Dot with butter, cover and bake at 170 °C (325 °F, gas 3) for 30–40 minutes.
Serves 4–6.

Variation

BAKED APPLES FLAMBÉ
Peel, core and slice 4 large Golden Delicious apples into eighths. Pack tightly into buttered 20-cm (8-in) pie dish. Sprinkle with 25 ml (5 tsp) lemon juice and 45 ml (3 tbsp) each sultanas and halved, toasted almonds. Dribble with 45 ml (3 tbsp) honey and sprinkle with 15 ml (1 tbsp) brown sugar and 2.5 ml ($^1/_2$ tsp) each ground cinnamon and ginger. Dot with slivers of butter and bake, covered, at 180 °C (350 °F, gas 4) for about 45 minutes. Remove cover, flame with 25 ml (5 tsp) brandy and serve hot with ice cream or cream.

Orange Crème Caramel

Caramel Crème Caramel

A light caramel in both colour and flavour, this is a velvet-textured ever popular pudding.

175 g (6 oz) sugar
25 ml (5 tsp) water
400 g (14 oz) canned condensed milk, caramelized (see Hint)
750 ml (1¹/₄ pints) hot water
6 eggs
pinch of salt
few drops of vanilla extract

In a heavy saucepan, over low heat, melt sugar with 25 ml (5 tsp) water. Do not keep stirring, simply shake the pan now and then until sugar has dissolved and the mixture turns a deep caramel colour. Being careful not to splash, pour into ovenproof soufflé dish, turning quickly to coat bottom and sides. (Individual ramekins may also be used, in which case reduce baking time by about 25 minutes.)

Empty condensed milk into a bowl and add hot water, whisking until well mixed. Beat eggs with salt. Slowly pour on the milk mixture. Add vanilla, then strain into caramel-coated dish. Place in baking dish with hot water coming halfway up the sides, and bake at 170 °C (325 °F, gas 3) for about 1 hour until just set. Cool, then chill thoroughly before unmoulding. Run a knife round the edges and invert onto platter.
Serves about 8.

Orange Crème Caramel

Another version of crème caramel, beautifully smooth and delicate, with a different flavour.

575 g (1¹/₄ lb) sugar
1.5 litres (2³/₄ pints) milk
grated rind of ¹/₂ large orange
8 eggs
45 ml (3 tbsp) orange-flavoured liqueur
pinch of salt

Melt 300 g (11 oz) sugar in a large, heavy frying pan over low heat. Spread it out evenly and stir now and then as it starts to dissolve. As soon as it is smooth and golden-brown in colour, remove from heat and carefully pour onto the base of 2–3 small soufflé dishes, or 12–16 ramekins, turning to coat sides evenly.

Scald milk with the orange rind. Beat remaining ingredients together. Pour hot milk onto egg mixture, then strain into moulds. Stand in pan of hot water to come halfway up the sides, and see that the dishes aren't touching. Bake at 150 °C (300 °F, gas 2) for about 45 minutes for ramekins, 1¹/₂ hours for larger dishes. When done, they'll still be a bit wobbly, but will firm up on standing. Cool, then chill very well. Unmould by running a knife round the edges, and inverting onto serving plates.
Serves 12–16.

Hint

To caramelize condensed milk, place a thick wad of newspaper in the bottom of a saucepan of hot water. Bring to the boil and stand can of condensed milk on the paper. Simmer for 3 hours, adding more water if necessary, and keeping can away from hot base and sides of saucepan.

Cheese Blintzes

Thin little pancakes, filled with low-fat soft cheese (in this case lightly flavoured with orange and orange liqueur), folded up, and traditionally fried in butter. However, as this involves standing over the cooker while everyone waits for their dessert, I prefer to make them in advance, chill them and then heat them through just before serving. Choose a light main course, as blintzes are rich and filling.

BLENDER CRÊPES
2 eggs
pinch of salt
125 g (4 oz) flour, sifted
125 ml (4 fl oz) water
125 ml (4 fl oz) milk
30 ml (2 tbsp) caster sugar
10 ml (2 tsp) brandy
10 ml (2 tsp) oil

FILLING
45 ml (3 tbsp) seedless raisins
250 g (9 oz) low-fat soft cheese
2.5 ml (^{1}/2 tsp) finely grated
    orange rind
45 ml (3 tbsp) icing sugar
15 ml (1 tbsp) orange-flavoured
    liqueur
1 egg yolk

melted butter or soured cream
30 ml (2 tbsp) soft brown sugar
generous pinch of ground
    cinnamon

Put ingredients for crêpes into blender. Blend well. Scrape down sides with rubber spatula and blend again. Cover and stand for about 1 hour. Blend again briefly before using to make thin pancakes in small pan lightly brushed with oil.

Plump raisins in boiling water, drain and mix with cheese, rind, sugar, orange liqueur and egg yolk. Put a heaped spoonful onto the centre of each crêpe. Flap sides over to middle and bottom ends up, to make a neat parcel. Arrange close together, in lightly buttered ovenproof dish (and it must be suitable for taking directly from refrigerator as the crêpes are not brought to room temperature.)

Just before baking, pour over either a little melted butter or soured cream, sprinkle with sugar and cinnamon and heat through at 180 °C (350 °F, gas 4) for 15 minutes. If using melted butter, serve a jug of soured cream separately. Serves 6–8.

Soufflé Grand Marnier

One of the few desserts in this book that can't be completed in advance, but a hot soufflé, served at its height, never fails to impress. The size of the dish is important to ensure a slightly creamy middle with a high, light-brown 'hat'.

45 g (1¹/₂ oz) butter
45 g (1¹/₂ oz) flour
300 ml (10 fl oz) milk
45 ml (3 tbsp) caster sugar
pinch of salt
3 egg yolks
45 ml (3 tbsp) Grand Marnier
2.5 ml (¹/₂ tsp) finely grated orange rind
4 egg whites

Melt butter, stir in flour, cook for a minute, then remove from heat and slowly add milk. Return to heat and cook, stirring with a balloon whisk, until very thick. Stir in sugar and salt until dissolved. Beat egg yolks, add a little of the hot sauce, mix well, then add the yolks to the sauce together with the Grand Marnier and orange rind.

When mixed, spoon into a large bowl. Whisk egg whites until stiff. Stir a quarter into egg sauce, then fold the remainder in gently but thoroughly. Grease a 14 x 7-cm (6 x 3-in) soufflé dish with butter and sprinkle with caster sugar. Pour mixture into prepared dish and bake at 180 °C (350 °F, gas 4) for about 30 minutes. Serve immediately. Serves 5–6.

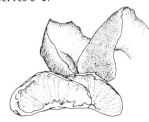

Spicy Peach and Nut Crumble

Another winter's pudding, first cousin to apple crumble.

800 g (1 lb 14 oz) canned peach slices
1 Granny Smith apple, peeled and cubed (optional)
5 ml (1 tsp) ground cinnamon

TOPPING
150 g (5 oz) self-raising flour
pinch of salt
45 ml (3 tbsp) brown sugar
60 g (2 oz) chopped walnuts
1 egg
generous pinch of ground cinnamon
2.5 ml (¹/₂ tsp) ground nutmeg
75 g (2¹/₂ oz) butter, melted

Lightly butter a deep 20-cm (8-in) pie dish. Spoon in the peach slices plus the syrup. Add the apple if using – it adds a nice tart touch – and sprinkle with cinnamon.

To make the topping, mix the flour, salt, sugar and nuts. Drop the unbeaten egg into the middle and, using a fork, mix until very well combined and crumbly. Sprinkle evenly over fruit. Sprinkle spices over topping and finally dribble the melted butter over.

Bake at 170 °C (325 °F, gas 3) for 50 minutes or until crisp and bubbling. Best served warm rather than very hot, with thick cream.
Serves 5–6.

Variation

GOOSEBERRY CRUMBLE
Make as for peach crumble, but for the filling substitute same quantity of gooseberries, undrained, and add 2 Golden Delicious apples, peeled and chopped. Reduce cinnamon to 2.5 ml (¹/₂ tsp). Omit nuts in the topping.

Grape Tart with Almond Pastry

A basic recipe, which is wide open to variations. The flan case, made with plenty of butter and ground almonds, is short and crisp, and may be made some days in advance, ready to be filled with any cream and fruit combination. I have used green and black grapes because they look so attractive – but any fruit may be used, and the filling spiked with complementary flavours: strawberries and Kirsch for example, or bananas and rum. The pastry is enough for two 20-cm (8-in) flan rings, the filling for one.

ALMOND PASTRY
250 g (9 oz) plain flour
45 g (1¹/₂ oz) icing sugar
generous pinch of salt
60 g (2 oz) ground almonds

200 g (7 oz) soft butter
1 egg yolk
2 drops of almond essence

FILLING
150 ml (5 fl oz) whipping cream
30 ml (2 tbsp) icing sugar
25 ml (5 tsp) Amaretto
7.5 ml (1¹/₂ tsp) powdered gelatine
25 ml (5 tsp) water
125 ml (4 fl oz) soured cream
1 egg white
pinch of salt

TOPPING
1 bunch green grapes
1 bunch black grapes
smooth apricot jam
toasted almonds

Make pastry by sifting flour, icing sugar and salt. Add ground almonds. Using an electric beater, work in the butter, egg yolk and essence. When very finely crumbled, form into a ball with your hands. Do not add any liquid. Press thinly into two ungreased 20-cm (8-in) loose-bottomed flan tins with fluted sides. Prick very well all over and bake at 180 °C (350 °F, gas 4) for 15 minutes. The pastry should not brown, but be a pale biscuit colour. Cool completely before removing the rings. The cases may now be stored in an airtight container, to be filled a few hours before dinner.

Whip cream, icing sugar and liqueur. Soften gelatine in water and dissolve over low heat. Stir into soured cream, and pour into a bowl. Whisk egg white with the pinch of salt and fold in together with whipped cream mixture. Now taste it – you may want it sweeter or sharper or more potent. Sprinkle base of flan case lightly with caster sugar to keep it crisp. Pour in filling and set in refrigerator.

Halve and seed grapes, but do not peel. Arrange rounded sides up, over cream filling in concentric circles, to cover completely. Melt a little smooth apricot jam with a little water. Using a pastry brush, brush glaze lightly over grapes until shiny. Tuck in a few toasted almonds. Return to refrigerator until required.
Serves about 8.

Strawberry Flan

Strawberry Flan

This flan looks every bit as professional as those on display in a pâtisserie: feather light pastry holding a creamy confection which is topped with bright, glazed strawberries.

PASTRY
100 g (3¹/₂ oz) butter, softened
45 ml (3 tbsp) icing sugar
1 egg yolk
few drops of vanilla extract
150 g (5 oz) plain flour
pinch of salt

FILLING
250–300 g (9–11 oz) strawberries
30 ml (2 tbsp) sugar
250 g (9 oz) cream cheese
200 ml (6¹/₂ fl oz) double cream
45 ml (3 tbsp) icing sugar
2.5 ml (¹/₂ tsp) finely grated orange rind
25 ml (5 tsp) Grand Marnier or few drops of vanilla extract

30 ml (2 tbsp) strawberry jam
5 ml (1 tsp) water
whipped cream and almond flakes to decorate

If possible, use an electric beater to make the pastry. Cream butter and icing sugar and beat in egg yolk and vanilla. Sift flour with salt and add. Dough will be soft. Form into a ball, wrap in waxed paper and chill for about 1 hour. Press thinly into 23-cm (9-in) loose-bottomed flan ring. Prick bottom and sides well and bake at 200 °C (400 °F, gas 6) for 10–12 minutes or until pale biscuit in colour – on no account must it brown. When cold, remove ring carefully and put flan onto serving plate.

Hull and wash strawberries and sprinkle with sugar. Leave to drain in a colander for about 15 minutes. Whisk cream cheese, cream, icing sugar, orange rind and liqueur or vanilla until thick. Spoon evenly into pastry shell.

Halve the strawberries and arrange on top of filling to cover completely.

Heat jam and water and pour into a small sieve. Glaze by holding sieve over berries and pushing liquid through, using back of spoon. Chill flan. It will hold well for about 4 hours without going soggy. Before serving, decorate with whipped cream piped in a lattice pattern. Fill the squares with toasted almond flakes.
Serves about 6.

Lychee Cobbler

575 g (1¹/₄ lb) canned, peeled and stoned lychees, drained
150 g (5 oz) plain flour
10 ml (2 tsp) ground ginger
generous pinch of salt
30 ml (2 tbsp) smooth peach jam
125 g (4 oz) butter, melted
5 ml (1 tsp) bicarbonate of soda

Chop lychees coarsely and cover bottom of lightly greased 20-cm (8-in) pie dish. Pour over 250 ml (8 fl oz) of the syrup. Sift together flour, ginger and salt. Add jam, then pour in melted butter and bicarbonate of soda dissolved in 30 ml (2 tbsp) hot water. Using a knife, mix until combined and then drop in dessertspoonfuls over lychees – do not try to cover them, the mixture will spread as it bakes. Bake on middle shelf of oven at 180 °C (350 °F, gas 4) for 30 minutes.
Serves 5–6.

Apple and Pear Tart with Soured Cream Topping

Baked in a fluted flan tin, this pastry case holds a fruity filling covered with a butterscotch-coloured, creamy topping. This is really quite a simple tart, using basic ingredients, but for sheer eye appeal it's hard to beat.

PASTRY
175 g (6 oz) plain flour
2.5 ml (¹/₂ tsp) baking powder
2.5 ml (¹/₂ tsp) salt
45 ml (3 tbsp) caster sugar
2.5 ml (¹/₂ tsp) ground mixed spice
100 g (3¹/₂ oz) butter
iced water

FILLING
375 g (13 oz) canned unsweetened apples
30 ml (2 tbsp) honey
45 ml (3 tbsp) seedless raisins
400 g (14 oz) canned pear pieces
2.5 ml (¹/₂ tsp) ground cinnamon

TOPPING
1 egg yolk
170–200 ml (5¹/₂–6¹/₂ fl oz) soured cream
30 ml (2 tbsp) light brown sugar
2.5 ml (¹/₂ tsp) ground cinnamon

Make pastry by sifting together the flour, baking powder, salt, caster sugar and mixed spice. Cut in butter until crumbly and slowly add enough iced water to bind. Mix quickly into a ball, wrap in greaseproof paper then chill about 1 hour. Roll out thinly on a floured board, and line a loose-bottomed 23-cm (9-in) fluted flan tin. Sprinkle base lightly with a little flour.

Chop apples into small pieces and mix with honey and raisins. Drain and chop pear pieces and add to apple mixture, then stir in the cinnamon. Spoon evenly into shell and bake at 200 °C (400 °F, gas 6) on middle shelf for 20 minutes.

Beat together ingredients for topping. Pour over fruit filling (be prepared for it to puff up a bit). Lower heat to 170 °C (325 °F, gas 3) and return tart to oven for 30 minutes. Remove and allow it to stand for about 10 minutes before lifting off the flan ring. Serve warm or at room temperature.
Serves 8–10.

Hint

For a more wholesome crust, brown flour may be substituted for half the flour. You will need about 45 ml (3 tbsp) iced water to bind this mixture, slightly less if using only white flour and about 60 ml (4 tbsp) if using only brown flour.

Baba au Rhum

Usually babas are baked in small dariole moulds, and savarins in rings, but personally I like the look of a ring, with the cream piled up in the middle. Deep muffin pans can be used if preferred.

25 ml (5 tsp) warm water
2.5 ml (^{1}/$_2$ tsp) sugar
10 ml (2 tsp) dried yeast
4 eggs
175 g (6 oz) plain flour (sifted before measuring)
90 g (3 oz) caster sugar
125 g (4 oz) butter, melted
whipped cream and/or strawberries to serve

SYRUP
500 ml (16 fl oz) water
160 g (5^1/$_2$ oz) sugar
75 ml (2^1/$_2$ fl oz) rum

Put water into a cup – it should not be hot, but warmer than lukewarm. Sprinkle in the sugar and dried yeast and leave for 15 minutes. Don't stir, just give it a shake now and then, and it will melt and start to bubble. Stir to a smooth cream just before using. Beat 3 eggs well. Warm flour in a very low oven, then stir into egg mixture, using a wooden spoon. Stir in the bubbly yeast. Beat well, still using a wooden spoon. The mixture will be tacky, like soft chewing gum. Cover and allow to rise in a warm place for about 25 minutes. When spongy and bubbly on the surface, add the remaining egg, beaten, the sugar and the melted butter. Beat again until well mixed – it will still be soft and tacky – then scoop into an oiled and floured 23-cm (9-in) ring mould. Cover, stand on a baking sheet, and return to a warm place for about 1 hour 20 minutes, until risen and spongy. Bake at 220 °C (425 °F, gas 7) for 10 minutes, then reduce heat to 200 °C

(400 °F, gas 6) and bake for 5 minutes more.

Meanwhile make syrup by boiling water and sugar rapidly for 5 minutes. Remove from stove and stir in rum.

Remove baba from oven, turn over, cover tin with 2 tea towels and leave for 5 minutes before loosening spring. Loosen edges with a knife and ease out gently onto a rack with a plate underneath. Prick all over with a skewer, then spoon syrup over slowly until it has all been absorbed, re-using any drips left on the plate. Cool, then fill centre with whipped cream, either plain or mixed with fresh strawberries. Serves 8–10.

Dutch Milk Tart

I have taken several liberties with this recipe. I have not, as in the traditional version, made a flaky pastry the night before, hung it up in a cloth and rolled it out at dawn. Nor have I flavoured it with tangerine peel. I have further broken with tradition by folding in the egg whites at the end, because I prefer the resulting lighter texture.

PASTRY
125 g (4 oz) butter, softened
45 ml (3 tbsp) caster sugar
1 egg
250 g (9 oz) plain flour
pinch of salt

FILLING
625 ml (1 pint) milk
1 cinnamon stick
30 g (1 oz) plain flour
60 g (2 oz) sugar
pinch of salt
30 g (1 oz) butter
3 eggs, separated
few drops of vanilla extract
3 drops of almond essence
**   (optional)**
ground cinnamon and sugar

To make the pastry, cream butter and sugar. Beat in egg. Sift in the flour and salt, form into a ball and chill while making the filling.

Using a heavy-based saucepan, scald 500 ml (16 fl oz) milk and cinnamon stick. Mix flour, sugar and salt to a paste with the remaining milk. Stir in the hot milk, then return to saucepan and cook until thick, stirring, and keeping heat low to prevent scorching. When thick and smooth, remove and add butter. Cool. Remove cinnamon stick and then beat in yolks, one at a time, using a wooden spoon. Add vanilla and almond essence. Whisk whites and fold in.

Press chilled dough evenly into 23-cm (9-in) pie dish – not too shallow as the filling puffs up. Cover base with a circle of greaseproof paper and weight with dried beans. Bake at 180 °C (350 °F, gas 4) for 10 minutes. Remove paper and beans and bake for further 5 minutes. Pour in filling and bake just below centre of oven for 20–25 minutes until set. Sprinkle generously with cinnamon and sugar.
Serves 8–10.

Pear Tart with Yoghurt

This tart has a very special appeal for those who are into health foods.

NO-ROLL CRUST
60 g (2 oz) wholemeal flour
60 g (2 oz) white flour
2.5 ml (¹/₂ tsp) salt
10 ml (2 tsp) caster sugar
100 g (3¹/₂ oz) butter
5 ml (1 tsp) lemon juice
45–60 ml (3–4 tbsp) cold water

FILLING
about 750 g (1³/₄ lb) nearly-ripe
    eating pears
2 egg yolks
250 ml (8 fl oz) plain drinking
    yoghurt
30 ml (2 tbsp) honey
10 ml (2 tsp) cornflour
15 ml (1 tbsp) light brown sugar
45 ml (3 tbsp) seedless raisins
5 ml (1 tsp) ground cinnamon
10 ml (2 tsp) brown sugar
30 ml (2 tbsp) honey
whipped cream to serve

To make the crust, use a flour sifter to sift both flours, salt and sugar into a bowl. Return husks to bowl, and rub in butter. Add lemon juice and cold water, just enough to be able to form a ball, using a knife and then your finger tips. Working quickly, press dough evenly into a loose-bottomed 23-cm (9-in) fluted flan tin. Chill while making the filling.

Peel, core and slice enough pears to give you 600 g (1 lb 5 oz), weighed after preparation. Beat egg yolks with yoghurt, honey and cornflour. Remove tart shell from refrigerator and sprinkle the 15 ml (1 tbsp) light brown sugar over the bottom (this helps to prevent the crust from becoming soggy). Cover with the thinly sliced pears.

Sprinkle with raisins, cinnamon and sugar and dribble with the honey. Pour the yoghurt mixture over. Put flan tin on a baking sheet and bake at 200 °C (400 °F, gas 6) just below the centre of the oven for 45 minutes. Remove and stand at room temperature until cool. Remove ring and serve with whipped cream.
Serves about 8.

Apple Crumble

High on the list of old-fashioned favourites, this apple crumble never fails to please. The apple juice ensures that it turns out juicy, and the nuts and spices add a tasty crunch.

750 g (1³/₄ lb) canned pie apples
200 ml (6¹/₂ fl oz) apple juice
 (or water)
45 g (1¹/₂ oz) white sugar
30 ml (2 tbsp) runny honey
45 ml (3 tbsp) sultanas
2–3 whole cloves (optional)
whipped cream to serve

TOPPING
125 g (4 oz) plain flour
5 ml (1 tsp) baking powder
75 g (2¹/₂ oz) brown sugar
10 ml (2 tsp) ground cinnamon
2.5 ml (¹/₂ tsp) ground nutmeg
60 g (2 oz) chopped walnuts
100 g (3¹/₂ oz) butter

Spread apples in buttered 23-cm (9-in) pie dish. Pour apple juice (or water) over. Sprinkle with sugar. Dribble with honey, add the sultanas and tuck in the cloves if you like it spicy.

For the crumble, mix flour, baking powder, sugar, spices and walnuts. Rub in butter. Sprinkle evenly over apples, then bake at 180 °C (350 °F, gas 4) for 45 minutes. Serve warm rather than bubbling, with a bowl of whipped cream.
Serves 6–8.

Note

As an alternative to serving whipped cream with sweet puddings, try the following: Stir 350 ml (11 fl oz) thick yoghurt until smooth. Whip 100 ml (3¹/₂ fl oz) whipping cream, and fold in. Cover and chill.

Apple Tart with Cinnamon Pastry

PASTRY
250 g (9 oz) plain flour
30 ml (2 tbsp) cornflour
125 g (4 oz) icing sugar
10 ml (2 tsp) ground cinnamon
10 ml (2 tsp) baking powder
pinch of salt
175 g (6 oz) butter, softened
1 egg, beaten
45 g (1¹/₂ oz) chopped nuts
few drops of vanilla extract

FILLING
750 g (1³/₄ lb) canned
 unsweetened pie apples
45 ml (3 tbsp) caster sugar
45 ml (3 tbsp) brown sugar
90 g (3 oz) sultanas
ground cinnamon
thick cream to serve

To make pastry, sift together flour, cornflour, sugar, cinnamon, baking powder and salt. Rub in butter until crumbly, then add egg, nuts and vanilla. Mix well, knead and form into a ball. Wrap in greaseproof paper and leave in freezer for a few hours until hard. Grate two-thirds of the pastry coarsely onto the bottom of an ungreased deep 23-cm (9-in) pie dish or loose-bottomed cake tin. Cover bottom completely, distributing dough evenly, but don't press down – use a fork to spread it around.

Chop apples and mix with sugars and sultanas. Spoon on top of pastry, top with a sprinkling of cinnamon, then grate remaining dough evenly over the top. Bake at 170 °C (325 °F, gas 3) for 1 hour. Serve hot or at room temperature, dusted with icing sugar, and with a bowl of thick cream. If baked in a cake tin, remove sides when quite cold.
Serves 8.

Upside-Down Apple Tart

Tarte des Demoiselles Tatin is a famous French dessert named after two ladies from Orléans. Traditionally, thinly sliced apples are arranged in carefully patterned circles in a tin lined with caramel, and then covered with a rich, sweet pastry. Tarte Tatin is always served upside down once baked. This is my simplified version of this excellent but tricky dessert.

PASTRY
125 g (4 oz) plain flour
generous pinch of salt
15 ml (1 tbsp) caster sugar
generous pinch of ground
** cinnamon**
60 g (2 oz) cold butter
30–45 ml (2–3 tbsp) iced water

FILLING
90 g (3 oz) light brown sugar
5 ml (1 tsp) ground cinnamon
45 g (1¹/₂ oz) chopped walnuts
** (optional)**
45 ml (3 tbsp) sultanas
500 g (18 oz) Granny Smith
** apples**

To make pastry, sift dry ingredients, rub in butter and slowly add enough water to bind. This may all be done using a hand-held electric beater. Form into a ball, wrap and chill briefly while preparing the tin and making the filling. It is essential to use a round 20-cm (8-in) cake tin, that is deep enough to take the filling and the crust.

Lightly oil the base and cover with a circle of greaseproof paper to fit. Butter the paper and the sides of the tin. Sprinkle with the sugar, pressing down firmly with the back of a spoon to make an even layer. Over this sprinkle the cinnamon, nuts and sultanas. Top with peeled and

thinly sliced apples – the slicing blade of a processor is perfect for the job. Press down firmly.

Roll out pastry on a floured board to a circle about 4 cm (1¹/₂ in) larger than the diameter of the tin, then place it directly onto the apples. Turn overlapping pastry inwards and press firmly against the inner edge of the tin. The pastry must rest on the apples. Bake at 180 °C (350 °F, gas 4) for 45 minutes. Stand at room temperature until cool. Unmould by running a knife round the edges, then put a large round plate on top and turn the tart upside down. Remove paper. The top should be toffee-coloured and juicy. Serve with whipped cream flavoured with brandy or rum.
Serves 6.

Baked Stuffed Apples

6 medium Granny Smith apples
60 g (2 oz) dates, chopped
60 g (2 oz) sultanas
45 ml (3 tbsp) chopped walnuts
1 large piece of preserved ginger,
** chopped**
15 ml (1 tbsp) honey
butter
250 ml (8 fl oz) unsweetened apple
** juice**
45 ml (3 tbsp) brown sugar
3 whole cloves
1 cinnamon stick
15 ml (1 tbsp) honey

Make large cavities in the apples. Remove a strip of peel around the middle of each. Mix dates, sultanas, walnuts, ginger and honey. Stuff apples and arrange in pie plate. Top each with a knob of butter. Heat remaining ingredients, pour around apples and bake at 180 °C (350 °F, gas 4) for about 1 hour or until soft, basting often. Serve at room temperature. Serves 6.

Fruit Flambé

Peach Küchen

The dish you use for this dessert is quite important – it can be square or round, but must be a bit larger than the average 20-cm (8-in) pie dish, with sides at least 3 cm (1¹/₄ in) high.

CRUST
**200 g (7 oz) flour
2.5 ml (¹/₂ tsp) baking powder
generous pinch of salt
30 ml (2 tbsp) caster sugar
125 g (4 oz) butter, softened
15 ml (1 tbsp) light brown sugar**

FILLING
**800 g (1 lb 14 oz) canned peach
  slices
30 ml (2 tbsp) light brown sugar
5 ml (1 tsp) ground cinnamon**

TOPPING
**1 egg yolk
250 ml (8 fl oz) soured cream
few drops of vanilla extract
5 ml (1 tsp) cornflour**

To make the crust, sift flour, baking powder and salt. Add caster sugar. Using an electric beater if possible, work in the butter. Beat until mixture is like fine cornmeal, and press into ungreased dish. No liquid must be added. Use the back of a spoon and press firmly to form a thin shell on the base and sides, but not on the rim. Sprinkle base with the light brown sugar.

Drain peaches very well and arrange on crust. Sprinkle with sugar and cinnamon. Bake at 200 °C (400 °F, gas 6) for 15 minutes.

Beat ingredients for topping together and pour evenly over peaches. Sprinkle with a little extra brown sugar and cinnamon, and return to oven to bake for another 15 minutes. Remove, and while still hot, neaten the edges of the crust. Serve warm or at room temperature, with or without cream. Serves about 8.

Fruit Flambé

A flexible pudding, using canned fruit, that can be prepared in advance. A good (and economical) combination is peaches and pears. The following is slightly more exotic.

**800 g (1 lb 14 oz) canned peach
  slices, drained
400 g (14 oz) canned fruit
  cocktail, drained
400 g (14 oz) canned lychees,
  drained, stoned and sliced
45 ml (3 tbsp) light brown sugar
1 knob preserved ginger,
  chopped
2.5 ml (¹/₂ tsp) finely grated
  lemon rind
few slivers of butter
45 ml (3 tbsp) brandy
125–250 ml (4–8 fl oz) double
  cream**

Mix fruits together. Sprinkle base of a large 23-cm (9-in) pie dish with the sugar. Spoon in the fruit. Add the ginger, sprinkle with lemon rind and dot with butter. Cover and leave at room temperature until required.

Bake, covered, at 170 °C (325 °F, gas 3) for 40 minutes. Remove and uncover. Have ready the warmed brandy in a small long-handled saucepan. Flame, then pour over the hot fruit. Swirl in the cream, and serve at once.
Serves 6.

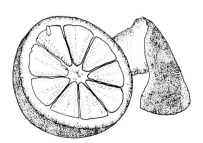

Jam Roly Poly

Jam Roly Poly

250 g (9 oz) plain flour
10 ml (2 tsp) baking powder
generous pinch of salt
30 g (1 oz) butter
1 egg
100 ml (3¹/₂ fl oz) milk or water
smooth apricot jam
chopped nuts

SYRUP
450 g (1 lb) sugar
15 g (¹/₂ oz) butter
5 ml (1 tsp) ground cinnamon
1 litre (1³/₄ pints) boiling water

Sift flour, baking powder and
salt. Rub in butter. Beat egg and
milk (or water) and add to flour
mixture. Mix to a soft, easy-to-
handle dough. Roll out about
5 mm (¹/₄ in) thick into a
30 x 23-cm (12 x 9-in) rectangle
on a floured board. Spread
liberally with jam and scatter
with nuts. Roll up from the long
side like a Swiss roll, pinching

edges together. With a sharp
knife cut into 2.5-cm (1-in) thick
slices and place in a single layer
in a 35 x 25 cm (14 x 10-in)
buttered baking dish, leaving
plenty of room for spreading.
    To make the syrup, put sugar,
butter and cinnamon into a bowl.
Add the boiling water, mix well,
then pour over rolled up dough
in baking dish. Bake at 180 °C
(350 °F, gas 4) for 35–40 minutes,
or until golden brown and well
risen. Serve hot with cream or
custard. Serves 10.

Variation

APPLE ROLY POLY
Substitute the following filling
for the apricot jam and nuts: Peel
and grate 2 large Golden
Delicious apples and mix with
45 g (1¹/₂ oz) sultanas, 30 g (1 oz)
chopped nuts and 30 ml (2 tbsp)
honey.

Orange Liqueur Crêpes

CRÊPES
2 eggs
10 ml (2 tsp) caster sugar
pinch of salt
125 ml (4 fl oz) milk
5 ml (1 tsp) oil
125 g (4 oz) plain flour, sifted
125 ml (4 fl oz) lukewarm water
125 ml (4 fl oz) soda water

SAUCE
45 g (1¹/₂ oz) butter
300 ml (10 fl oz) fresh orange
   juice
2.5 ml (¹/₂ tsp) finely grated
   orange rind
10 ml (2 tsp) honey
45 ml (3 tbsp) orange-flavoured
   liqueur
sugar
2.5 ml (¹/₂ tsp) ground cinnamon
5 ml (1 tsp) brown sugar
30 ml (2 tbsp) warmed brandy

Make crêpes by whisking eggs
with sugar. Add salt, milk and oil
and whisk again. Add flour,
water and soda water and beat
until well mixed, then cover and
stand for 1 hour. Whisk briefly
before using to make thin
pancakes, preferably in a non-
stick pan. Fold each in four, and
arrange close together in a
shallow baking dish – a 23-cm
(9-in) pie dish is a good size. The
batter will make 12 large or 18
medium crêpes.
    To make the sauce, melt butter
and allow it to brown lightly.
Remove from heat and add
orange juice and rind, honey,
liqueur and a little sugar if
necessary. Pour over crêpes,
sprinkle with cinnamon and
sugar and cover.
    Bake, covered, at 170 °C
(325 °F, gas 3) for about
30 minutes or until very hot.
Remove, uncover and flame with
warmed brandy. Serve with
vanilla ice cream. Serves 6.

Ginger Brandy Torte

Ginger Brandy Torte

This is a strange looking pudding, as puddings go, but then so is Spotted Dick – and it's much, much nicer. The base can be made a day or two in advance and stored in an airtight container.

4 egg whites
2.5 ml (¹/₂ tsp) cream of tartar
2.5 ml (¹/₂ tsp) salt
175 g (6 oz) caster sugar
few drops of vanilla extract
5 ml (1 tsp) ground ginger
16 gingernut biscuits, finely crushed
45 g (1¹/₂ oz) walnuts or pecans, chopped

TOPPING
5 ml (1 tsp) powdered gelatine
45 ml (3 tbsp) water
200 ml (6¹/₂ fl oz) whipping cream

45 ml (3 tbsp) icing sugar
15 ml (1 tbsp) brandy
preserved ginger to decorate

Beat egg whites with cream of tartar and salt until soft peaks form. Slowly add caster sugar, beating constantly, and continue beating until stiff. Whisk in vanilla. Fold in ginger, biscuits and walnuts. Spoon evenly into a lightly oiled and floured, loose-bottomed 23-cm (9-in) cake tin, and bake at 180 °C (350 °F, gas 4) for 25 minutes. Cool for 5 minutes, then invert and cool on rack.

For the topping, soften gelatine in the water and dissolve over low heat. Whip cream with icing sugar, and gradually beat in dissolved gelatine. Add brandy and whip until thick. Spread over cold cake base. Decorate with slivers of preserved ginger and refrigerate for a few hours before serving.
Serves about 8.

Tipsy Tart

A traditional old favourite, this time with a hint of orange.

125 g (4 oz) stoned dates, chopped
2.5 ml (¹/₂ tsp) bicarbonate of soda
125 ml (4 fl oz) boiling water
45 g (1¹/₂ oz) butter
60 g (2 oz) sugar
1 egg
125 g (4 oz) flour
5 ml (1 tsp) baking powder
pinch of salt
5 ml (1 tsp) finely grated orange rind
2.5 ml (¹/₂ tsp) vanilla extract
45 g (1¹/₂ oz) chopped walnuts

SYRUP
125 ml (4 fl oz) water
nut of butter
60 g (2 oz) sugar
30-45 ml (2-3 tbsp) brandy
30-45 ml (2-3 tbsp) orange-flavoured liqueur

Put dates into bowl, sprinkle with bicarbonate of soda and pour boiling water over. Cool, stirring and mashing a bit. Cream butter and sugar, add egg and beat well. Sift flour, baking powder and salt. Add dates to egg mixture, then stir in flour mixture. Add orange rind, vanilla and nuts. Pour evenly into greased 20-cm (8-in) pie dish and bake at 180 °C (350 °F, gas 4) on middle shelf for 25 minutes.

Meanwhile, make the syrup by boiling water, butter and sugar for 3 minutes. Stir at first to dissolve the sugar, and then boil rapidly. Remove from heat, add brandy and liqueur. Prick the hot tart when it is taken from the oven and pour syrup over slowly until it is all absorbed. Leave for a day to mature, if possible, then serve at room temperature, with a bowl of thick cream.
Serves 6–8.

Cinnamon-Coffee Hot Water Sponge

A light and spicy cake in pale café au lait.

3 eggs, separated
225 g (8 oz) caster sugar
175 g (6 oz) plain flour
generous pinch of salt
5 ml (1 tsp) ground cinnamon
2.5 ml (½ tsp) ground nutmeg
30 g (1 oz) butter
125 ml (4 fl oz) very hot, strong
　　black coffee
15 ml (1 tbsp) baking powder

ICING
325 g (11½ oz) sifted icing sugar
45 g (1½ oz) butter, softened
2.5 ml (½ tsp) ground cinnamon
5 ml (1 tsp) instant coffee
　　powder
about 45 ml (3 tbsp) milk or
　　single cream
walnuts to decorate

Using an electric beater, whisk
egg yolks and sugar until thick
and pale. Sift together flour, salt
and spices. Add to first mixture
and beat again – the mixture will
be crumbly. Melt butter in coffee
and add to cake mixture, beating
just until smooth. Fold in the
stiffly whisked egg whites and
lastly the baking powder.
　　Pour batter into two 20-cm
(8-in) oiled and floured cake tins.
Bake at 180 °C (350 °F, gas 4) for
25–30 minutes. Cool for 5
minutes, then invert onto cake
rack.
　　To make the icing, beat icing
sugar, butter, cinnamon and
coffee powder dissolved in 5 ml
(1 tsp) hot water, and then add
enough milk or cream to
moisten. Fill and ice cake, and
decorate with walnuts.

Variation

NUTMEG-BRANDY ICING
450 g (1 lb) sifted icing sugar
45 g (1½ oz) butter, softened
freshly grated nutmeg to taste
30 ml (2 tbsp) brandy
30 ml (2 tbsp) milk

Beat icing sugar with butter and
nutmeg, then add brandy and
milk. Mix to a creamy
consistency.

Beat and Bake Coffee-Pecan Cake (left) and Instant Spice Cake (right)

Instant Spice Cake

A large, moist, stick-to-the-ribs sort of cake, with a delicious flavour. One of my favourites, especially when in a hurry, as it is mixed in minutes.

10 ml (2 tsp) baking powder
350 g (12 oz) brown sugar
2 eggs
450 g (1 lb) sifted flour
345 ml (11 fl oz) buttermilk
250 ml (8 fl oz) oil
10 ml (2 tsp) ground nutmeg
5 ml (1 tsp) ground cinnamon
generous pinch of ground cloves
10 ml (2 tsp) bicarbonate of soda
175 g (6 oz) seedless raisins
125 g (4 oz) chopped nuts

ICING
100 g (3¹/₂ oz) butter
520 g (18 oz) sifted icing sugar
10 ml (2 tsp) mixed spice
about 15 ml (1 tbsp) orange-
    flavoured liqueur
single cream to moisten

Put baking powder, sugar, eggs, flour, buttermilk, oil, spices and bicarbonate of soda into a large mixing bowl. Mix with electric beater on medium speed for about 1 minute or until well blended. Fold in raisins and nuts and pour into a deep, oiled 23-cm (9-in) ring tin. Bake at 180 °C (350 °F, gas 4) for 1 hour. Stand for 5 minutes before inverting onto cake rack.

To make the icing, cream butter and icing sugar. Add mixed spice, liqueur, and cream. Ice top and sides of cake, swirling with prongs of fork dipped in hot water. Cover and stand for a day if possible.

Beat and Bake Coffee-Pecan Cake

This is a marvellously quick and versatile recipe. Oil is used instead of butter, so there's no creaming, and the flavours may be changed by omitting cinnamon, coffee and pecans and substituting vanilla extract, or grated lemon or orange rind. Altogether a real boon for the busy cook.

3 eggs, separated
175 g (6 oz) caster sugar
100 ml (3¹/₂ fl oz) oil
2.5 ml (¹/₂ tsp) salt
150 ml (5 fl oz) milk
175 g (6 oz) plain flour
10 ml (2 tsp) baking powder
5 ml (1 tsp) ground cinnamon
10 ml (2 tsp) instant coffee
    powder
5 ml (1 tsp) water
45 g (1¹/₂ oz) chopped pecan nuts

ICING
10 ml (2 tsp) instant coffee
    powder
30 ml (2 tbsp) water
60 g (2 oz) butter, softened
390 g (13¹/₂ oz) sifted icing sugar
few drops of vanilla extract

Put egg yolks into bowl and add all the ingredients, except the egg whites, coffee, water and nuts, in the order listed. Dissolve coffee in water and add. Mix on medium speed for 90 seconds. Fold in stiffly whisked egg whites and nuts. Pour into two greased and lined 18-cm (7-in) cake tins and bake at 180 °C (350 °F, gas 4) in the centre of the oven for 30 minutes. Stand for 5 minutes, then invert onto cake rack, remove paper, and cool.

Make icing by dissolving coffee in water, adding remaining ingredients and creaming, adding a little more water if necessary. Decorate with pecan halves.

Carrot Cake with Cream Cheese Icing

Some carrot cakes are too dry, some too sticky. After endless creating and baking and sifting and sorting, this one has emerged as my favourite, which may be served iced or plain.

3 eggs
350 g (12 oz) sugar
250 ml (8 fl oz) oil
125 g (4 oz) plain flour
125 g (4 oz) sifted wholemeal
  flour
5 ml (1 tsp) bicarbonate of soda
10 ml (2 tsp) baking powder
7.5 ml (1½ tsp) ground
  cinnamon
5 ml (1 tsp) ground nutmeg
pinch of ground cloves
4 medium carrots, coarsely
  grated
150 g (5 oz) seedless raisins
60 g (2 oz) chopped walnuts

ICING
390 g (13½ oz) sifted icing sugar
45 g (1½ oz) butter, softened
about 90 g (3 oz) cream cheese or
  low-fat soft cheese
few drops of vanilla extract

Beat eggs and sugar until pale, then beat in oil. Sift dry ingredients and add. Mix well, then add carrots, raisins and walnuts. Line base of 20–22-cm (8–9-in) square tin with greaseproof paper and oil lightly. Pour in cake mixture, which will be thickish and tacky. Spread evenly, and make a small depression in the centre. Bake at 170 °C (325 °F, gas 3) for 1¼ hours or until firm and brown. Stand for 5 minutes before turning out onto cake rack. Remove paper, then ice when cold.

Using a wooden spoon, mix icing sugar and butter. Slowly beat in just enough cream or low-fat cheese to give a spreading consistency. Add vanilla. To ice, turn cake right side up onto serving plate. Cover top and sides with icing, decorate with nuts, if desired, and cut into squares to serve.

Chocolate Chiffon Cake

This light cake is baked in a ring tin and covered with a creamy chocolate icing spiked with rum.

125 ml (4 fl oz) oil
175 g (6 oz) caster sugar
4 eggs, separated
125 ml (4 fl oz) water
125 g (4 oz) plain flour
5 ml (1 tsp) instant coffee powder
15 ml (1 tbsp) baking powder
45 ml (3 tbsp) cocoa powder
generous pinch of salt
few drops of vanilla extract

ICING
390 g (13$^1/_2$ oz) sifted icing sugar
45 g (1$^1/_2$ oz) butter, softened
45 g (1$^1/_2$ oz) plain chocolate
30 ml (2 tbsp) dark rum
few drops of vanilla extract
about 30 ml (2 tbsp) milk

Stir oil and sugar together until creamy. Add yolks one at a time, beating well. Slowly beat in the water. Sift together the flour, coffee powder, baking powder and cocoa three times, and fold in. Stiffly whisk egg whites with the salt and fold in. Finally add the vanilla. Pour into a deep, ungreased 20-cm (8-in) ring tin and bake at 180 °C (350 °F, gas 4) in the centre of the oven for 1 hour.

Turn upside down on cake rack. Air must circulate freely around cake. Leave until absolutely cold, then ease out of tin and ice, using a knife dipped in hot water.

For the icing, cream icing sugar with butter. Melt chocolate in the rum over hot water and add. Stir in vanilla and just enough milk to give a spreading consistency. Ice top and sides, roughing up with prongs of a fork, and garnish with shaved chocolate or walnut halves.

Feather Sponge Cake

This is quite the lightest of cakes. Usually, sponges are made with just three ingredients – flour, eggs and sugar – but Americans often include a raising agent, as in this recipe. It rises dramatically in the oven, but will settle, once cooled, into the traditional, flat-topped sponge. This type of cake should be eaten very fresh, as raising agents tend to make sponges dry.

4 eggs, separated
100 g (3$^1/_2$ oz) caster sugar
45 g (1$^1/_2$ oz) cornflour
30 g (1 oz) plain flour
2.5 ml ($^1/_2$ tsp) bicarbonate of soda
5 ml (1 tsp) cream of tartar
pinch of salt
few drops of vanilla extract
strawberry jam
sweetened whipped cream
icing sugar

Using an electric whisk, beat egg whites until stiff but not dry. Slowly add sugar and beat until very stiff. Add yolks one at a time, beating well. Sift dry ingredients twice, fold in very lightly and quickly, and then fold in vanilla. Turn into two 20-cm (8-in) cake tins, lined with rounds of greaseproof paper and lightly oiled and floured. Bake at 180 °C (350 °F, gas 4) in the centre of the oven for 20 minutes. Stand for 2 minutes, then turn out onto a cake rack to cool.

Spread with warmed strawberry jam, and sandwich together with whipped cream. Position a paper doily on the top layer, dust with icing sugar, and then carefully remove doily to create an attractive design.

Coffee Liqueur Cream Cake

This is a rich and tipsy sponge, doused with coffee and liqueur and covered with whipped cream. It may be served as a dessert or take pride of place at a lavish tea, where calorie-counting doesn't matter.

100 g (3¹/₂ oz) butter, softened
90 g (3 oz) caster sugar
125 g (4 oz) self-raising flour
2.5 ml (¹/₂ tsp) ground cinnamon
generous pinch of salt
2 eggs
45 g (1¹/₂ oz) coarsely crushed pecans (optional)
10 ml (2 tsp) instant coffee powder
170 ml (5¹/₂ fl oz) cold water
75 ml (2¹/₂ fl oz) Tia Maria
cream

Cream butter and sugar until very light. Sift flour, cinnamon and salt. Add eggs to creamed mixture, one at a time, together with 5 ml (1 tsp) of the flour mixture. Fold in remaining flour and pecans, if using. Spread batter, which will be stiffish, into an 18-cm (7-in) cake tin, base lined with greaseproof paper and oiled. Bake at 180 °C (350 °F, gas 4) for 25–30 minutes. Stand for 5 minutes before turning out onto cake rack. Remove base paper and cool, then tip back into tin.

Mix coffee powder, water and liqueur and slowly spoon over cake, as evenly as possible. It will be a tight fit, as the cake swells, but this is correct for in this way all the liquid will be absorbed. Turn out onto serving dish. Whip cream stiffly with a little icing sugar and, if desired, flavour with coffee. Cover cake with cream and decorate with a few pecan halves.

Dark Chocolate Cake

This cake is of the old, family favourite variety. It's not as light as a hot milk sponge, but then it's beautifully moist and keeps well.

125 g (4 oz) butter, softened
225 g (8 oz) caster sugar
3 eggs, separated
30 g (1 oz) cocoa powder
125 ml (4 fl oz) boiling water
250 g (9 oz) plain flour
5 ml (1 tsp) cream of tartar
5 ml (1 tsp) bicarbonate of soda
5 ml (1 tsp) instant coffee powder
2.5 ml (¹/₂ tsp) salt
125 ml (4 fl oz) yoghurt

ICING
260 g (9 oz) sifted icing sugar
15 g (¹/₂ oz) cocoa powder
45 ml (1¹/₂ oz) butter, softened
5 ml (1 tsp) rum or few drops of vanilla extract
little milk or cream

Cream butter and beat in sugar. Add yolks one at a time, beating well between each addition, adding at the same time 5 ml (1 tsp) of the flour with each egg. Dissolve cocoa in boiling water and beat in slowly. Sift dry ingredients and add alternately with yoghurt, beginning and ending with flour. Whisk egg whites stiffly and fold in. Spoon mixture, which will be thickish, into two 18-cm (7-in) oiled and floured cake tins, and bake at 180 °C (350 °F, gas 4) for 25–30 minutes. Stand for 5 minutes, then invert onto cake rack to cool.

Mix icing ingredients to desired consistency. Sandwich layers and ice the top, roughening with a fork, then decorate, if desired, with chocolate curls.

Orange, Date and Rum Cake (left) and Brandy Syrup Cake (right)

Orange, Date and Rum Cake

300 g (11 oz) plain flour
5 ml (1 tsp) baking powder
2.5 ml (¹/₂ tsp) salt
5 ml (1 tsp) ground cinnamon
5 ml (1 tsp) ground ginger
2.5 ml (¹/₂ tsp) ground nutmeg
250 g (9 oz) stoned dates,
chopped
60 g (2 oz) walnuts or pecan nuts,
chopped
250 g (9 oz) butter, softened
175 g (6 oz) caster sugar
2 eggs
250 ml (8 fl oz) buttermilk
5 ml (1 tsp) bicarbonate of soda
5 ml (1 tsp) finely grated orange
rind
few drops of vanilla extract
175 g (6 oz) sugar
200 ml (6¹/₂ fl oz) fresh orange
juice
about 45 ml (3 tbsp) dark rum

Sift together the flour, baking powder, salt and spices. Mix dates and nuts, toss with a little of the flour mixture and set aside. Cream butter and caster sugar. Add eggs one at a time, beating well between additions. Mix buttermilk with bicarbonate of soda and add to creamed mixture alternately with flour mixture, beginning and ending with flour. Finally stir in orange rind, vanilla, dates and nuts.

Spoon into a deep, oiled and floured 23-cm (9-in) ring tin, spreading batter evenly. Bake at 170 °C (325 °F, gas 3) on middle shelf for 1 hour. Five minutes before cake is ready, mix the 175 g (6 oz) sugar and orange juice in a saucepan and bring to the boil slowly, stirring to dissolve the sugar. Remove from heat and stir in the rum. Cool cake for 5 minutes before turning out onto large plate. Prick top with a skewer and slowly trickle the hot syrup over until it is all absorbed.

Brandy Syrup Cake

300 g (11 oz) plain flour
5 ml (1 tsp) baking powder
2.5 ml (¹/₂ tsp) ground cinnamon
2.5 ml (¹/₂ tsp) ground nutmeg
2.5 ml (¹/₂ tsp) salt
100 g (3¹/₂ oz) stoned dates,
chopped
60 g (2 oz) seedless raisins
45 g (1¹/₂ oz) chopped walnuts or
pecan nuts
12 glacé cherries, chopped
125 g (4 oz) butter
225 g (8 oz) caster sugar
2 eggs
5 ml (1 tsp) bicarbonate of soda
250 ml (8 fl oz) skimmed milk
soured with 5 ml (1 tsp)
vinegar
few drops of vanilla extract

SYRUP
250 ml (8 fl oz) water
125 g (4 oz) sugar
75-100 ml (2¹/₂-3¹/₂ fl oz)
brandy

Sift flour with baking powder, spices and salt. Add dates, raisins, nuts and cherries. Cream butter with caster sugar until light. Add eggs one at a time, beating well, adding 5 ml (1 tsp) of the flour mixture with each egg. Stir bicarbonate of soda into soured milk and add to creamed mixture alternately with flour. Finally add vanilla.

Spoon into an oiled and floured 23-cm (9-in) ring tin. Smooth top and bake at 170 °C (325 °F, gas 3) for 50–60 minutes or until done.

Just before cake is done, make the syrup by boiling the water and sugar together rapidly, uncovered, for 5 minutes. Remove from stove and add brandy. Pour hot syrup slowly over cake in tin, waiting as each spoonful is absorbed. Cool cake in tin for about an hour, then invert and release spring. Stand for about 8 hours for flavour to mellow, then serve with whipped cream.

Last Minute Cake

Dark and moist, this cake can be made the week before Christmas.

125 g (4 oz) butter
500g (18 oz) mixed dried fruit
125 g (4 oz) dates, stoned and
  chopped
210 g (7¹/₂ oz) brown sugar
5 ml (1 tsp) bicarbonate of soda
200 ml (6¹/₂ fl oz) water
2.5 ml (¹/₂ tsp) ground mixed
  spice
5 ml (1 tsp) ground cinnamon
90 g (3 oz) glacé cherries,
  chopped
60 g (2 oz) nuts, chopped
45 ml (3 tbsp) brandy
250 g (9 oz) plain flour
pinch of salt
2 eggs, beaten
5 ml (1 tsp) baking powder

Melt butter. Add washed dried fruit, dates, sugar, bicarbonate of soda stirred into the water, and spices. Bring to the boil, then cover and simmer for 15 minutes. Leave in a mixing bowl overnight. Next day add cherries, nuts and brandy. Sift flour with salt and fold in. Add eggs and finally add baking powder.

Line a deep 20-cm (8-in) cake tin with one layer of foil, shiny-side down, and two layers of greaseproof paper, and brush base and sides with oil. Spread batter evenly and make a small dent in the middle. Place a small cake tin filled with water on the bottom shelf of the oven, to prevent the cake from drying out. Bake at 150 °C (300 °F, gas 2) on middle shelf for a total of about 2¹/₂ hours – test with a skewer – and cover top loosely with foil after 1 hour. Cool in tin before turning out, then dose with a little sherry or brandy before wrapping in greaseproof paper and storing.

Light Fruit Cake

The word light in the title refers only to the colour – for this cake is very fruity, large and moist, with a lovely flavour.

360 g (12¹/₂ oz) plain flour
2.5 ml (¹/₂ tsp) salt
10 ml (2 tsp) baking powder
250 g (9 oz) butter
225 g (8 oz) sugar
finely grated rind of 1 orange
few drops of vanilla extract
3 eggs
500 g (18 oz) mixed dried fruit,
  washed and dried
90 g (3 oz) glacé cherries,
  chopped
2 large rings glacé pineapple,
  finely chopped
60–125 g (2–4 oz) nuts, chopped
250 ml (8 fl oz) milk
45 ml (3 tbsp) brandy

Sift flour, salt and baking powder. Cream butter, sugar, orange rind and vanilla until light. Add eggs one at a time, beating well between additions and adding 5 ml (1 tsp) of the flour mixture with each egg. Stir in the sifted dry ingredients, all the fruit and nuts. The mixture will be very stiff. Slowly stir in milk until completely absorbed, and finally add brandy.

Line a deep 23-cm (9-in) cake tin with one layer of foil, shiny-side down, and two of grease-proof paper. Brush well with oil, and spoon in cake mixture. Place a cake tin of water on the shelf below the cake, to prevent it drying out while baking. Bake at 150 °C (300 °F, gas 2) on middle shelf for 2–2¹/₄ hours, covering loosely with foil after 1¹/₂ hours. Test with a skewer before removing from oven. Cool in tin before turning out.

Variation

Sift 10 ml (2 tsp) ground mixed spice with the flour and add a knob of slivered, preserved ginger with the fruit.

Favourite Fruit Cake

Favourite Fruit Cake

Like all good fruit cakes, this one needs to be unwrapped and dosed with a dash of brandy or sherry. Serve plain or covered with almond paste and royal icing.

500 g (18 oz) mixed dried fruit, washed
100 g (3¹/₂ oz) glacé cherries, chopped
2 knobs preserved ginger, chopped
100 ml (3¹/₂ fl oz) sherry
125 g (4 oz) butter
150 g (5 oz) light brown sugar
few drops of vanilla extract
30 ml (2 tbsp) orange marmalade
2 eggs
200 g (7 oz) plain flour
5 ml (1 tsp) baking powder
pinch of salt
5 ml (1 tsp) ground cinnamon
2.5 ml (¹/₂ tsp) ground nutmeg
generous pinch of ground cloves
100 g (3¹/₂ oz) nuts, chopped

Put dried fruit, cherries and ginger into bowl. Pour sherry over and leave overnight.

Cream butter, sugar, vanilla and marmalade. Drop in eggs, one at a time, beating well after each addition and adding 5 ml (1 tsp) of the flour with each egg. Sift flour, baking powder, salt and spices and fold into creamed mixture alternately with fruit. Finally add nuts.

Line a deep, round 20-cm (8-in) cake tin with one layer of foil, shiny-side down, topped with two layers of greaseproof paper. Brush base and sides with oil. Spoon in the cake mixture, and level top with the back of a spoon dipped in hot water. Place a cake tin of water in the oven on the shelf below the fruit cake and bake at 150 °C (300 °F, gas 2) on the middle shelf for about 2¹/₂ hours or until done. Cool in tin. Turn out, sprinkle with brandy or sherry and store, well wrapped in waxed paper.

Quick Coffee Cake

This type of cake does not contain coffee. The name is derived from the fact that it is meant to be served, freshly baked and cut into squares, with morning coffee. The texture is light and moist and it does not require icing.

125 g (4 oz) plain flour
2.5 ml (¹/₂ tsp) salt
5 ml (1 tsp) ground mixed spice
5 ml (1 tsp) bicarbonate of soda
5 ml (1 tsp) baking powder
125 g (4 oz) wholemeal flour
75 g (2¹/₂ oz) seedless raisins
225 g (8 oz) sugar
chopped nuts (optional)
250 ml (8 fl oz) buttermilk
2 eggs
125 ml (4 fl oz) oil
cinnamon/sugar

Sift plain flour with salt, spice, bicarbonate of soda and baking powder. Add wholemeal flour.

Stir in raisins, sugar and nuts if using. Beat together the buttermilk, eggs and oil. Stir into dry ingredients and mix very lightly and quickly, as though making muffins.

Line base of a 20-cm (8-in) square pan with greaseproof paper and brush with oil. Pour in cake mixture, spreading evenly, dust top with a little cinnamon/sugar and bake at 180 °C (350 °F, gas 4) on middle shelf of oven for about 35 minutes – test with a skewer. Stand for a few minutes before inverting onto cake rack. Cut into squares to serve.
Makes 16 squares.

Orange Loaf Cake

250 g (9 oz) plain flour
175 g (6 oz) caster sugar
10 ml (2 tsp) baking powder
generous pinch of salt
125 ml (4 fl oz) oil
125 ml (4 fl oz) fresh orange
   juice
5 ml (1 tsp) finely grated orange
   rind
2 eggs
few drops of vanilla extract

ORANGE GLAZE
30 ml (2 tbsp) orange juice
15 g (¹/₂ oz) butter
120 g (4 oz) sifted icing sugar

Sift dry ingredients into bowl.
Add oil, juice and rind. Using an
electric beater, mix for 1 minute
on medium speed. Add eggs and
vanilla. Beat for 45 seconds until
well mixed. Pour into oiled,
floured and lined 23 x 9 x 7-cm
(9 x 3¹/₂ x 3-in) loaf tin and bake
at 170 °C (325 °F, gas 3) on
middle shelf for 1 hour. Stand for
5 minutes, turn out and cool on
cake rack.
  Heat butter and juice in small
saucepan, add icing sugar and
stir over very low heat until
smooth. Pour over top of cold
cake, allowing glaze to trickle
down the sides.

Nutty Dark Gingerbread

210 g (7¹/₂ oz) brown sugar
125 g (4 oz) butter
30 ml (2 tbsp) syrup or honey
30 ml (2 tbsp) molasses
45 ml (3 tbsp) milk
45 ml (3 tbsp) water
125 g (4 oz) brown flour
125 g (4 oz) plain flour
2.5 ml (¹/₂ tsp) salt
2.5 ml (¹/₂ tsp) ground nutmeg
15 ml (1 tbsp) ground ginger
7.5 ml (1¹/₂ tsp) baking powder
2.5 ml (¹/₂ tsp) bicarbonate of
   soda
60 g (2 oz) hazelnuts, chopped
1 egg, beaten

Heat the sugar, butter, syrup,
molasses, milk and water gently.
Mix remaining ingredients,
except egg. Pour the hot, melted
ingredients into dry ingredients
and mix well. Stir in egg. Pour
into oiled and floured
20 x 9 x 7.5-cm (8 x 3¹/₂ x 3-in)
loaf tin and bake at 180 °C
(350 °F, gas 4) for 45 minutes.

Lemon Coconut Loaf

A butter-rich, lemony loaf.
Serve plain.

125 g (4 oz) butter
210 g (7¹/₂ oz) caster sugar
225 g (8 oz) plain flour
10 ml (2 tsp) baking powder
generous pinch of salt
2 eggs
finely grated rind of 1 lemon
45 g (1¹/₂ oz) desiccated coconut
125 ml (4 fl oz) water
125 ml (4 fl oz) milk
few drops of vanilla extract

Cream butter and sugar until
light. Sift flour, baking powder
and salt. Add eggs to creamed
mixture, one at a time, together
with 5 ml (1 tsp) of the sifted
mixture. Mix in sifted mixture
and then add remaining
ingredients, beating until just
mixed. Pour into oiled, floured
and base-lined 23 x 7.5 x 7.5-cm
(9 x 3 x 3-in) loaf tin. Smooth the
top with the back of a spoon
dipped in hot water. Sprinkle
with extra coconut and bake at
180 °C (350 °F, gas 4) for 1 hour.
Stand for 5 minutes, then turn
out and cool on cake rack.

Variation

This mixture may also be used to
make small, flat-topped cup
cakes. Make as above and use to
fill 24 patty pans, two-thirds full.
Omit coconut topping. Bake for
20–25 minutes and allow to cool
for a few minutes before
removing. Ice, if desired, with
butter icing flavoured with
grated lemon rind.

Banana Loaf

Banana loaves are all much the
same, but this is the one I like
best, especially with the addition
of a handful of chopped walnuts.
The flour used may be either
white or plain brown.

250 g (9 oz) plain flour
10 ml (2 tsp) baking powder
generous pinch of bicarbonate
  of soda
2.5 ml (¹/₂ tsp) salt
5 ml (1 tsp) ground cinnamon
125 g (4 oz) butter
225 g (8 oz) sugar
2 eggs
4 large, ripe bananas, mashed
60–125 g (2–4 oz) nuts, chopped
  (optional)
few drops of vanilla extract

Sift flour with baking powder,
bicarbonate of soda, salt and
cinnamon. Cream butter and
sugar until light. Add eggs, one at
a time, beating well between
additions and adding 5 ml (1 tsp)
of the flour mixture with each
egg. Add flour mixture to
creamed mixture alternately with
bananas, beating well until
smooth. Stir in nuts and vanilla.

Pour into a lined and lightly
oiled 25 x 9 x 7.5-cm
(10 x 3¹/₂ x 3-in) loaf tin. Smooth
top and bake at 180 °C (350 °F,
gas 4) in centre of oven for
50 minutes to 1 hour. Turn out,
remove paper and cool. Serve
sliced and buttered.

Spiced Carrot and Raisin Loaf

A large, moist loaf. Serve in slices, lightly buttered.

690 ml (22 fl oz) water
390 g (13¹/₂ oz) light brown sugar
250 g (9 oz) seedless raisins
5 medium carrots, coarsely
    grated
30 g (1 oz) butter
5 ml (1 tsp) ground cinnamon
2.5 ml (¹/₂ tsp) ground nutmeg
pinch of ground cloves
450 g (1 lb) plain flour †
10 ml (2 tsp) bicarbonate of soda
10 ml (2 tsp) baking powder
generous pinch of salt
125 g (4 oz) walnuts or pecan
    nuts, chopped

Combine water, sugar, raisins,
carrots, butter, cinnamon,
nutmeg and cloves in a large
saucepan. Bring to the boil,
cover and simmer for

10 minutes. Pour into large
mixing bowl and leave until
completely cooled. Sift dry
ingredients. Stir into carrot
mixture and add the nuts.
    Pour into a base-lined and
lightly oiled 25 x 9 x 7.5-cm
(10 x 3¹/₂ x 3-in) loaf tin. Bake
at 170 °C (325 °F, gas 3) for
1 hour or until firm. Turn out on
cake rack and cool.

† Brown or wholemeal flour
may be substituted for some or
all of the flour.

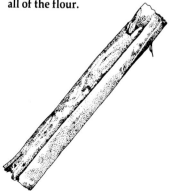

Brown Fruit Loaf

A simple, reliable loaf to serve
sliced and buttered for tea or for
packed lunches.

250 g (9 oz) mixed dried fruit
210 g (7¹/₂ oz) brown sugar
250 ml (8 fl oz) water
45 ml (3 tbsp) oil
2.5 ml (¹/₂ tsp) ground nutmeg
5 ml (1 tsp) ground cinnamon
2.5 ml (¹/₂ tsp) ground ginger
2.5 ml (¹/₂ tsp) salt
45 g (1¹/₂ oz) walnuts, pecan nuts
    or brazil nuts, chopped
125 ml (4 fl oz) yoghurt
1 egg
5 ml (1 tsp) bicarbonate of soda
250 g (9 oz) brown bread flour
5 ml (1 tsp) baking powder
few drops of vanilla extract

Put dried fruit, sugar, water, oil,
spices and salt into a saucepan,
bring to the boil and simmer for 5
minutes. Cool thoroughly. Add
nuts. Beat yoghurt, egg and

bicarbonate of soda and add to
fruit mixture alternately with
flour. Finally add baking powder
and vanilla.
    Spoon into oiled and floured
20 x 9 x 7.5-cm (8 x 3¹/₂ x 3-in)
loaf tin and smooth top with
back of spoon dipped in hot
water. Bake at 170 °C (325 °F,
gas 3) for about 45 minutes or
until skewer comes out clean.
Invert and cool on cake rack.

Note

The flavour of freshly grated
nutmeg is far superior to that of
pre-ground nutmeg. Buy the
nutmegs whole and grate as
needed – small nutmeg graters
are manufactured specially for
this purpose.

Courgette Tea Loaf

Serve this large, spicy loaf sliced and buttered.

3 eggs
250 ml (8 fl oz) oil
225 g (8 oz) sugar
few drops of vanilla extract
300 g (11 oz) courgettes
250 g (9 oz) flour (half brown
    flour may be used)
5 ml (1 tsp) bicarbonate of soda
5 ml (1 tsp) baking powder
2.5 ml ($^1/_2$ tsp) salt
5 ml (1 tsp) ground cinnamon
5 ml (1 tsp) ground mixed spice
60–125 g (2–4 oz) pecans or
    walnuts, chopped

Beat eggs, oil, sugar and vanilla together until light. Trim, peel and coarsely grate raw courgettes and stir in. Sift dry ingredients together and add. Finally stir in nuts. Combine thoroughly and turn into a base-lined, oiled and floured 25 x 9 x 7.5-cm (10 x 3$^1/_2$ x 3-in) loaf tin. Bake at 180 °C (350 °F, gas 4) on middle shelf of oven for 1 hour to 1 hour 10 minutes. Cool for 5 minutes, then turn out onto cake rack, remove paper and cool.

Date and Pecan Loaf

250 g (9 oz) stoned dates, finely
    chopped
30 g (1 oz) butter
210 g (7$^1/_2$ oz) light brown sugar
2.5 ml ($^1/_2$ tsp) bicarbonate of
    soda
250 ml (8 fl oz) boiling water
250 g (9 oz) flour (half brown
    flour may be used)
generous pinch of salt
5 ml (1 tsp) baking powder
few drops of vanilla extract
60 g (2 oz) pecans, chopped

Put dates into bowl with butter and sugar. Sprinkle with bicarbonate of soda and pour boiling water over. Leave to cool, stirring occasionally. Sift flour, salt and baking powder. Add cooled date mixture. Add vanilla and pecans and mix well. Pour into oiled and base-lined 20 x 9 x 7.5 cm (8 x 3$^1/_2$ x 3-in) loaf tin. Level top with back of spoon dipped in hot water and bake at 170 °C (325 °F, gas 3) in the centre of the oven for 1 hour. Turn out onto cake rack, remove paper and cool.

Wholemeal Scones

Wholemeal Scones

Raisins, dates, orange rind,
or nuts may be added.

300 g (11 oz) wholemeal flour
20 ml (4 tsp) baking powder
2.5 ml ($^1/_2$ tsp) salt
1 egg
75 ml ($2^1/_2$ fl oz) milk
75 ml ($2^1/_2$ fl oz) water
30 ml (2 tbsp) honey
45 ml (3 tbsp) oil

Mix flour, baking powder and
salt in a bowl. Beat remaining
ingredients together. Add to
flour mixture and mix to a soft
dough with a fork. Turn onto a
floured board and pat into a
round, adding more flour if
necessary, to make a manageable
dough. Brush surface with milk
or eggwash and cut into
8 wedges with a knife. Place on
oiled baking sheet and bake at
220 °C (425 °F, gas 7) for
12 minutes. Makes 8.

Cheese Scones

125 g (4 oz) plain flour
15 ml (1 tbsp) baking powder
2.5 ml ($^1/_2$ tsp) salt
10 ml (2 tsp) sugar
5 ml (1 tsp) dry mustard
125 g (4 oz) wholemeal flour
45 g ($1^1/_2$ oz) butter
100 g ($3^1/_2$ oz) Cheddar, grated
1 egg
45 ml (3 tbsp) milk
45 ml (3 tbsp) water

Sift plain flour, baking powder,
salt, sugar and mustard. Add
wholemeal flour. Rub in butter,
add cheese. Beat egg, milk and
water and add. Mix with a fork
and then lightly form into a ball,
adding, if necessary, an extra 5–
10 ml (1–2 tsp) water. Pat out
lightly and cut into squares. Place
on oiled baking sheet. Brush tops
with eggwash. Sprinkle with
paprika and bake at 220 °C
(425 °F, gas 7) for 12 minutes.
Makes 9.

Quick Breakfast Scones

The only time-consuming aspect
of this recipe is heating the oven.
After that, these feather-light
'drop' scones are made and baked
in a jiffy.

250 g (9 oz) plain flour
15 ml (1 tbsp) baking powder
5 ml (1 tsp) sugar
2.5 ml ($^1/_2$ tsp) salt
5 ml (1 tsp) dry mustard
60 g (2 oz) mature Cheddar
   cheese, grated
1 egg
100 ml ($3^1/_2$ fl oz) milk
100 ml ($3^1/_2$ fl oz) water
45 ml (3 tbsp) oil
paprika

Sift flour, baking powder, sugar,
salt and mustard. Add cheese.
Beat egg, milk, water and oil.
Make a well in centre of dry
ingredients and pour in the
liquid. Mix quickly to a soft
dough, using a fork. Drop
spoonfuls onto oiled baking
sheet, dust tops with paprika
and bake at 220 °C (425 °F,
gas 7) for 10–12 minutes.
Serve hot with butter.
Makes 12.

Wholemeal Nutty Pulled Breads

Crisp and wholesome, these can be dunked in hot drinks at teatime.

1 kg (2¹/₄ lb) wholemeal flour
225 g (8 oz) plain flour
225 g (8 oz) sugar
5 ml (1 tsp) salt
10 ml (2 tsp) baking powder
5 ml (1 tsp) bicarbonate of soda
5 ml (1 tsp) cream of tartar
250 g (9 oz) butter, melted
125 g (4 oz) seedless raisins
60 g (2 oz) pecan nuts, chopped
500 ml (16 fl oz) buttermilk
2 eggs
200 ml (6¹/₂ fl oz) oil

In a large bowl mix flours, sugar, salt, baking powder, bicarbonate of soda and cream of tartar. Stir in butter. Add raisins and nuts. Beat buttermilk, eggs and oil. Stir into dry mixture, knead into a

dough and roll into balls a little bigger than a golf ball. Pack closely into two base-lined and oiled 23 x 9 x 9-cm (9 x 3¹/₂ x 3¹/₂-in) loaf tins.

Bake at 180 °C (350 °F, gas 4) for 1 hour. Turn out, break apart, nick in half and then carefully break again. Use a knife to help, but don't actually slice them – for some reason they are always better if broken. Arrange on flat baking sheets and dry out in a very low oven of 120–140 °C (250–275 °F, gas ¹/₂–1). They taste even better if allowed to toast slightly.
Makes about 72.

Old-fashioned Buttermilk Pulled Breads

1,5 kg (3 lb) self-raising flour
10 ml (2 tsp) salt
225 g (8 oz) sugar
375 g (13 oz) butter
500 ml (16 fl oz) buttermilk
3 eggs

Mix flour, salt and sugar in a large mixing bowl. Rub in the butter – or if you're in a hurry you can melt the butter first. Mix well. Beat buttermilk with eggs and add. Knead well – the more you knead, the higher they'll rise. If the dough seems a little dry, rinse the buttermilk carton out with a little water and add to the mixture to make a medium-soft but not a slippery dough. Continue kneading until the dough forms a ball and leaves the sides of the bowl

clean, then roll into balls about twice the size of golf balls and pack closely into two base-lined, oiled and floured 25 x 9 x 7.5-cm (10 x 3¹/₂ x 3-in) loaf tins.

Bake at 200 °C (400 °F, gas 6) for 30 minutes, then reduce heat to 180 °C (350 °F, gas 4) and bake for a further 30 minutes. Turn out and break apart and then, with the help of a knife, break into pieces. Arrange on biscuit trays and dry out at 120 °C (250 °F, gas ¹/₂) or in a warming drawer.
Makes 84–96.

Date, Nut and Oat Biscuits

125 g (4 oz) butter
125 g (4 oz) sugar
1 egg, beaten
125 g (4 oz) stoned dates,
    chopped
60 g (2 oz) walnuts, chopped
125 g (4 oz) brown flour
2.5 ml (¹/₂ tsp) baking powder
2.5 ml (¹/₂ tsp) bicarbonate
    of soda
pinch of salt
90 g (3 oz) porridge oats
45 g (1¹/₂ oz) desiccated coconut
few drops of vanilla extract

Melt butter, add sugar and mix
well. Pour into mixing bowl and
add egg. Stir in dates together
with walnuts.

Sift flour, baking powder,
bicarbonate of soda and salt and
add to above mixture, tipping in
any bran left in sieve. Add
porridge oats, coconut and
vanilla. Mix thoroughly – the
mixture will be soft but firms up
on cooling. Form into about 30
balls and place on lightly oiled
baking sheets, not too close.
Flatten lightly with a fork and
bake at 180 °C (350 °F, gas 4) for
12 minutes or until golden
brown. Cool on cake rack.
Makes about 30.

Cinnamon Jam Bars

250 g (9 oz) butter, softened
165 g (5¹/₂ oz) sugar
1 egg
few drops of vanilla extract
300 g (11 oz) plain flour
5 ml (1 tsp) baking powder
pinch of salt
5 ml (1 tsp) ground cinnamon
175 g (6 oz) smooth apricot jam
80 g (3 oz) desiccated coconut

Cream butter and sugar. Beat
egg with vanilla and add. Sift dry
ingredients and add. Work into a
soft dough and pinch off two
thirds. With floured hands, press
into lightly greased 33 x 20-cm
(13 x 8-in) Swiss roll tin.

Spread evenly with jam. Add
coconut to remaining dough and
mix in thoroughly. Grate
coarsely over top of jam. Dust
with a little cinnamon and bake
at 180 °C (350 °F, gas 4) for
20–25 minutes until golden
brown. Cut into small bars and
allow to cool in tin, then remove
to cake rack and leave until cold.
Makes 32.

Cinnamon Squares

Chocolate Crunchies

A different method and a different flavour from the usual brown crunchie. The recipe is easily doubled for a larger batch.

125 g (4 oz) sugar
125 g (4 oz) white or brown flour
90 g (3 oz) desiccated coconut
30 ml (2 tbsp) cocoa powder
2.5 ml (½ tsp) bicarbonate of soda
90 g (3 oz) porridge oats
125 g (4 oz) butter, softened
few drops of vanilla extract
60 g (2 oz) nuts, chopped (optional)
few squares of plain chocolate

In a large mixing bowl, combine sugar, flour, coconut, cocoa, bicarbonate of soda and porridge oats. Using an electric beater, mix in butter and vanilla. When well mixed, add nuts, if using. Press into a greased 33 x 20-cm (13 x 8-in) Swiss roll tin and top with coarsely grated chocolate. Bake at 180 °C (350 °F, gas 4) for 20 minutes, cut into squares and leave to cool in tin.
Makes 24–30.

Note

If preferred, chocolate topping may be omitted and replaced by mixing 240 g (8½ oz) icing sugar with 20 ml (4 tsp) cocoa and just enough boiling water to make it spreadable. Spread evenly over slightly cooled crunchies and cut into squares when set.

Cinnamon Squares

125 g (4 oz) butter, softened
210 g (7½ oz) light brown sugar
1 egg, beaten
125 g (4 oz) brown flour
90 g (3 oz) porridge oats
75 g (2½ oz) muesli
30 g (1 oz) desiccated coconut
60 g (2 oz) seedless raisins
5 ml (1 tsp) baking powder
7.5 ml (1½ tsp) ground cinnamon
60 g (2 oz) Brazil nuts, chopped

Using an electric beater, cream butter and sugar. Add egg, and beat well. Add remaining ingredients and mix to a fairly soft dough. Press out flat into a lightly oiled biscuit tray or large Swiss roll tin, and bake at 180 °C (350 °F, gas 4) for 20 minutes. Cut into large squares and remove from tin when cooled, then leave on cake rack until cold. Makes 20.

Crunchies

175 g (6 oz) porridge oats
150 g (5 oz) sugar
125 g (4 oz) white or brown bread flour
90 g (3 oz) desiccated coconut
150 g (5 oz) butter
30 ml (2 tbsp) golden syrup
5 ml (1 tsp) bicarbonate of soda

Mix porridge oats, sugar, flour and coconut. Melt butter, stir in syrup, then add bicarbonate of soda. When mixture foams, stir into dry ingredients, mix well and press into a medium-sized, greased baking tray. Bake at 180 °C (350 °F, gas 4) for 15 minutes or until lightly browned. Cut into squares and remove from tin when cold.
Makes 30.

Variation

Add a handful of seedless raisins and/or sunflower seeds to dry mixture.

Coconut Slices

Spiced Pecan Crisps

Coconut Slices

150 g (5 oz) butter, softened
225 g (8 oz) sugar
1 egg
few drops of vanilla extract
250 g (9 oz) plain flour
generous pinch of salt
2.5 ml ($^1/_2$ tsp) bicarbonate
  of soda
90 g (3 oz) desiccated coconut

Cream butter and sugar until
light. Add egg and vanilla and
beat well. Sift flour with salt and
bicarbonate of soda and mix into
creamed mixture, then add
coconut. Roll dough into two
3-cm (1$^1/_4$-in) wide sausages.
Wrap in greaseproof paper and
chill for 1 hour. Using a sharp
knife, cut into 5-mm ($^1/_4$-in) slices
and place fairly far apart on an
ungreased baking sheet. Bake at
170 °C (325 °F, gas 3) in the
centre of the oven for about 12
minutes. Makes about 60.

Spicy Brown Biscuits

Economical, Continental-type
biscuits.

125 g (4 oz) butter, softened
175 g (6 oz) sugar
1 egg, beaten
45 ml (3 tbsp) golden syrup
375 g (13 oz) plain flour
5 ml (1 tsp) bicarbonate of soda
2.5 ml ($^1/_2$ tsp) salt
5 ml (1 tsp) ground cinnamon
10 ml (2 tsp) mixed ground spice
whole cloves

Cream butter, sugar, egg and
syrup. Sift dry ingredients
together and add. Mix into a
ball, pinch off pieces and place on
oiled baking sheet. Press a clove
into the middle of each and bake
in the centre of the oven at
180 °C (350 °F, gas 4) for
12 minutes, or until lightly
browned. Store in airtight tin for
a few days for best flavour.
Makes 40.

Spiced Pecan Crisps

125 g (4 oz) butter
210 g (7$^1/_2$ oz) light brown sugar
1 egg
few drops of vanilla extract
275 g (10 oz) plain flour
2.5 ml ($^1/_2$ tsp) baking powder
generous pinch of bicarbonate
  of soda
5 ml (1 tsp) ground cinnamon
2.5 ml ($^1/_2$ tsp) ground nutmeg
60 g (2 oz) pecan nuts, chopped

Cream butter with sugar until
fluffy. Beat in egg and vanilla.
Sift dry ingredients and add to
creamed mixture, combining
thoroughly. Lastly stir in pecans.
Form into sausages, wrap in
greaseproof paper and freeze for
about 45 minutes, until firm.
  To bake, slice into fairly thin
rounds and place on lightly oiled
baking tray. Bake at 180 °C
(350 °F, gas 4) for 12–15 minutes,
until a pale golden brown. Makes
about 54.

Chocolate Kisses

When the tiny meringues are
cold, carefully pierce the
bottoms to form hollows. Fill
with whipped cream, then
sandwich two together.

125 g (4 oz) caster sugar
10 ml (2 tsp) cocoa powder
2 egg whites

Mix sugar and cocoa. Whisk egg
whites with a pinch of salt until
stiff but not dry. Gradually beat
in half the sugar-cocoa mixture.
When very stiff, fold in the
remainder, using a metal spoon
and being careful not to over-
mix. Lightly oil a large baking
sheet, sprinkle with cornflour,
dust off excess. Pipe or drop
teaspoonfuls of meringue onto
prepared sheet and bake in
centre of oven at 120 °C (250 °F,
gas $^1/_2$) for 2 hours. Turn off heat
and leave in oven until cold.
Makes 24.

Walnut Fridge Crisps

Delicious, crisp cookies.

250 g (9 oz) plain flour
5 ml (1 tsp) baking powder
generous pinch of salt
2.5 ml (¹/₂ tsp) bicarbonate
of soda
5 ml (1 tsp) ground mixed spice
125 g (4 oz) butter
90 g (3 oz) light brown sugar
125 g (4 oz) caster sugar
1 egg
few drops of vanilla extract
60 g (2 oz) finely chopped
walnuts

Sift flour, baking powder, salt, bicarbonate of soda and mixed spice. Cream butter and slowly add brown and white sugar, beating well. Beat egg with vanilla and add to butter mixture, then mix in the flour mixture – an electric beater is perfect for the job. Lastly add walnuts.

Form into 2 long sausages, wrap in greaseproof paper and chill until firm enough to slice. Cut into thin rounds and bake on an ungreased baking sheet at 180 °C (350 °F, gas 4) for about 15 minutes. Cool on cake rack. Makes about 54.

Hint
Lightly toasting nuts before using brings out the flavour. Using the grinding blade, chop coarsely in a food processor, taking care not to reduce to a fine powder – which can happen very quickly. Spread them out on baking sheets and place in a moderate oven until lightly browned. Pecan and Brazil nuts respond particularly well to toasting, although, when nibbled purely for nourishment, nuts should be eaten fresh.

Orange Wafers

Thin, feather-light biscuits to serve with delicate desserts or ice cream.

125 g (4 oz) butter, softened
125 g (4 oz) caster sugar
30 ml (2 tbsp) orange-flavoured
liqueur
125 g (4 oz) plain flour
45 ml (3 tbsp) cornflour
pinch of salt
5 ml (1 tsp) finely grated orange
rind

Cream butter, sugar and liqueur until fluffy. Sift flour, cornflour and salt and blend into butter mixture. Mix in orange rind and shape into a ball, then roll into a long, smooth sausage. Wrap in greaseproof paper and chill for about 1 hour. Slice thinly, using a sharp knife, and arrange on an ungreased baking sheet, leaving plenty of room for spreading. Bake at 180 °C (350 °F, gas 4) for

10–12 minutes, or until pale gold. Dust with caster sugar and leave on baking sheet to cool slightly, then lift carefully onto cake rack and leave until cold. Makes 42–48.

Note
When grating orange rind, be sure not to include any of the white pith. Half an orange should provide 5 ml (1 tsp) finely grated rind.

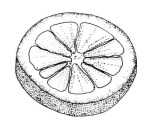

Oat Cookies

Large, crunchy biscuits.

250 g (9 oz) butter, softened
210 g (7¹/₂ oz) light brown sugar
125 g (4 oz) plain brown flour
  (not wholemeal)
200 g (7 oz) porridge oats
90 g (3 oz) desiccated coconut
2.5 ml (¹/₂ tsp) salt
few drops of vanilla extract
2.5 ml (¹/₂ tsp) bicarbonate of
  soda
45 ml (3 tbsp) hot water

Cream butter and sugar very
well. Add flour, porridge oats,
coconut, salt and vanilla.
Dissolve bicarbonate of soda in
the hot water and add. Mix well.
Roll into balls or push from
teaspoon into rough heaps on
oiled baking sheet and flatten
slightly with a fork. Leave plenty
of room for spreading. Bake at
180 °C (350 °F, gas 4) for
15 minutes or until a pale brown
colour. Remove carefully with a
spatula and leave to crisp on
cake rack. Makes 36.

Wholemeal Raisin Drops

125 g (4 oz) butter, softened
15 ml (1 tbsp) honey
90 g (3 oz) light brown sugar
1 egg
60 g (2 oz) plain flour
pinch of salt
5 ml (1 tsp) bicarbonate of soda
5 ml (1 tsp) ground mixed spice
60 g (2 oz) wholemeal flour
100 g (3¹/₂ oz) porridge oats
45 g (1¹/₂ oz) desiccated coconut
90 g (3 oz) seedless raisins
chopped nuts (optional)

Cream butter with honey and
brown sugar. Add egg and beat
well. Sift flour, salt, bicarbonate
of soda and mixed spice, add to
creamed mixture and beat. Add
wholemeal flour, porridge oats,
coconut, raisins and nuts, if
using. Mix well and then push off
the end of a teaspoon onto a
lightly oiled baking sheet, leaving
room for spreading. Bake at
180 °C (350 °F, gas 4) for
15 minutes, until browned. Cool
on cake rack, then store in
airtight container with a little
sugar sprinkled between layers.
Makes 30.

Oat Cookies (top) and Wholemeal
Raisin Drop Cookies (bottom)

Namib Knobs

Crisp little cakes, stuffed with dates, and very like mince pies in appearance.

PASTRY
225 g (8 oz) plain flour
45 ml (3 tbsp) cornflour
45 ml (3 tbsp) icing sugar
175 g (6 oz) butter
1 egg
few drops of vanilla extract

FILLING
250 g (9 oz) stoned dates, chopped
5 ml (1 tsp) lemon juice
45 ml (3 tbsp) water
45 g (1¹/₂ oz) walnuts, chopped

First make the filling. Put dates, lemon juice and water into a small saucepan and heat gently until dates are soft enough to be mashed with a wooden spoon. Add nuts and set aside to cool.

Sift flour, cornflour and icing sugar. Rub in butter. Beat egg and vanilla and add. Mix well and then knead into a ball with your hands – do not add any liquid. Roll out thinly on a floured board and cut into 5–7.5-cm (2–3-in) circles. Re-roll off-cuts until all the dough has been used. Place a heaped spoon of filling in the middle of each pastry round, cover with a second round and press edges together with the prongs of a fork. Prick each top twice. Arrange on oiled baking sheet and bake at 180 °C (350 °F, gas 4) for 18–20 minutes or until pale gold. Remove to cake rack and dust thickly with sifted icing sugar.
Makes about 14.

Hint
A light dusting of sugar between the layers of biscuits in a tin will help to keep them crisp.

Butter Cookies

125 g (4 oz) butter, softened
175 g (6 oz) caster sugar
1 egg
few drops of vanilla extract
225 g (8 oz) flour (half brown flour may be used)
5 ml (1 tsp) cream of tartar
2.5 ml (¹/₂ tsp) bicarbonate of soda
halved almonds or glacé cherries

Cream butter with sugar until light. Add egg and vanilla and beat well. Sift dry ingredients, add to creamed mixture and knead until smooth. Form into walnut-sized balls and place on oiled baking sheet, leaving room for spreading. Flatten lightly with a fork and top each with an almond or cherry. Bake at 180 °C (350 °F, gas 4) for 12–15 minutes until golden brown. Cool on cake rack.
Makes 30.

Chocolate Cookies

100 g (3¹/₂ oz) porridge oats
150 g (5 oz) plain flour
90 g (3 oz) desiccated coconut
225 g (8 oz) sugar
generous pinch of salt
125 g (4 oz) butter, softened
1 egg
15 ml (1 tbsp) honey
2.5 ml (¹/₂ tsp) bicarbonate of soda
25 ml (5 tsp) boiling water
25 ml (5 tsp) cocoa powder

Mix oats, flour, coconut, sugar and salt. Rub in butter. Mix in egg beaten with honey. Dissolve soda in boiling water. Add to cocoa, mix to a thick paste, then combine with flour mixture. Roll into small balls, place on oiled baking sheet and flatten with a fork. Bake at 180 °C (350 °F, gas 4) for 12–15 minutes. Cool on rack.
Makes 40.

Shortbread Biscuits

Shortbread Biscuits

Crisp, buttery biscuits served in wedges like shortbread.

250 g (9 oz) plain flour
30 ml (2 tbsp) cornflour
pinch of salt
100 g (3¹/₂ oz) icing sugar
175 g (6 oz) butter
few drops of vanilla extract

Sift together the flour, cornflour, salt and icing sugar. Rub in butter until crumbly. Add vanilla. Knead well, then roll out to about 10-mm (¹/₂-in) thickness onto the ungreased base of a loose-bottomed 23-cm (9-in) cake tin. Crimp the edges, prick well and mark into 12 wedges. Bake at 150 °C (300 °F, gas 2) for 45 minutes and allow to crisp on tin for 5 minutes before cutting through slices and removing. Makes 12.

Coconut Shortbread Fingers

250 g (9 oz) plain flour
120 g (4 oz) caster sugar
90 g (3 oz) desiccated coconut
125 g (4 oz) butter, softened

Mix dry ingredients. Rub in butter thoroughly until mixture has a fine, crumbly consistency, then knead for 5–10 minutes until dough clings together and forms a smooth ball. Press evenly into an ungreased 20-cm (8-in) square tin. Mark into fingers and prick well. Bake on the middle shelf of oven at 150 °C (300 °F, gas 2) for 50–60 minutes. Cut into fingers, sprinkle with extra caster sugar and leave in tin to cool. Remove to cake rack and leave until cold and crisp before storing in airtight tin. Makes 21 fingers.

Coconut Tartlets

Sweet and delicious: crisp pastry shells hold a dollop of jam and a coconut-meringue topping.

PASTRY
125 g (4 oz) butter
90 g (3 oz) caster sugar
2 egg yolks
few drops of vanilla extract
175 g (6 oz) flour
5 ml (1 tsp) baking powder

FILLING
smooth apricot jam
2 egg whites
90 g (3 oz) desiccated coconut
75 g (2¹/₂ oz) caster sugar
few drops of vanilla extract

Cream butter and sugar, add yolks one at a time, beating well. Add vanilla. Sift flour and baking powder, add and mix to a dough. Knead, adding a little more flour if necessary. Roll out thinly on a floured board, cut out circles, and line oiled patty pans. Put 5 ml (1 tsp) jam in the centre of each.

Whisk egg whites with a pinch of salt until stiff. Gradually beat in coconut, sugar and vanilla. Cover jam with meringue mixture and bake at 200 °C (400 °F, gas 6) for 16–18 minutes until lightly browned. Leave for a few minutes before removing to cake rack. Makes 18 medium tartlets.

American-style Overnight Muffins

American-Style Overnight Muffins

125 g (4 oz) wholemeal flour
125 g (4 oz) plain flour
125 g (4 oz) sugar
60 ml (4 tbsp) oil
few drops of vanilla extract
7.5 ml (1¹/₂ tsp) bicarbonate of soda
1 egg, beaten
generous pinch of salt
250 ml (8 fl oz) milk
5 ml (1 tsp) ground cinnamon
2.5 ml (¹/₂ tsp) ground nutmeg
125 g (4 oz) seedless raisins
60 g (2 oz) walnuts, chopped

Mix together all the ingredients, except raisins and nuts. Stir in raisins and nuts. Mix, cover and leave in refrigerator overnight. Fill greased muffin pans three-quarters full, and bake at 200 °C (400 °F, gas 6) for 15–20 minutes, until well risen and browned. Makes about 18.

American-Style Jam Muffins

250 g (9 oz) plain flour
45 ml (3 tbsp) sugar
15 ml (1 tbsp) baking powder
generous pinch of salt
5 ml (1 tsp) finely grated orange rind
125 ml (4 fl oz) milk
125 ml (4 fl oz) water
60 ml (4 tbsp) oil
1 egg
jam or marmalade
cinnamon/sugar

Stir dry ingredients. Add rind. Beat together milk, water, oil and egg and pour into a well in the centre of sifted mixture. Mix quickly and lightly. Drop a little batter into oiled muffin pans, add 5 ml (1 tsp) jam, cover with more batter and top with a little cinnamon/sugar. Bake at 200 °C (400 °F, gas 6) for 25 minutes. Makes 12–16.

Spiced Raisin Bars

Soft bars with a cake-like texture, which may be served either plain, dusted with sifted icing sugar, or topped with vanilla or orange butter icing.

60 g (2 oz) butter
45 g (1¹/₂ oz) light brown sugar
45 ml (3 tbsp) golden syrup
2 eggs
few drops of vanilla extract
125 g (4 oz) flour (half brown flour may be used)
5 ml (1 tsp) baking powder
2.5 ml (¹/₂ tsp) ground cinnamon
2.5 ml (¹/₂ tsp) ground nutmeg
pinch of ground cloves
125 g (4 oz) seedless raisins
chopped nuts (optional)

Cream butter and sugar until light. Add syrup, eggs and vanilla and mix well. Sift dry ingredients, toss in the raisins, and stir into creamed mixture. Add nuts, if using. Line base of a 20-cm (8-in) square tin with greaseproof paper and brush with oil. Pour in mixture and spread evenly. Bake at 180 °C (350 °F, gas 4) for 25 minutes. Turn out carefully onto cake rack, remove paper and cool. Turn right side up, spread with icing, if using, and, using a sharp knife, cut into bars. Makes 24.

Flour-Topped Rolls

These are soft, floury rolls similar to the baps which the Scots serve warm for breakfast.

200 ml (6$^{1}/_{2}$ fl oz) milk
100 ml (3$^{1}/_{2}$ fl oz) water
5 ml (1 tsp) sugar
7.5 ml (1$^{1}/_{2}$ tsp) dried yeast
450 g (1 lb) plain flour
5 ml (1 tsp) salt
45 g (1$^{1}/_{2}$ oz) butter, softened

Scald milk with water and leave until lukewarm. Sprinkle in the sugar and yeast, stir, then cover and leave until frothy. Sift flour and salt into a large bowl. Rub in butter. Pour yeast mixture into the centre, mix and then knead very well until smooth and pliable, adding a little extra warm water if necessary. Return to bowl, brush top with oil, then cover with a cloth and leave to rise in a warm place for 1$^{1}/_{2}$ to 2 hours, until doubled.

Punch down, knead briefly, and divide into 12 pieces. Flatten between the palms of the hands into rounds, then using a rolling pin roll lightly into ovals and place on a baking sheet dusted with flour. With your thumb make a deep dent in the centre of each, then leave to rise for about 25 minutes, preferably in the warming drawer below the preheated oven. Just before baking, brush with milk and, using a sieve, sift a little flour evenly over the tops. Bake in centre of oven at 220 °C (425 °F, gas 7) for 10 minutes.
Makes 12.

Hint

Dried yeast stays fresh for much longer than cubes of fresh yeast. Never leave the container standing open, and store in the refrigerator, where it will keep for a few months if kept dry and tightly covered.

Brown Soda Bread

Brown Soda Bread

175 g (6 oz) white bread flour
250 g (9 oz) wholemeal flour
2.5 ml (^{1}/$_2$ tsp) salt
5 ml (1 tsp) brown sugar
5 ml (1 tsp) bicarbonate of soda
345 ml (11 fl oz) buttermilk
milk or egg yolk

Mix both flours, salt and sugar.
Stir bicarbonate of soda into
buttermilk until dissolved, then
add to flour mixture and mix to
a soft dough. Shape into a large
round with floured hands, and
place on an oiled and floured
baking sheet.

Brush with milk or beaten egg
yolk and score into quarters or
eighths with the back of a knife.
Bake at 200 °C (400 °F, gas 6) for
about 40 minutes or until crusty
and brown. Serve as soon as
possible, broken into sections.
Serves about 8.
Makes 1 round loaf.

Wholemeal Pitta

5 ml (1 tsp) instant dried yeast
5 ml (1 tsp) sugar
175 g (6 oz) wholemeal flour
175 g (6 oz) plain flour
15 ml (1 tbsp) oil
250 ml (8 fl oz) warm water
2.5 ml (^{1}/$_2$ tsp) salt

Mix ingredients. Knead well for
5–10 minutes, adding extra flour
if necessary, to make a soft,
pliable dough. Place in bowl and
brush top with oil. Cover and
leave to rise in a warm place for
about 1 hour until doubled.
Punch down, divide into 8 and
shape into balls. Roll into flat
ovals and place on baking sheets
dusted with flour. Cover and
leave until slightly risen and
puffy. Bake at 240 °C (475 °F,
gas 9) for 10 minutes. Wrap in
cloth to keep soft.

Old-Fashioned Wholemeal Bread

**This takes a bit of mixing and
kneading, but the result is a
large, crunchy loaf with that
traditional humped top.**

15 g (^{1}/$_2$ oz) instant dried yeast
1 kg (2^1/$_4$ lb) wholemeal flour
7.5 ml (1^1/$_2$ tsp) salt
625 ml (1 pint) warm water
15 ml (1 tbsp) honey
25 ml (5 tsp) oil
250 g (9 oz) plain flour
125 g (4 oz) crushed wheat
10 ml (2 tsp) water
5 ml (1 tsp) sugar

In a large bowl mix yeast, 375 g
(13 oz) wholemeal flour and the
salt. Mix together the 625 ml
(1 pint) warm water, honey and
oil. Stir thoroughly into the flour
mixture to make a sloppy,
porridge-like dough. Cover and
leave in a warm place for

15 minutes. Add the plain flour,
crushed wheat and the remaining
wholemeal flour, and knead very
well until mixture makes a firm,
smooth ball. You may have to
add a little more water or a little
more flour, as flours differ in
their absorption capacity.

Shape dough into a loaf to fit
one large or two medium oiled
and floured loaf tins. Cover and
leave in a warm place for
40 minutes to 1 hour, until well
risen. Mix the 10 ml (2 tsp) water
with the sugar and brush the top
to give it a good colour when
baked. Bake at 200 °C (400 °F,
gas 6) for 30 minutes, then at
180 °C (350 °F, gas 4) for another
30 minutes. Turn out – the loaf
should sound hollow when
rapped on the bottom. Cool on
cake rack.
Makes 1 large or 2 medium
loaves.

Wholemeal Nut and Raisin Bread

A very wholesome and spicy loaf.

450 g (1 lb) wholemeal flour
5 ml (1 tsp) salt
7.5 ml (1¹/₂ tsp) ground
   cinnamon
2.5 ml (¹/₂ tsp) ground nutmeg
generous pinch of ground cloves
30 ml (2 tbsp) oil
30 ml (2 tbsp) honey
60 g (2 oz) brown sugar
90 g (3 oz) seedless raisins
60 g (2 oz) walnuts, pecan nuts
   or Brazil nuts, chopped
500 ml (16 fl oz) yoghurt or
   buttermilk
10 ml (2 tsp) bicarbonate of soda

Put flour, salt, 5 ml (1 tsp)
cinnamon, nutmeg, cloves, oil,
honey, 45 ml (3 tbsp) brown
sugar, raisins and nuts into a
large bowl and mix with a
wooden spoon. Beat yoghurt or
buttermilk with bicarbonate of
soda. Pour into flour mixture
and mix well. Spoon into an
oiled and floured 23 x 9 x 7.5-cm
(9 x 3¹/₂ x 3-in) loaf tin. Sprinkle
the top with remaining brown
sugar and cinnamon and bake at
180 °C (350 °F, gas 4) for 1 hour.
Turn out and cool on cake rack,
then serve sliced and buttered.
Makes 1 loaf.

Nutty Wholemeal Bread

This is a quick, yeast bread, which requires no kneading.

425 ml (14 fl oz) warm water
5 ml (1 tsp) honey
10 ml (2 tsp) dried yeast
375 g (13 oz) wholemeal flour
60 g (2 oz) plain flour
175 g (6 oz) crushed wheat
7.5 ml (1¹/₂ tsp) salt
10 ml (2 tsp) brown sugar
5 ml (1 tsp) mixed dried herbs
   (optional)
15 ml (1 tbsp) oil
60 g (2 oz) sunflower seeds

Mix 250 ml (8 fl oz) warm water
with the honey. Sprinkle in dried
yeast, stir, cover and leave to
froth. Mix both flours, crushed
wheat, salt, sugar, herbs (if
using) and oil. Stir in dissolved
yeast and sunflower seeds. Add
just enough of the remaining
warm water to make a soft
dough. Spoon into an oiled
and floured 23 x 9 x 7.5-cm
(9 x 3¹/₂ x 3-in) loaf tin, patting
in firmly.
   Sprinkle top with more
sunflower seeds and leave to rise
in a warm place for about 1 hour.
Bake at 200 °C (400 °F, gas 6)
for 45 minutes.
Makes 1 medium loaf.

Hint

When using sunflower seeds in
one of these quick-bread recipes,
use buttermilk, not yoghurt, for
the liquid – the latter tends to
turn the sunflower seeds green.

Wholemeal Health Bread (left) and White Bread (right)

Wholemeal Health Bread

250 g (9 oz) wholemeal flour
125 g (4 oz) brown flour
75 g (2¹/₂ oz) porridge oats
5 ml (1 tsp) salt
30 ml (2 tbsp) honey
90 g (3 oz) sunflower seeds
60 g (2 oz) mixed nuts, chopped
500 ml (16 fl oz) buttermilk
7.5 ml (1¹/₂ tsp) bicarbonate
  of soda

Mix both flours, porridge oats, salt, honey, sunflower seeds and nuts. Beat buttermilk with bicarbonate of soda and stir into dry mixture. Add a little water if necessary, to make softish dough. Spoon into oiled and floured loaf tin. Make a deep groove down centre, to prevent humping. Sprinkle with extra sunflower seeds and bake at 180 °C (350 °F, gas 4) for 1 hour.
Makes 1 loaf.

White Breads

The following basic bread dough can be used for loaves, rolls or plaits. Allow plenty of time for rising, and be prepared for some vigorous kneading. The reward is the matchless aroma of home-baked bread.

875 g (1 lb 12 oz) sifted white
  bread flour
10 ml (2 tsp) salt
30 ml (2 tbsp) melted butter
15 ml (1 tbsp) dried yeast
10 ml (2 tsp) sugar
500 ml (16 fl oz) warm water

Sift flour again with salt and add melted butter. Sprinkle yeast and sugar onto 250 ml (8 fl oz) water (which should be just a little warmer than lukewarm), stir, cover and leave to froth. Make a well in the flour, pour in bubbly yeast, mix, and add the rest of the water. † Knead very well until smooth and elastic, adding up to 125 ml (4 fl oz) extra warm water if necessary. Shape into a ball, put back in bowl, brush top with oil, cover and leave to rise in a warm place for 1¹/₂ to 2 hours, depending on room temperature, until doubled. Punch down and knead very well. Shape into loaves, rolls or plaits. The above quantity will make 1 very large loaf (for a 35 x 10 x 10-cm (14 x 4 x 4-in) tin), 1 medium loaf and 1 plait, or about 20 rolls.

For the plait, pinch off one third of dough and roll into 3 long sausages. Pinch together at one end, plait, and pinch to close. Place on oiled baking sheet, cover lightly and leave to rise for 45 minutes to 1 hour, until doubled. Brush with milk and sprinkle with poppy seeds. Bake at 220 °C (425 °F, gas 7) for 10 minutes, then reduce heat to 180 °C (350 °F, gas 4) and bake for 20 minutes longer.

Shape the remaining dough into a loaf and place in oiled 23 x 9 x 9-cm (9 x 3¹/₂ x 3¹/₂-in) loaf tin. Cover and leave to rise for 1 to 1¹/₂ hours – a good second rising is important. For a crusty top, brush with a mixture of generous pinch of salt dissolved in 5 ml (1 tsp) water and then bake at 220 °C (425 °F, gas 7) for 15 minutes. Reduce heat to 200 °C (400 °F, gas 6) and bake for a further 35 minutes. Turn out and cool on cake rack – to test, rap on the bottom – if bread is done, it will sound hollow. The same method is used for 1 very large loaf.

Bake rolls at 220 °C (425 °F, gas 7) for 10 minutes and then at 180 °C (350 °F, gas 4) for 10 minutes.
Makes 1 large loaf or 1 medium loaf and 1 plait or 20 rolls.

†250 ml (8 fl oz) milk, scalded and cooled to lukewarm may be used instead of the second addition of water.

Buttermilk Herb Bread

This is one of those great stand-by recipes - a soft-textured, aromatic loaf, stirred up in just a few minutes and excellent with soup, cheese or a meaty pâté.

500 g (18 oz) self-raising flour
90 g (3 oz) crushed wheat (optional)
5 ml (1 tsp) dried oregano
5 ml (1 tsp) dried thyme
5 ml (1 tsp) salt
45 g (1¹/₂ oz) parsley, finely chopped
500 ml (16 fl oz) buttermilk
1 egg
2 garlic cloves, crushed
paprika and grated Cheddar or Parmesan cheese for topping

Mix dry ingredients, including parsley. Beat buttermilk with egg and garlic. Stir into dry ingredients and mix well to a tacky dough. Spoon evenly into a lightly oiled and floured 23 x 9 x 9-cm (9 x 3¹/₂ x 3¹/₂-in) loaf tin. Smooth the top and sprinkle with paprika and cheese. Bake at 180 °C (350 °F, gas 4) for 1 hour.
Makes 1 loaf.

Variation

CORNMEAL BREAD
500 g (18 oz) self-raising flour
10 ml (2 tsp) mixed dried herbs
400 g (14 oz) canned sweetcorn kernels, drained
5 ml (1 tsp) salt
45 g (1¹/₂ oz) parsley, chopped
500 ml (16 fl oz) buttermilk

Mix dry ingredients, add parsley and corn. Add buttermilk and then proceed as above.

Rosemary Milk Rolls

Light, white herb rolls. Best served hot from the oven, but may be reheated.

250 ml (8 fl oz) milk (either low-fat, or use half milk and half water)
15 g (¹/₂ oz) butter
5 ml (1 tsp) sugar
2.5 ml (¹/₂ tsp) salt
1 large fresh rosemary sprig
375 g (13 oz) flour
5 ml (1 tsp) instant dried yeast
crushed dried rosemary

Scald milk, add butter, sugar and salt, stir to dissolve and leave until lukewarm. Chop rosemary needles finely and mix with flour and yeast. Add milk mixture, mix well and then knead well on a floured board, adding extra flour as needed to make a pliable dough. Shape into a ball and place in a bowl, brush top with oil, cover and leave to rise in a warm place for about 1 hour, until doubled.

Punch down and shape into 8–10 rolls, plaits or crescents. Arrange on oiled baking sheet, brush tops with milk and sprinkle with dried rosemary. Cover lightly and leave to rise for 20–30 minutes.

Bake for 10 minutes at 200 °C, (400 °F, gas 6) then reduce heat to 180 °C (350 °F, gas 4) and bake for 10 minutes more.
Makes 8–10 rolls.

Rum Truffles

End the evening on a really sweet note.

45 g (1¹/₂ oz) plain chocolate
45 g (1¹/₂ oz) milk chocolate
25 ml (5 tsp) single cream
45 g (1¹/₂ oz) sifted icing sugar
few drops of vanilla extract
20 ml (4 tsp) dark rum
cocoa powder or chocolate vermicelli

Melt chocolate over simmering water – don't allow it to get too hot. When melted, stir in cream, icing sugar, vanilla and rum. When smooth, turn onto a plate, spreading about 2.5 cm (1 in) thick. Place a sheet of greaseproof paper directly on the surface and chill for a few hours until firm. Roll into small balls and then roll the balls in cocoa powder or chocolate vermicelli. Place in small paper cups, and keep in refrigerator. Makes 12.

Caramel Fudge

675 g (1¹/₂ lb) sugar
30 ml (2 tbsp) golden syrup
400 g (14 oz) canned condensed milk
125 ml (4 fl oz) milk
125 ml (4 fl oz) water
45 g (1¹/₂ oz) butter
few drops of vanilla extract

Put all ingredients, except vanilla, into a saucepan with a thick, heavy base. Stir slowly over low heat so that sugar melts before mixture boils, then boil gently over low heat for about 15–20 minutes. Take care that the mixture does not catch on the bottom. When ready, a drop should form a firm ball in cold water. Remove from heat and add vanilla. Beat with a wooden spoon until very thick and creamy, then pour into a buttered, 25 x 15-cm (10 x 6-in) tin, and cut into small squares as it cools. Makes about 40 squares.

Coffee Caramel Fudge with Liqueur

Much smarter than ordinary fudge, these sweet and fattening delights will round off a special dinner on a delicious note.

400 g (14 oz) canned condensed milk
30 ml (2 tbsp) golden syrup
575 g (1¹/₄ lb) sugar
45 g (1¹/₂ oz) butter
125 ml (4 fl oz) water
125 ml (4 fl oz) milk
few drops of vanilla extract
10 ml (2 tsp) instant coffee powder
45 ml (3 tbsp) Tia Maria

Put condensed milk, syrup, sugar, butter, water and milk into a deep saucepan with a heavy base. Stir over low heat to dissolve sugar before mixture comes to the boil, then continue to boil over medium heat for 15–20 minutes until a drop forms a firm ball in cold water. Stir frequently, but not frantically, and check that it doesn't burn on the bottom.

When ready, remove from heat and add vanilla and coffee powder, then carefully and slowly beat in liqueur. Continue beating until creamy and very thick, then pour into a buttered 20-cm (8-in) square pan and cut into small squares as it sets. Makes 36.

To cook dried beans

HARICOT BEANS: Soak overnight in plenty of cold water. Drain, rinse and place in saucepan. Cover with water and simmer until soft, adding salt after 45 minutes. An alternative method is to bring the beans to the boil in a generous quantity of water, and then leave to soak for 2 hours. Drain and rinse, cover with fresh water and boil until soft.

CHICKPEAS: Soak overnight in plenty of cold water. Drain, rinse and simmer, covered with water for 2½–3 hours until soft, adding salt after 1 hour. Pour off cooking liquid and reserve if required. Tip chickpeas into a large bowl, add cold water and rub them between the palms of your hands to remove the skins – as skins float to the top, pour off and repeat several times.

SOYA BEANS: Soak overnight in plenty of cold water. Drain and tip into a large bowl. Add plenty of fresh water and then rub beans between palms of hands to remove skins. As skins float to the top, pour off and repeat several times. To cook, simmer soya beans in water for about 3 hours, adding salt towards the end of the cooking period.

How to use phyllo pastry

The day before using, transfer the phyllo to the refrigerator to thaw. Unwrap and lay out on a dry tea towel. Cover with another dry towel and then with a damp towel, and leave to stand for 10 minutes before using, always keeping the sheets you are not working with covered in this way. They quickly become brittle and dry when exposed to air. Brush each sheet lightly with melted butter (for sweet or savoury dishes) or oil (for savoury dishes) before using.